RACINE

BRITANNICUS

RACINE

*

BRITANNICUS

INTRODUCTION, NOTES AND
GLOSSARY BY
PHILIP BUTLER

Professor of French
University of Wisconsin

CAMBRIDGE UNIVERSITY PRESS

CAMBRIDGE
LONDON · NEW YORK · MELBOURNE

Published by the Syndics of the Cambridge University Press
The Pitt Building, Trumpington Street, Cambridge CB2 1RP
Bentley House, 200 Euston Road, London NW1 2DB
32 East 57th Street, New York, NY 10022, USA
296 Beaconsfield Parade, Middle Park, Melbourne 3206, Australia

Library of Congress catalogue card number: 68-10026

ISBN 0 521 29197 6

First published 1967
Reprinted 1977

First printed in Great Britain in the City of Oxford
at the Alden Press
Reprinted in Great Britain at the
University Press, Cambridge

CONTENTS

CONTENTS

vi

PREFACE

Racine's academic admirers have, in the course of the last three centuries, done him an injury from which he is only now beginning to recover. By insisting, up to a comparatively recent time, that he had established a model, valid for all times, of what a tragedy should be, they have aroused in France and abroad understandable protests. Their peremptory statements about his 'classical perfection' have encroached upon the reader's freedom, blunted his curiosity, distorted his natural approach to a genuine poet, and succeeded in creating misapprehensions as to the very notion of classicism. For Racine's greatness must ultimately be measured by what he comes to mean to each one of us; and he is no more a 'model' to a twentieth-century dramatist, critic, or spectator, than Aeschylus or Shakespeare. Even worse perhaps, in asserting that Racine's style illustrated the French language in its absolute purity, they have made it appear dull and lifeless. For the truth is that the French language has kept growing and changing, and that Racine's French is no longer our French. The angry legionaries who groan at carrying the Roman eagles in front of a woman do not make *speeches* about it ('toute autre se serait rendue à leurs discours', 1249); and it is not only Néron's 'ennui', or 'les fiers Domitius' which do not mean what they seem to mean. Since the seventeenth century scores of expressions have changed their meaning slightly or not so slightly, lost some of their force, or some of their sheen. Just like the brown varnish that dims the hues of an old master, the thin film of centuries that tarnishes some of Racine's words has to be cleaned before they can reappear with the original freshness of their colours. And we have to grasp with as much precision as we can the seventeenth-century intention of his theatre before we may become fully aware of its modern implications.

I hope this edition of *Britannicus* will be useful to university students and to sixth-formers. The text is followed by a fairly extensive *Glossary* of seventeenth-century words and expressions (marked by an asterisk *), and by *Notes* which provide information concerning Racine's own special use of some words, passages which present difficulties, historical allusions. On this last point, however, it seemed that Tacitus, who so fired Racine's imagination, was too great a writer to be doled out in snippets; that he should be able to make his own powerful impact, and long extracts from Books XII, XIII, and XIV of the *Annals* will be found in an *Appendix*—which is what Racine himself wanted to provide. I have considered myself fortunate to have at my disposal Michael Grant's modern, racy translation; I gratefully acknowledge the permission given by Penguin Books, Ltd. to reproduce parts of his *Tacitus: The Annals of Imperial Rome*. In the Notes will be found too, on characters and situations, a running commentary which I have tried to keep discreet, for the discovery of Racine must be left to the reader himself, under the teacher's guidance, and an edition must not become a conducted tour. In the Introduction that precedes the text I have tried to give information of a more general character, and to take a broader view of the author and the play. I should like also to acknowledge the help I have received from Professor Stewart Maguinness, King's College, London, a French as well as a Classical scholar, and from the staff of the Cambridge University Press.

Except for the punctuation, the text is, as in all modern editions, that of 1697, the last one published in Racine's lifetime, to which are added the *Epître* and *Préface* of the first edition, and the variants of 1670, 1676, 1687, as well as a scene first published by Racine's son in 1747, in his *Mémoires sur la vie de Jean Racine*. Racine's spelling, however, is still surprisingly archaic, and might easily cause regrettable confusion in the minds of learners of French. Mesnard's solution, on the other hand, no longer seems acceptable: his otherwise admirable edition of *Les Grands Ecrivains de la France* retains some archaisms and drops the others; it represents nothing but the nineteenth-century convention in dealing with seventeenth-century texts. I have instead followed the example set by Raymond Picard in his *Pléiade* edition, and modernized the text altogether. As for the punctuation in the original editions, I felt I could not disregard it as entirely as did Mesnard, who obviously took it to mean nothing but the printer's whim. It is true that it is often inconsistent or careless, but its purpose is different from ours, and it probably affords hints on the way the verse was spoken. I have altered it where it directly clashed with modern usage, or might have disconcerted, even in cases in which it may not be without significance ('Mais crains, que l'avenir détruisant le passé, . . .', 'Je sais, que j'ai moi seule avancé leur ruine . . .'). Whenever possible I have tried to preserve it: I have refrained from sprinkling the text with commas, which make 'l'analyse logique' easier but break the rhythm of the line, or from re-grouping Racine's lines with the help of colons and semicolons. In a passage like the following one, the slow initial movement of the verse and its sudden acceleration are lost if the distribution of commas and full stops is disturbed:

> Burrhus ne pense pas, Seigneur, tout ce qu'il dit.
> Son adroite vertu ménage son crédit.
> Ou plutôt ils n'ont tous qu'une même pensée,
> Ils verraient par ce coup leur puissance abaissée,
> Vous seriez libre alors, Seigneur, et devant vous
> Ces maîtres orgueilleux fléchiraient comme nous.   (Text of 1670–1687)

It was said that for the benefit of his greatest actress Racine used to write down like music the inflexions of the voice for every line: however faint the echo of his voice in the text, nothing must be done to mute it.

INTRODUCTION

1. *13 December 1669*

On that winter afternoon of 13 December 1669, in the long, rectangu-
lar room of the Hôtel de Bourgogne—the longest established and
still the main theatre of Paris—there was, in spite of the usual
hubbub, a curious atmosphere of tension and expectation. Most of
the two tiers of boxes which surrounded the room on three sides were
still empty, but in the pit a very mixed audience had begun assemb-
ling a couple of hours before the play was due to start. They were
mostly middle-class people of some substance, merchants from the
smart shopping centre of the Rue Saint-Denis, soberly dressed
bourgeois and *rentiers*; but artisans, shop-keepers and shop-assistants,
lackeys and servants were also present, as well as pages, guardsmen
and guards officers from the Palace. The theatre was very dark: it
had no windows, and was only dimly lit by a few candles. There
were no seats but for a couple of benches against the wall, where
people could sit down for a while when they were getting too tired
of standing. This had an obvious advantage for the management:
the number of customers could be increased almost indefinitely;
no wonder that some of them fainted sometimes in the heat and
press, or were almost crushed to death. On less crowded days, the
spectators could move freely, greeting acquaintances and con-
versing together.

The theatre was not very large (about fifty feet long and forty-five
wide), and it was not filling very fast: a public execution was taking
place on that very day, and the expectation of seeing the executioner
on his scaffold beheading his victim—a nobleman—in the full view
of the crowd had drawn a good many of the *bons bourgeois* of the
neighbourhood. Fifty years before, tragedy had attempted to rival
such thrills as in the more gory Elizabethan plays; by the 1660s it
scorned even to try. At the first arrivals in the boxes, curious heads
were turned, names whispered. Whereas black, and brown and
grey were the dominant colours in the pit, the newcomers wore
richly coloured velvets and brocades, long, full coats with a profusion
of ribbons, cuffs and frills of white embroidery. Under their arms
they carried hats covered with feathers; the younger ones wore their

long curly hair flowing over their shoulders, following the fashion
set by the young King; their barbers had provided the not so young
with wigs, which were in a few years to be worn by all, and to take
extravagant dimensions. They hardly glanced into the pit, at the
parterre, which eyed them with reluctant admiration; they talked
among themselves, loudly, with ease and confidence and with
elaborate marks of respect to the women, whose long skirts and
trains matched the magnificence of their companions. These were
the people who could afford half a *louis d'or* for their seat—perhaps
the equivalent of fifteen guineas or thirty dollars, and double price
for the *premières*. They were the courtiers from the Louvre, the lords
and the ladies of a much envied and still highly glamorous aristocracy.

Suddenly there was a hush in the pit as well as in the boxes. A
man had walked into one of the *loges*, and sat down quietly, all by
himself. There was nothing very striking about him: he looked
awkward and ill at ease, as he acknowledged the respectful bows of
spectators; yet this shy old man with a defensive look in his eyes was
the most illustrious writer in France. For the last forty years he had
been without an equal, indeed without a rival. He had created the
model of witty, romanesque, entertaining comedy, as well as that of
tragedy in the grand manner. His plays had not always been successful, but nothing had made Paris forget the wonder and delight of
Le Cid; and *Horace, Cinna, Polyeucte, Pompée, Nicomède, Rodogune,
Œdipe* had been applauded by two generations of Frenchmen
united in admiration for the man who, in his own lifetime, was already
le grand Corneille. And now the tension grew, and could be sensed by
all. Here and there in the pit small groups started forming; sharp-
profiled, often black-clothed, shabby-looking men exchanged crisp
remarks, like officers on the battle-field. For it was a battle that was
to be fought that night, and the presence of Corneille gave the evening its full historical dimension. Another drama was beginning,
apart from the one the spectators would watch on the stage. Two
men confronted each other on that evening, two generations, almost
two ages, and two deeply conflicting views of tragedy, and of life,
and man's condition. For tonight, with all the arrogance of youth
and genius, Racine had openly challenged Corneille.

The young author was nowhere to be seen. No doubt he was
behind the stage, feverishly giving the nervous actors his last
instructions. Racine was not thirty yet, and he was already famous.
He was tall, strikingly handsome, and contemporaries had noted

his odd resemblance to the King. His success had been swift: an orphan of modest origin, he had been, only a few years before, a penniless youth who had gone all the way to Provence in the hope of a dingy Church living, which had after all not been forthcoming. Almost at once after his return to Paris we find him at Court, and in 1664 his first play, *Les Frères ennemis*, had been produced by the most famous actor-author of the day, Molière. The following year, *Alexandre le Grand* was a triumph: it was performed in the presence of the King and his Court, and received with the most flattering applause; furthermore the monarch had graciously accepted the *Dédicace* of the play, in which the young writer expressed in a fulsome, but undoubtedly sincere, manner his loyal admiration for Louis. *Les Frères ennemis* and *Alexandre* showed promise: *Andromaque* was a major literary event. Few people fully realized the originality of the play, but most of them felt its novelty, and they vigorously reacted for or against Racine: there was in 1667 a 'Querelle d'*Andromaque*', just as, thirty years before, there had been a 'Querelle du *Cid*'.

Much of the criticism directed against *Andromaque* was the expression of petty jealousy, or the reluctance to consider on its own merits something that was new. But one point recurred again and again: the excessive importance (as well as the nature) of love. Now love had always been an ingredient of French seventeenth-century tragedy, even of Corneille's tragedy, but it was supposed to be a subordinate interest. Grandeur was what was expected from tragedy; it showed high-ranking people, often great historical figures, whose decisions affected the fate of empires, powerful wills who fought down their opponents, as well as their own passions: 'Je suis maître de moi comme de l'univers', Augustus said in *Cinna*. When in the 1650s Quinault made love the mainspring of his tragi-comedies, people flocked to be entertained by his lively, unlikely plots, to sympathize with his tender heroes, to listen to his agreeable, rather flaccid verse. But no one would have thought of comparing him with Corneille. Was Racine just another Quinault? Was he one of those 'doucereux' whom Corneille despised? The older generation, unable or unwilling to conceive tragedy except on Corneille's model, the 'vieille Cour', whose ideals and passions he had so magnificently portrayed, looked upon the newcomer with anger and annoyance: love, nothing but love, *All for love*, as in Dryden's play, that did not add up to a tragedy. Let Racine prove himself; let him show that he could recreate on the stage the deeds of Augustus, Caesar, Pompey, or

3

Cleopatra, that he had the insight and genius to understand, and give new life and meaning to, the great crises of history. Racine took up the challenge, and he wrote *Britannicus*, a political play, the subject of which was taken from Tacitus.

This was a daring move: in fighting Corneille on his own ground, was not Racine running the risk of sacrificing his originality, of becoming a mere follower of the established master of the *genre*? Could Racine really write a Cornelian play better than Corneille? Racine had no intention of writing a Cornelian play, but the stakes were high for both poets on that winter afternoon in 1669. It was nearly five now, and the play was about to start. The candles of the chandeliers had all been lit, and they would remain lit during the whole representation, shedding their soft light on spectators and actors alike. Suddenly the curtain that divided them went up (it would not come down before the end of the last Act), and the play began:

Quoi! tandis que Néron s'abandonne au sommeil. . . .

What did a tragedy look like in 1669? The idea has sometimes been expressed that a classical tragedy was an austere experience of the mind, which should spurn any visible means of arousing the imagination, something to be listened to seriously, composedly, almost with closed eyes, like a sermon. In fact it has often been considered best to produce Racine's tragedies without *décors*, in front of brown curtains, with actors vaguely draped in neutral-coloured costumes of Republican simplicity. This is a respectable view. But it would have filled Racine with dismay. It certainly was not the way he meant his plays to be performed, nor the way they were performed in his time. The setting did not change in the course of the five acts of the tragedy, but when, as in *Britannicus*, this setting was a chamber, or rather an antechamber, in the Emperor's palace, pillars and columns with richly ornamented capitals, ancient statues and marbles aimed at recalling to the spectator's mind the wealth and the power of Rome. The costumes of the actors would have looked bizarre to us: they were originally derived from the statues of Roman Emperors, with their armour moulding, or imitating, the human torso, their short tunic leaving the arms and legs bare. But this was oddly combined with elements of seventeenth-century costume: the armour had become a close-fitting garment of richly embroidered material; the sleeves and the tunic were adorned with ribbons; the actor wore long stockings and high-laced boots of soft leather; his hat had a profusion of feathers; sometimes he even wore gloves. This baroque attire—each costume was worth a small fortune— which was, historically speaking, neither Roman nor French, has been dismissed as an example of the lack of historical sense in the seventeenth century. Yet the least experienced producer knows that his job is not that of an historian or an archaeologist; *décors* and costumes to him are only a means of creating an atmosphere. He is not professing a course on Roman costume in A.D. 56, but collaborating with the poet. He is not trying to teach the spectator, but to arouse his imagination. This the seventeenth-century costume achieved for a seventeenth-century audience: other means would be required today. All that must be retained from the original production is its intention: the suggestion of a stylized Antiquity, the impression of stately dignity, solemn magnificence. This is but the outer shell of classical tragedy, but such was the splendid setting for Racinian simplicity.

2. *Racine and his critics*

What was the outcome of the great duel between Racine and Corneille? Heated discussions, apparently, started the very moment the play ended, and even before. And it seems that Corneille himself, who in his great position should have shown reserve, made some unfavourable comments. Hence—in his First Preface—Racine's furious reactions against the 'malevolent old poet', a fury thinly disguised under the veil of a Latin quotation. Racine had his enthusiastic supporters, but, as is often the case, the partisans of the old and proved way were more numerous. Besides, Racine was not liked: he was too ambitious, too successful, too young; he was also too sarcastic, too witty, too resentful of criticism. *Britannicus* had only five (perhaps eight) representations. At a time when twenty meant a great success, this was not so bad as it looks, but for a playwright of Racine's fame it was failure, and he acknowledged it, bitterly, in his First Preface: 'Whatever care I took in working on this tragedy, it seems that, hard as I tried to make it good, some people tried just as hard to denigrate it. There is no cabal they have not contrived, no disparagement they have not brought up.' And when the tide had turned, he recalled it with quiet but crushing pride in the Second Preface: 'Success did not at first fulfil my hopes. Hardly had this

5

tragedy appeared on the stage when there arose a great deal of criticism that would, it seemed, destroy it. . . . But the fate of this play has been that of all productions that have some value: criticism has faded away, the play has endured.'

The critics Racine so harshly dismissed were often limited and ill-informed. But their reactions are not entirely useless if we are to understand the originality of the play. Boursault, a contemporary playwright who has left us an account of the first representation, was no friend of Racine's, but he tried to be fair. He praised the style; everybody did: on this point Racine's mastery could not be denied: had even Corneille ever written verse of such concentrated energy, as that in which Agrippine's sardonic wit alternated with truly Roman *gravitas*? With less candour Boursault praised the acting: everybody knows a good actor can make almost anything sound good. . . . The first Act to him seemed the best: it silenced all critics, and apparently compelled reluctant admiration even from enemies. As a dramatic *exposition*, as a lucid unravelling of a very complex situation, as a presentation of three of the chief characters, Agrippine, Britannicus, and, through Agrippine, Néron, the first Act was indeed a masterpiece, and such *tours de force* could be immediately understood by spectators used to Corneille's plays. The second Act was almost as good. Why 'almost'? Too much love-making, perhaps; too much of that passion which, Corneille thought, was not grand enough to be given pride of place in a tragedy. The third Act appeared 'weak', and this to us seems incredible: Agrippine's outburst of hurt pride and jealousy, the clash of the two rivals, Néron for the first time shaking off all restraint, how could all this appear 'weak'? And yet this is no individual blind spot of the critic, but a likely reaction of part of the audience. For they liked to imagine the tragic hero as dignified, self-controlled, and above all preoccupied with the exclusive demands of his 'duty', that is to say with the demands of his rank and his ambition. Now it was clear that the great Agrippine, screaming abuse, her Machiavellian plans all but forgotten, was no Cornelian heroine. Britannicus, an Imperial prince, was caught by his rival in a somewhat undignified position, and Néron, the ruler of a vast empire, calling upon his guards to arrest him for the sake of his love, looked more like one of Quinault's heroes in *Astrate* than a great figure in Roman history. The play, the Cornelians felt, was losing its dignity and its grandeur: Racine could not keep it up; they had always predicted he could not.

The fourth Act was better: plenty of history and politics; serious stuff. And Burrhus at least was a character one could admire, who said the things one expected to hear in a political tragedy: his pleas for clemency, his invective against tyranny, such things had been heard before, and could be fitted into a known frame. The fifth 'faisait pitié': it was below everything. The moving scene of Junie's and Britannicus' last farewell left Boursault cold; even Agrippine's curse upon her son, eloquent enough for Corneille, it seems, could not redeem the failure of the *dénouement*. Such contempt is partly explained by Racine himself in his Preface: *Britannicus* was said by its opponents not to follow the proper rules of good drama, which should bring the plot to its climax, and leave it there; the climax is Britannicus' death; all that comes afterwards is of no interest; in the view of the 'cornéliens' it exposed Racine's poor craftsmanship. This purely 'dramatic' conception of tragedy, which was no longer that of Racine, makes this criticism significant, as we shall see later.

Far more important than Boursault's, more balanced and more thoughtful too, was the opinion of a man who was to be for the rest of his life an exile in England, but who still had considerable influence in Paris, Saint-Evremond. Saint-Evremond expressed great admiration for Racine; he even found in *Britannicus* that somewhat elusive quality of 'le sublime', the elevated and the elevating, the sense of uplift and pride the readers felt 'as if we had ourselves produced the very thing we heard' (Montani). He went so far as to imply that Racine was the only poet in the same class as Corneille, that he could, one day, become a worthy successor of Corneille. But Racine, he felt, had not equalled Corneille, and his play was, ultimately, unsatisfactory. The reason lay in the choice of the subject and the nature of the characters, neither of which was fit for a tragedy. 'I deplore', he wrote, 'this author's misfortune, which is to have worked in a praiseworthy manner on a subject that cannot be represented in a pleasing way. For the idea we have of Narcissus, of Agrippina, of Nero, is so black and horrible that it cannot be erased from the spectator's memory; and however hard he tries to put out of his mind the thought of their cruel deeds, the horror they arouse in him wrecks and somehow destroys the whole play.' At first sight this may seem disconcerting and timid: should Iago, Richard III, even Macbeth be debarred from tragedy because they are too wicked and too cruel? In principle, however, Saint-Evremond's idea is a sound one: if a character arouses nothing but horror,

7

his triumph will cause indignation, his downfall satisfaction—but neither feeling is a 'tragic' one. This Racine knew, and showed that he knew, as well as his critic, and Saint-Evremond should have perceived it.

The lukewarm reception given by the public and the critics to a play that was too original and too controversial to be accepted at once, was not the end of the story. For Racine had his main supporters among the new generation of the 'jeune Cour', and his powerful protectors did not let him down. When at the beginning of 1670 Racine published his play, it was preceded by an *Epître* addressed to the friend of his youth, the young Duke of Chevreuse, who had just married Colbert's daughter. This *Dédicace* gave Racine the opportunity not only of praising Colbert but of informing his critics that the King's principal minister, one so feared by the courtiers and so unapproachable that they had nicknamed him 'le Nord', had taken time to listen to his tragedy, to discuss and consider it, and Colbert, Racine implied, knew more about politics than Boursault, Saint-Evremond, and all the 'doctes' together. But this was not enough. If Racine was not above crushing his *literary* critics under the weight of his *political* protectors, he was not one to leave their criticism unanswered. Behind the steady flow of disparaging comments that had finally compromised the success of his play Racine knew there was the rival, coherent conception of Corneille's tragedy; and behind much of the unfair or unintelligent criticism he had been submitted to, he thought he saw the hand of Corneille. In the counterattack of the 1670 Preface it was at Corneille he struck, and struck hard.

Dealing first with the tiresome quarrels about historical accuracy (the 'doctes' could always catch out the poets on some minor points, and thus parade their own erudition), Racine answers them by quoting to his critics their respected model. The real Narcisse had had nothing to do with Britannicus' death, and Britannicus in his play lives two years longer than he actually did: but has not Corneille done much worse in *Héraclius*, in which he upsets the whole chronology of the Emperors' reigns? His Junie is not quite like the historical Junie: what about Corneille's Emilie in *Cinna*, or his Sabine in *Horace*, sheer inventions in those so-called historical plays? These are but skirmishes; when it comes to fundamentals Racine really lets fly. The image he presents of Corneille's drama is at first sight unrecognizable; unfair as it is, if we consider Corneille's theatre as a whole, it is not, unfortunately, as inaccurate as it may appear. For in his long career Corneille had widely experimented. It is true that, in some of his plays, the plot is so 'extraordinaire' as to have nothing that could be called 'naturel': in *Héraclius* Martian, unaware that he is Martian, addresses the pseudo-Martian, not knowing him to be Héraclius, who alone knows his own identity, and indulges on the subject in a number of ambiguous remarks and witticisms. It is true that in *Héraclius* or *Œdipe* so many things take place that the pretence that the play does not last more than a day becomes laughable. Finally, it is true that Corneille had deliberately created a drama in which suspense was more important than the psychological interest, a drama that relied on the amazing, the incredible, the *invraisemblable*, that he had even stated that a tragedy should not be *vraisemblable*. Such features, which are not so obvious in his greatest plays, were not so much his own as those of his time—of the Baroque age of Rotrou, Du Ryer, or Tristan—and it is probable that Racine's last strictures ('un conquérant qui ne débiterait que des maximes d'amour', 'une femme qui donnerait des leçons de fierté à des conquérants') are directed not at Corneille but, in the first instance, at Quinault, in the second one at Thomas Corneille (see *Notes* to the *Première Préface*). The two Corneilles and Quinault were the three most successful playwrights of the time: if this interpretation is correct Racine's Preface could be considered not only a caustic attack against Corneille but a kind of manifesto against the reigning type of tragedy.

This manifesto, however, had its positive aspects. To his contemporaries Racine offered different models; instead of Corneille, Sophocles, twice mentioned, and the greatest among the poets of antiquity—Homer and Virgil. Because at the time of the Romantics the 'imitation of the ancients' had become an obstacle to originality, it is sometimes assumed that this is necessarily the case; but Greek and Latin poetry were more often an inspiration than an obstacle. Because Racine and La Fontaine loved and enjoyed the ancient writers, it is often assumed that this was general in the seventeenth century, or even that Racine meekly followed the accepted models of his time. This is almost the reverse of the truth. In the Jesuits' colleges Latin literature—much bowdlerized—was, it is true, the basis of education. But most writers in the seventeenth century were hostile to the ancients, and after the enthusiasm of the Renaissance the study and knowledge of Greek had sharply declined. Those who, like Racine, had a genuine love and understanding of Sophocles, Euripides, Homer,—because they could read the originals—were few. In presenting them as his chosen models Racine was challenging the dominant taste of his time; he was being as polemical and provocative as in the rest of his Preface.

But he was not being merely provocative. He also gave in his First Preface a brief but positive definition of his own conception of tragedy: 'une action simple, chargée de peu de matière, telle que doit être une action qui se passe en un seul jour, et qui s'avançant par degrés vers sa fin, n'est soutenue que par les intérêts, les sentiments et les passions des personnages.' Simplicity, continuity, concentration—this is of course very different from Shakespearian tragedy. If Shakespeare had written a play on a similar subject, he would have shown, in a series of discontinued scenes, *all* the highlights in Agrippina's career: Messalina's execution and Agrippina's marriage with her uncle, Claudius' murder and Nero's accession, Britannicus' death, and her own, at the hands of the assassins sent by her son. Out of this long, epic fresco Racine selects one day and one episode. All that comes before is suggested, not shown. Only the decisive moment in Nero's life and Agrippina's career, only the moment of crisis interests him, the moment when Nero becomes himself, rejecting his mother's authority, and asserting his own, through the murder of his rival. Fifteen or eighteen hours are all that Racine requires. There are, it is true, a number of events in his play: it begins shortly after Junie's kidnapping with Agrippine's unsuccessful attempt at seeing her son, and Britannicus' incautious arrival. The conspiracy with Pallas, and the Emperor's swift reaction, the quick succession of scenes between Néron and Junie, Junie and Britannicus, Britannicus and Néron can all take place in a few hours, while Agrippine raves at her disgrace. Her last attempt at re-establishing her ascendancy over her son, Néron's final hesitations, protracted as they are, and in the fifth Act the parting of the lovers and the murder—all this makes up a very full day, a day of feverish activity, but only at the end perhaps, with Junie's retreat, Narcisse's lynching, Néron's despair, do we feel that the rhythm of time is accelerating.

All the same, those who have struggled with the complexities of the politics in *Britannicus*, as well as of the relationships between the characters, may wonder a little about Racine's vaunted 'simplicity'. *Britannicus* of course is not simple in the way of *Bérénice*, which consists of little more than one action between two characters. In a way, there are several 'actions' in *Britannicus*: the conflict between Néron and Agrippine, the rivalry between Britannicus and Néron, the love of Junie and Britannicus, Néron's love for Junie; but all those actions are so closely interwoven and integrated that none can be dispensed with, or separated from the others: all are made into one single whole. In such a play the plot still matters, but the main interest is shifted to the characters. It is not so much what happens as why it happens that matters, and in that sense it can be said that Racine's tragedy 'n'est soutenue que par les intérêts, les sentiments, et les passions des personnages'. In his Preface to *Bérénice* Racine repeats many of his assertions, adding to his definition of tragedy that feeling of inevitable doom, that growing premonition of destruction which his heroes face without unseemly cries or vulgar demonstrations of grief, and which is the essence of tragedy, 'cette tristesse majestueuse qui fait tout le plaisir de la tragédie'.

In the Second Preface, written for the 1676 edition of his tragedies, nothing remains of the searing attacks of the first. *Britannicus* was now acknowledged by all as a masterpiece. By that time Racine could relax. He could afford to be generous too: Corneille, discouraged by an uninterrupted succession of failures, had finally ceased to write, and on the French tragic stage Racine no longer had any rival.

3. *Racine before 'Britannicus'*

In one of his more flippant moments, Jean Giraudoux in his *Racine* (translated by Mansell Jones) suggested that the poet who created some of the most tragic plays ever conceived lived himself the quiet, sheltered life of a sensible *bourgeois*. With all due respect to a great modern playwright, this is nonsense. If exotic travels and warlike exploits are needed to make a life eventful, Racine's was not. But his life is not exempt from the violence and passion of his plays, and his career is in some ways more astonishing than if he had, like his contemporary Bernier, explored the India of the Moguls. He was born in December 1639 in a tiny, sleepy town of provincial France, La Ferté-Milon, east of Paris, and his father was a petty official without standing or fortune even in his limited surroundings. Who could have predicted, in the rigid, caste-ridden society of Richelieu and Louis XIII, that Jean Racine would end his life as a wealthy nobleman, a gentleman of the Chamber in the almost mythical splendours of Versailles, and, in the middle of thousands of courtiers, one enjoying the particular favour of the *Roi-Soleil*?

Yet everything seemed to be against him. Before he was two he lost his mother; before he was three his father died. We know now that, to an infant child, these are traumatic shocks, deep injuries the scars of which Racine carried throughout his life. To them, perhaps, should be ascribed his extreme sensitivity, his morbid susceptibility, even, partly, the psychic depression which was brutally to interrupt his career for many years. Contemporaries tell us that while following the funeral of Mademoiselle Du Parc, a great actress he had loved, Racine was beside himself with grief, and had almost to be carried by his friends. Much later, towards the end of his life, when one of his daughters took the veil, her father wept irrepressibly during the whole impressive ceremony. The same man could write the most biting epigrams against those who stood in his way, and like Boileau or Voltaire, make obscure scribblers immortal.

The little orphaned family—Jean Racine had a sister to whom he remained attached—was shared between the paternal and maternal grandparents. The boy went to the Racines, but his grandfather died after a short time, and old Madame Racine (whom in his letters he always calls 'ma mère'), lonely, and probably in financial straits, soon retired to the convent of Port-Royal near Versailles, where her daughter, Sister Agnès, was a nun. The grandmother and the aunt brought up the child, and it seems now certain that he spent all his childhood at Port-Royal, that his earliest memories were of Port-Royal. But Port-Royal provided him not only with a home, but with a larger family, a background, an education. For Port-Royal was not only a convent: the 'Messieurs de Port-Royal', who lived in its vicinity, were laymen or ecclesiastics who devoted themselves to meditation, study, education—and also to violent polemics against their arch-enemies, the Jesuits. Port-Royal played a great part in the religious history of France, and it was the centre of the religious and political sect of the Jansenists. The 'Messieurs' adopted the orphan; they admitted him to their classes, the 'Petites-Ecoles', in which those learned, dedicated men educated in small groups a limited number of children (there were never more than fifty altogether, and often fewer). Such an education, even if it was not given for profit, was very expensive: it was given free to this obviously gifted child. Racine saw in Port-Royal some of the eminent men of his time, Arnauld and Pascal. For Hamon, the physician of the convent, he developed a passionate affection: half a century later, he was to ask in his will to be buried at the feet of Hamon. Lemaître and Nicole were his teachers, and we still have a letter addressed by Lemaître to 'le petit Racine', and signed 'votre papa'.

The Petites-Ecoles catered for younger children. When he was fourteen Racine left them and spent two years in another college at Beauvais. When he came back in 1656 he found the place in total confusion. The struggle with the Jesuits was reaching its climax, and in his *Lettres Provinciales*, Pascal had dealt them such mighty blows that to this day they have not quite recovered from them. In retaliation the Jesuits had had the Messieurs expelled from Port-Royal, and the Petites-Ecoles closed down, by order of Cardinal Mazarin. The children were being sent away, back to their parents, or to friends of the sect. Racine had no parents, but he had a cousin, Nicolas Vitart, who was to be a faithful friend to him, and who was the steward of a great and wealthy lord, the Duke of Luynes. The Duke had for many years lived the humble life of the Messieurs—or 'Solitaires'—and he had now built near the convent a small but beautiful castle, the Château de Vaumurier; and to Vaumurier Racine went. There he was to study with the Duke's son (the future Duke of Chevreuse, to whom *Britannicus* was dedicated), under Lancelot, also one of the Messieurs and probably the greatest hellenist in France. His initiation to Greek culture was the last, and the most priceless, gift Port-Royal conferred upon Racine. Throughout his life he went on reading and annotating Homer, Aeschylus, Sophocles, Euripides. Two of his later tragedies, *Iphigénie* and *Phèdre* are directly inspired by Greek plays. In Greek poetry he found a corrective to what was over-refined and over-elaborate in the poetry of his time, a justification of his instinctive dislike of rhetoric and bombast, and the suggestion of a type of tragedy that Corneille had not suspected, a tragedy with a new sense of fatality and a more poignant pathos. But of course Latin authors, Virgil and Tacitus, were important to him too. And of course Racine's tragedies are very different from Greek tragedies.

Port-Royal, then, played a most important part in Racine's life. To the moral severity of Jansenism, no doubt, to its insistence on seeing through the disguises in which men clothe their selfishness,

Racine's psychological insight is to some extent due. To the Jansenists' harsh conception of God and life (their enemies accused them of professing Calvin's predestination) can be partly traced Racine's pessimistic view of man's condition. But Racine was a poet, not a theologian; his plays cannot be bound within the narrow range of a system, and his experience and intuition of life were wider and deeper than those of Arnauld or Nicole. When all is said, Jansenism does not, in my opinion, give us the key to Racine's tragic universe, and it would be unprofitable to dwell on it too long. If it can be granted that Racine would not have been Racine without Port-Royal, it is even more certain that Racine would never have become Racine if he had not broken away from Port-Royal. But when he had come back from his disappointing journey to Provence Racine's mind was made up: he would not live the austere life of a 'Solitaire'.

Already he had made several, unsuccessful, dramatic attempts. He was now busy writing *Les Frères ennemis*. He was also frequenting actors and actresses. In Port-Royal there was pious anxiety. All theatre to the Jansenists was abomination: 'a novelist and a playwright', Nicole had written, 'are public poisoners, not of the bodies, but of the souls'. After several warnings Sister Agnès, Racine's aunt, delivered an ultimatum: either he would give up his shameful life, or they would not see him any more. The ultimatum was ignored.

These were anxious, crucial times to the twenty-three-year-old rebel. He had no profession, and no resources whatsoever; he was existing on loans from his cousin. On his return to Paris the Duke of Luynes again gave him hospitality; even more important he, or his friend the Duke of Liancourt, introduced him to Court. Already Racine had composed poems in praise of Louis or his Queen; he had received gifts from the King, and was soon to receive a pension. But all this did not make a career. The remarkable phenomenon of Jean Racine's career was due to his talent, no doubt, but also to a single-minded ambition, born of a kind of desperation, a resolve not to fall back into the suffocating life from which he had escaped. His first play, *La Thébaïde, ou les Frères ennemis* (1664), owed a great deal to Rotrou's *Antigone*; it told the story of Oedipus' children; as is sometimes the case in a beginner's play, Racine had rather overdone the horror, and all the characters died a violent death; the style could hardly be called Racinian, but the outlines of what was to become Racinian tragedy were already there. *Alexandre le*

Grand (1666), which takes place in an India of which Racine knew nothing, was much better written, but less original. It is one of the least Racinian of Racine's plays. Yet its success is easily explained, so well had Racine caught the prevailing mood of the elegant, sensuous, pleasure-loving Court that surrounded the King, and that very success perhaps encouraged him to be himself. *Andromaque* (1667) had a most ingenious plot, and its dramatic progress was most cleverly contrived: Oreste loves Hermione, who loves Pyrrhus, who loves Andromaque, Hector's widow, who can never forget that Pyrrhus' father killed the only man she ever loved. Exasperated, Pyrrhus is now threatening the life of Andromaque's and Hector's son. The whole play revolves around Andromaque's hesitations: whenever she refuses to listen to the destroyer of Troy, Pyrrhus in anger goes back to Hermione, and Oreste is in despair. When Andromaque remembers the danger to her son, she tries to placate Pyrrhus, who turns away from Hermione, to her fury, and to the joy of Oreste. But now love, hatred, and jealousy spoke with new voices. For the first time in Racine's dark, implacable world, passion sang its anguished music.

Andromaque was followed by *Les Plaideurs* (1668), Racine's only comedy, and a farce rather than a comedy. It was inspired by Aristophanes' *Wasps*, but gave Racine an opportunity to make fun of the legal profession—who happened to be very discontented with Colbert's and the King's policy. *Les Plaideurs* makes little attempt at *vraisemblance*: in its conception it looks back to Scarron and Desmarets rather than to Molière, and the acrobatics of its style, its verbal humour, its buffoonery leave it far below Molière's great comedies. And then came *Britannicus*.

At the time of *Alexandre* Racine had quarrelled with Molière. Dissatisfied with Molière's production of his play, he took it to the rival company of the Hôtel de Bourgogne, which from now on was to perform all his tragedies. He also took away from Molière one of his best actresses, Mademoiselle Du Parc. She became his mistress. They had a child, a little girl, who was secretly baptized and brought up in the country. Then a second child was on its way. What happened next is not clear. Perhaps Mademoiselle Du Parc died in childbirth. Perhaps Racine sought the aid of a doubtful character, the woman Voisin, who provided all sorts of drugs, and the attempted abortion went wrong. . . . It is strange to think of the brilliant courtier, the famous author, the King's friend, mixed up with the Paris underworld. What is certain is that at once—stupidity or blackmail?—ugly rumours began to circulate: Racine had hidden away his mistress; he had robbed her; he had poisoned her.... This was the time when Racine wrote *Britannicus*. For years he must have lived in dread. And the time came when his worst fears nearly came true. In 1679, an enormous scandal burst out in Paris: it became known that 'la Voisin', who has remained more notorious even than 'la fameuse Locuste' of *Britannicus* (l. 1392), had sold poisons to large numbers of people; even great names were involved.... Under torture, the poisoner accused Racine. The order for his arrest was prepared; it was never carried out. It seems likely that only his great protectors saved Racine from disaster.

After *Britannicus*, Racine wrote another Roman play, *Bérénice* (1670). It is the most often quoted, but not the most representative, example of Racinian simplicity; in it Racine boasted that he had made 'something out of nothing', for the whole tragedy consists of the separation of Titus and Bérénice. The part of Bérénice was created by another great actress, Mademoiselle de Champmeslé; she consoled him for the loss of Mademoiselle Du Parc, but also gave him first-hand experience of the jealousy he was to describe so often in his plays. *Bajazet* (1672) is very different from *Bérénice*: whereas no blood is shed in *Bérénice*, *Bajazet* is, as Madame de Sévigné called it, 'une grande tuerie'. Its source is a contemporary episode in Turkish history, and it takes place in Constantinople. With *Mithridate* (1674) we remain in the East but go back to antiquity; it tells the story of an old man's love for a girl, and of his rivalry with his own sons. *Iphigénie à Aulis* (1675) is based on the famous legend of the human sacrifice which the gods exacted from the Greeks before they allowed their ships to sail against Troy; Racine, unexpectedly, saves Iphigénie, although an alternative victim is found. *Phèdre* (1677) is Racine's most celebrated play; never before had Racine created such strident, almost unbearable tragedy, or such compelling poetry. What happened after he wrote *Phèdre* we do not know, but it seems certain that Racine passed through a profound crisis. Soon after he ceased to write tragedies, became reconciled with Port-Royal (he was soon to become one of their leaders), and married a girl who had never read a line of his plays and gave him six children, all brought up along the strictest Jansenist lines (Racine begged his elder son never to show himself in a theatre). He was still in great favour at the Court; he was the King's historiographer, the *protégé* not only of the Colberts but of Madame de Maintenon, whom the King secretly married. Only at Madame de Maintenon's express prayer did he write two more plays, both derived from the Bible: *Esther* (1689), which can hardly be called a tragedy, and the powerful drama of *Athalie*, in which Racine showed he was still himself. Both plays use music and song. Both were written for amateur actresses, and never performed publicly in Racine's lifetime. He died in 1699.

4. 'Britannicus' and its sources

A full survey of the sources of *Britannicus* has no place in an Introduction of this kind, for an attempt at reconstructing the genesis of the play should consider all the texts which may have set the poet's imagination in motion, the differences as well as the resemblances, and space does not allow for such a detailed comparison. There were of course in the seventeenth century a number of plays dealing with Imperial Rome, and several which portrayed Nero: Tristan's *La Mort de Sénèque* is centred on a conspiracy against the Emperor; Gilbert's *Arie et Pétus* tells the story of 'un amour de Néron', and rails at his artistic pretensions; Corneille's *Othon* contains numerous references to Nero's reign, and evokes the implacable rivalries of a world in which, as Corneille puts it with sombre energy, 'Il faut, quoi qu'il arrive, ou périr ou régner' (236). But in none of these plays do we find equivalents of Agrippine, Junie, or Britannicus, or none of them contains any suggestion of what is perhaps the central theme of Racine's *Britannicus*, the birth of Néron's character, *le monstre naissant*. And even if Gilbert and Corneille played their part in directing Racine's attention towards the period and the subject he chose, as soon as he had made up his mind to write a play about Néron, Agrippine, and Britannicus, he went back to the original texts, like the true humanist his teachers at Port-Royal had made him, and Tacitus' *Annals* became his chief inspiration, with Seneca a secondary but not unimportant one, and a few suggestions from Suetonius.

With Tacitus Racine fell in love: he is, he says, 'le plus grand peintre de l'antiquité'. 'Il n'y a presque pas un trait éclatant dans ma tragédie', he declares in his *Seconde Préface*, 'dont il ne m'ait donné l'idée'. Racine was not content to read the few chapters devoted in the *Annals* to Britannicus' murder and to the events that led up to it; he often makes use of passages and pieces of information which are in other parts of the *Annals*, subtly altering them to fit them into the pattern of his play, and a careful study of *Appendix I* would be instructive from that point of view. In fact the whole historical background in *Britannicus* is borrowed from Tacitus, as well as allusions to people, events, customs, and to the peculiar institutions of the Roman 'Republic' under the first Emperors, whose power ultimately depended on the army, and more immediately on those picked legionaries encamped at the gates of Rome, shock-troops and body-guards: the praetorians. No wonder the commander of the guards—Burrhus in the play—is now a power in the State, and Agrippine, whose father Germanicus the soldiers still remember with affection, can threaten to rouse them and have Néron dethroned. In spite of all this it cannot be said that Racine has simply distributed into acts and scenes the matter provided by Tacitus. His chief innovation was the introduction of Junie. It is true that, to confound his critics, he managed to find some kind of historical justification for her existence (see the two Prefaces). But Junie's character has nothing whatsoever in common with Junia Calvina; the whole story of her love for Britannicus has no historical basis, nor was she ever loved by Nero. The double rivalry of the two youths is an invention of Racine, and the tangle of passion and ambition in which Néron, Junie, Britannicus, and Agrippine are inextricably involved, and which constitutes the essence of the drama, is therefore of Racine's making. However accurate the allusions to contemporary history, however carefully the poet has inserted his tragedy into the reality of the time, it is not exaggerated to say that *Britannicus* is the creation of Racine's imagination.

It may be granted, though, that Racine invents in the spirit of history, for there *was* a woman Néron loved, to the jealous fury of Agrippine. But, unlike Junie, Acte was no Princess of the Blood: a former slave, she loved Néron humbly and truly, to the last; after Néron's horrible end, she it was who gave the abandoned corpse of the still young Caesar a decent burial. Of the other characters Agrippine is the one who remains nearest to Tacitus: her genius for intrigue, her courage, her cruelty, her outbursts of temper, her shrewdness, and her blindness are all in the *Annals*; even her posses-sive love for her son has its basis in the sinister suggestions of incest which the seventeenth-century *bienséances* did not allow Racine to

mention openly. The ambitious Britannicus is in Tacitus; Britannicus the lover is, as we saw, Racine's invention. And Racinian
too is the compassion the character arouses, for Tacitus, in spite
of a few words of sympathy (XII, 25; XIII, 15), concludes with some
surprisingly harsh remarks: Britannicus, he says, would have come
to no good, being too thoroughly stained by a corrupt Court and its
corrupt ruler. As for Néron, we know that the general feeling was
that Racine had made him too mild, and his Néron, compared to
Tristan's or to Gilbert's, must appear scrupulous and timid. Yet
Racine's treatment of the character, far from being timid, was daring
in the extreme, for it flew in the face of deeply rooted traditions and
emotions. Nero had been the first of the Christians' cruel perse-
cutors, and he had always remained in the imagination of men the
predestined enemy of God's working in this world, an almost
Luciferian power, the earthly incarnation of Satan. This supernatural vision Racine had the audacity to conceive and recreate as a
human being, and by and large his approach to his character is that
of Tacitus. Tacitus dwells even more than Racine upon Nero's
moderation in the first years of his reign, and Britannicus' murder is
briefly but clearly motivated: the co-existence of two rivals with such
valid claims was not a good prospect for the tranquillity of Rome;
Agrippina's terrible threats upset the young Emperor all the more
because he was aware that Britannicus was neither resigned to his
fate nor devoid of courage or intelligence. And from that point he
had no hesitation: he had sensed the danger, made his decision,
and he pressed and bullied his killers relentlessly. Here the Racinian
Néron's protracted resistance to Narcisse is a significant change which
gives the character an entirely new dimension. But generally
speaking, Tacitus, while not concealing his distaste and horror at
Nero's crimes, is careful to preserve an open mind: there is no
evidence, he says, that Nero killed Burrhus; it is very doubtful that
he instigated the burning of Rome; Agrippina's murder is connected
with the alleged incest, of which she was said to have boasted; not
morality but superstition might have taken fright at such a sacrilege
and caused the fall of the Emperor; in more ways than one Agrippina
was a public menace. In their final farewell Nero embraced her for
a long time: crowning piece of hypocrisy? or genuine emotion?
Tacitus wonders. When the first attempt had failed sheer terror
caused the second one, for Agrippina was capable of everything....
Racine was infected by Tacitus' determination to understand, to

get at the elusive truth hidden in the hearts of men. Insight took the place of religious bias, moral indignation, and baroque rhetoric.

Narcisse and Burrhus have little to do with their historical name-sakes in Tacitus. The real Narcisse, one of the 'trois affranchis' (200) who ruled Rome under Claudius, was killed by Agrippina's order at the very beginning of Nero's reign; he was never a tutor to Britannicus or an informer to Nero; the whole part is of Racine's invention. To some extent the same could be said of Burrhus. Of Nero's two 'gouverneurs', whose dramatic functions might have overlapped, Racine kept only one: 'J'ai choisi Burrhus', he says in his Preface, 'et je l'ai choisi plutôt que Sénèque. . . .' But has Racine really chosen Burrhus? Burrhus' profile is, in Tacitus, briefly but deeply engraved: his physical courage and the cruel mutilation he had suffered at war, his harshness (Nero stood in fear of him) were only one side of the man; there was in him the innocent craftiness of the regular soldier. When Agrippina made him commander of the guards he knew what was expected of him. But this did not trouble him because as a soldier he was used to obeying his superiors' orders without asking himself or anybody awkward questions. He was a practical man, and a simple man devoid of any petty *amour-propre*. Such a character belonged to a level of reality which had no place in Racinian tragedy: he was at the same time too homely and too stark, too cynical and too rugged. But Seneca had different disadvantages; he was a philosopher, with a doctrine and a system, a sage, given to sententiousness and finger-waving, a 'square' in the world of teenagers of *Britannicus*. To Racine and to Racine's public he would have been, in 1669, a bore. Neither Seneca nor Burrhus then would do, and Racine chose neither: he chose both and made them into one. As an 'honnête homme' Burrhus would serve his purpose, but the rough, one-handed veteran, the strict disciplinarian used to the clipped orders and military brusqueness of the guard-room and the camp was conveniently dropped. What was needed was a character with Burrhus' courage and loyalty, who could, under the impulse of strong emotion, invent or rediscover, draw from himself, so to speak, those political principles which could be found in Seneca's *De Clementia*. A soldier with a clear, coherent policy, a regular whose life-long experience of war would not have clouded his vision of the ideal State and the ideal ruler, and who would know how to express it with polished yet moving eloquence; an intellectual soldier and a passionate philosopher; at any rate a soldier-philosopher, in short: Seneca-Burrhus.

For if Tacitus' influence is all-important in Britannicus, Seneca's is also present. In his *De Clementia ad Neronem*, composed for, and addressed to, Nero in the first year of his reign as a kind of advisory manifesto of his political principles, Seneca constantly opposes the unhappiness of the tyrant to the serenity of the good ruler, the security which is brought about by lenient government to the perpetual fear which harshness and violence produce, the infamy that will be the lot of the despot, to the benevolent king's enduring glory. The tyrant is caught in a vicious circle of crimes: 'For this is the worst thing about cruelty: one must go on with it; it offers no way back to better things; crimes must be upheld by crimes (*scelera enim sceleribus tuenda*)', (XIII, 2). 'For the tyrant is hated because he is feared, and he wants to be feared because he is hated' (XII, 4). 'He does not know what blind fury is aroused in men when hatreds go beyond measure. . . . The most dauntless courage is the one that is born of dire necessity. . . .' Then 'men rejoice in facing dangers and throw away their lives as if they were not their own' (XII, 4, 5,). 'The harsh, bloodthirsty tyrant, his own mercenaries hate him. . . . He who rules by murder and violence, who no longer trusts the fidelity of his friends and his children's love . . . lives in fear of death, and more often wishes for it' (XIII, 1, 3). All these ideas reappear in Burrhus' impassioned plea to Néron (1343–54. Cf. too 1684–6), and so does the praise of clemency (1355–64): the ruler's security, Seneca said, depends on clemency, but so does his felicity (XIII, 1, 4,); his final reward is in the love of his subjects: '. . . the ruler who cares for the good of each and all . . . people do not on his passage (*eo procedente*) flee as they would from an evil, dangerous beast sallied from its den; they fly towards him (*advolant*), struggling as if to contemplate a bright and beneficent star' (III, 3). Finally the *De Clementia* was certainly in Racine's mind when he wrote the first and second scenes of his first Act. Twice Néron is compared to Augustus (30, 84), whom Seneca constantly offers as a model to his pupil (IX, X, etc.). But Seneca's admiration is not uncritical: he dwells at length on the violence upon which Octavian established his rule, on the civil war, the murders, the proscriptions. This in Racine will become Agrippine's sinister premonition that Néron's reign might end as that of Augustus had begun (34). Another reminiscence of the *De Clementia* explains Racine's reference to Néron as father of his people (29, 47), an unexpected expression for a youth of eighteen. Suetonius only briefly mentions the fact that Nero refused the title of *Pater Patriae*; it is Seneca who develops at length the idea that the ruler must be, as Augustus was, a father to his subjects (XIV, 1).

Not to the *De Clementia* but to Seneca's *Apokolokyntosis* should be referred Racine's repeated allusions (202, 214) to the freedom and happiness of Rome after the end of a tyrannical reign. On the day of Claudius' funeral, Seneca says, 'The Roman people walked like free men' (XII, 2). And three times in the *Apokolokyntosis* (which Racine also quotes in his Preface when referring to Junia Calvina, 'the liveliest of girls'), there is a mention of Silanus' death (VIII, 2; XI, 4; XIII, 5). Finally Seneca praises without irony Nero's poetical gifts as well as his physical comeliness. Much of this could be found in Tacitus, but this youthful Nero, seen in a hopeful light at a time when no one could predict his career of crime, must have helped Racine to approach his character with a fresh vision.

Certainly there is a link too between *Britannicus* and the tragedy of *Octavia*, written in the first century A.D. by an anonymous contemporary and imitator of Seneca (in what follows for 'Seneca' read 'Pseudo-Seneca'), and many ideas of the *De Clementia* have found their way into *Octavia*. Some lines in *Britannicus* are clear reminiscences from the Latin play:

> Seul reste du débris d'une illustre famille (556

calls to mind the Senecan

> Magni resto nominis umbra (71)
> (I am left the mere shadow of a great name)

> Eussiez-vous pu prétendre
> Qu'un jour Claude à son fils dût préférer son gendre? (1143)

can be referred to the Senecan Claudius

> qui nato suo
> Praeferre potuit sanguine alieno satum. (139)
> (who to his own son
> Could prefer the scion of an alien race.)

> Genitamque fratre coniugem captus sibi
> toris nefandis flebili iunxit face. (141)
> (His brother's daughter he made his wife, she lured
> [him
> to a baneful bed, to grievous nuptials.)

clearly suggests *Britannicus* 1133–37. But in the plot or in the characters, the relationship between the two plays becomes elusive or dubious. In *Octavia* only the ghost of Agrippina appears on the stage; Britannicus has been dead for years, and it is highly artificial to take the wholly passive, purely pathetic Octavia as a model for the firm, clear-sighted Junie. The significance of Seneca lies elsewhere. Tacitus, for all the potential drama and tragedy in the *Annals*, remains aloof and strives never to allow his feelings to cloud his judgment. With Seneca, Tacitus' grim struggle for power and for life passes into the realm of poetry. With Seneca, with Racine in a deeper manner, Tacitus' concrete, historical individuals rise above the level of the particular to assume their full poetical dimensions. The murder of Britannicus is not just an incident in the harsh fight for survival at the Roman Court. It becomes, in the Senecan vision of Agrippina's ghost risen from Tartarus, as in the Racinian curse of the mother upon her son, the first momentous step into an abyss of horror, loneliness, and death. The weaker Britannicus is not only the expected loser in his violent collision with Néron; he is, in Seneca and in Racine, the pitiful youth marked out with all his youthful hopes for inevitable death, the *infelix puer*, whose harrowing memory will forever haunt Junie, as it haunts Octavia: 'Britannicus, o brilliant star, ... now but a handful of dust, a melancholy ghost'. And Agrippine's curse encompasses Néron's whole life, as if, like the Senecan ghost, she could see it at one glance from outside time and outside life, from the timelessness of her own death.

Other texts no doubt played their part in the creation of *Britannicus*; so did other kinds of influences: the political situation in Racine's own time, his own life, conscious and unconscious (Mauron). But here the scholar is on treacherous ground: obvious resemblances may be purely coincidental; what had really stirred the poet's imagination may have been so completely transposed as to be unrecognizable. The study of sources is not only an endless task; in so far as it takes us *away* from the text, it is beyond a certain point an unrewarding and unprofitable one.

5. *'Une action simple ... qui n'est soutenue que par les intérêts, les sentiments, et les passions des personnages.'*

A tragedy was first of all, according to Aristotle's definition, 'the imitation of an action'. Authors and critics, the poets as well as the 'doctes', always eager to retain from Aristotle what suited them and to ignore the rest, were quick to accept the apparent primacy

Aristotle gave to the *action*. Tragedy to them was above all *drama*, whether this meant a succession of changes in the balance of power between the conflicting wills of the play, as in Corneille, or, as in Quinault and others, an uninterrupted cascade of incidents, an ever-moving kaleidoscope of swiftly changing situations. Racine was too much of his own time, wished too keenly for success, not to give great care to the workings of drama in his tragedy. With him, however, the emphasis is no longer on suspense but on insight and understanding, and the feelings and passions of the characters are now in the foreground. This does not mean that a Racinian tragedy consists of psychological analysis, or even that it can be assimilated to a 'roman d'analyse' like *La Princesse de Clèves*, or *Adolphe*. The characters express, reveal, or betray themselves rather than explain themselves: even when they do explain themselves, it does not follow that they understand themselves; it is for us to draw the conclusions. Lucid and perceptive as they often are, Racine's heroes can also be amazingly blind and headstrong. Nevertheless Racine possessed a sense of the inner life, an immediate intuition of human behaviour which is without parallel in the seventeenth century. An understanding of his characters is therefore fundamental, the first and essential step in the understanding of his drama, his poetry, his tragedy.

Agrippine

'It is Agrippine above all whom I have tried to portray most faithfully', Racine says in his Second Preface, 'and my tragedy deals no less with Agrippine's disgrace than with Britannicus' death.' And in fact the whole tragedy could be read as the gradual decline of Agrippine's power, slowly eaten up from the inside, until it is but an empty shell that collapses into dust. But this complex character is revealed to us little by little. In the first Act Agrippine is a proud, self-assured, apparently invincible fighter; an aggressive, power-hungry woman, whose ambition could never stop short of supreme authority; a Lady Macbeth who will never be troubled by remorse, or haunted by the blood on her hands. To her powerful, calculating mind murder is only a means to an end; blood lust is as alien to her as rancour or remorse; she strikes when she has to, and goes her way without a further thought for the fallen victims; but she is just as ready to reverse her alliances, and support those she has brought down. A proud patrician whose ancestors have ruled Rome for centuries, she has grown up in the middle of soldiers, and is at ease among the praetorians. Yet when power is to be gained Agrippine does not shrink from 'lowering her pride', and offering herself to a former slave ('Je fléchis mon orgueil, j'allai prier Pallas', 1129. Racine's phrase was hardly a euphemism in a society as caste-conscious as seventeenth-century France). There does not seem to be a chink in the armour of this relentless, ever-resourceful, ever-watchful character, 'l'implacable Agrippine'.

The story of her slow ascent to power she tells herself, in memorable lines, in the second scene of the fourth Act (1123–1194). For years she had foreseen every obstacle, prepared for every eventuality, gradually suppressing or removing all opponents, filling with her own devotees Claudius' government, his palace, his guard, his bedroom, patiently biding her time, and when the time was ripe, striking quickly, decisively, without the shadow of a scruple, at the old man whose love she had deliberately aroused and exploited. No wonder Burrhus is appalled at the apparent levity with which Néron challenges such a dangerous enemy:

> Agrippine, Seigneur, est toujours redoutable.
> Rome et tous vos soldats révèrent ses aïeux; ...
> Elle sait son pouvoir; vous savez son courage, ... (768)

Against Agrippine Néron's rebellion seems futile; Seneca, Burrhus, Narcisse are lightweights; Britannicus is but a child; how could they hope to shake Agrippine's power? Yet at the end of the play that power lies in ruins; her cunning plot to play Britannicus against Néron has been brutally exploded; Néron's long dependence is at an end; and in a sudden intuition, which is not dissimilar to the prophetic vision of another of Racine's great fallen Queens, Athalie, Agrippine foresees her own doom:

> Ta main a commencé par le sang de ton frère.
> Je prévois que tes coups viendront jusqu'à ta mère. (1675)

How was such a reversal made possible? Circumstances have changed, but Agrippine has changed too. The Agrippine we see in *Britannicus* is but a shadow of the great Agrippine of the past. Then her goal was simple, well defined, and, however ambitious, attainable: the substitution of Néron for Britannicus as heir presumptive, and the elimination of the ageing Claudius. Now it is no longer enough for her to have made an Emperor; she herself must rule the Empire and the Emperor. Against the secular tradition of

25

Rome she claims the eagles and the fasces; she claims dominance over the ancient seat of Roman power, the Senate; she, a woman, seeks to rule that world of men. And against the very course of nature she strives to keep her son in the everlasting dependence of childhood: 'Dans une longue enfance ils l'auraient fait vieillir', Burrhus says of those unworthy tutors he does not want to resemble; consciously or not, Agrippine has no other purpose. When the play begins there is in the Empress Mother's policy more than a touch of megalomania, a *hubris*, a defiance not of the gods, for there are no gods in *Britannicus*, but of a certain natural order of things; a warped view of what is possible and what is not, of what is, and of what might be. Even what seems—and to some extent is—a sharp insight into the future ('Contre Britannicus Néron s'est déclaré') is, at this stage, a premature conclusion, which will hasten what Agrippine wishes to avoid.

Above all Agrippine, incomprehensibly at first, seems to have forgotten all her craft and her wisdom. In her long ascending march to the throne she never seemed to put one foot wrong; in the play she never puts one right. Her daring plan to hold the balance between Britannicus and Néron made sense only on the assumption that Néron would yield at once, that he would not, and could not, defy her power. When he does, Agrippine is compelled to persist in a course which becomes more and more dangerous to herself. Even the inexperienced Britannicus sees his chance: he does his best to compromise the Empress, and making use of her great name quickly gathers a party of discontented senators. But he succeeds only too well: Agrippine suddenly takes fright and withdraws. Later she will explain, or rationalize, her retreat: what could she expect from the Emperor Britannicus, whose father she has murdered, or from his wife, the Empress Junie, when she has caused the death of her two brothers? In fact the plot with which she tried to blackmail Néron into submission has backfired; her bluff has been called; her great design was still-born. Agrippine instinctively shrinks from the abyss she herself has opened under her own feet, and she sends Britannicus away with vague promises about his sister.

Such incoherent marches and counter-marches like those of an incompetent general will soon become clear. Ever since Junie's appearance Agrippine's behaviour can no longer be explained in terms of power politics, is no longer commanded in fact by motives of mere ambition. It is not just the cold, ruthless will to preserve her

power that makes her plot against the Emperor, any more than it is
caution alone, and political acumen that make her withdraw her
support from Britannicus. When in a fit of uncontrollable passion
Agrippine says loud and clear that Néron's adoption is invalid, that
Britannicus is the rightful heir to the throne, when she threatens to
take him to the praetorians' camp, and throwing in the balance the
immense prestige of her name and her father's name, to have him
proclaimed Emperor, the consequences of such a move are clear to
any listener: Agrippine, who in a few hours will curse Néron's
parricide, is now plotting the downfall and inevitable death of her
son. At that moment even the awareness of her own danger ('Quand
je devrais du Ciel hâter l'arrêt fatal . . .') cannot stop her: self-interest
and self-preservation have gone by the board; reason in the service
of ambition no longer guides the Empress; passion and jealousy have
taken over. Whatever Agrippine may say at times, Néron is not to
her a mere tool of her ambition, a replaceable cog in the vast
machinery of her plans (she could not have ruled more completely
than she did through Claudius). Her love, though demanding and
imperious, is love all the same, and in the very first lines of the play
she claims Néron's love as of right ('Il me le doit, Albine'). But in the
dictatorial soul of Agrippine love must imply dependence; there is
between her son and her a deep sense of identity, almost a physical
tie; Néron is an extension of herself, he is part of herself, but it must
be a subordinate part. When Néron resentfully states that 'Vous
n'*avez* sous mon nom travaillé que pour vous', and Agrippine
dramatically replies: 'O Ciel . . . T'ai-je fait quelques vœux qui ne
fussent pour lui?' they are both saying the same thing. In the third
Act Agrippine's possessive love unexpectedly explodes into fierce
jealousy of the woman who will detract from her honours (but it
seems incredible that Agrippine has never considered the eventuality
of Néron falling in love, never taken it into account in her plans),
jealousy above all of the woman who will steal from her the love
of her son. The words she uses are not those of a crafty politician
but of a betrayed lover:

> C'est à moi qu'on donne une rivale. . . .
> Ma place est occupée . . .
> Une autre de César a surpris la tendresse,
> Elle aura le pouvoir d'épouse et de maîtresse, . . .
> Que dis-je? l'on m'évite, et déjà délaissée . . .
> Néron, l'ingrat Néron . . .
>
> (880)

If jealous love, not merely calculating ambition, turns into blind and self-destroying hatred, it is love again—self-love in a way, love of her own flesh and blood—and not only the clear perception of her own peril, that stays Agrippine's hand, and reduces to empty words her promises and her threats. But it is too late: nothing now can undo them, and if Burrhus no doubt refrained from betraying the Empress, others did not. Néron cannot ignore them: he must and will draw the consequences, to Britannicus first:

> Et je ne prétends pas que sa coupable audace
> Une seconde fois lui promette ma place. (1319)

and to Agrippine later. After her open challenge to Néron Agrippine has only one way open to her (and the old Agrippine would have known and accepted the fact): she must follow it up to the bitter end, to the utter destruction of Néron. She cannot, except at her extreme peril, retrace her steps: she must now conquer, or be conquered. 'Men become enemies', Machiavelli says, 'for the sake of hatred, or of fear. The Ruler must destroy those who are likely, or bound, to cause him harm.' From the harsh logic of this conclusion Agrippine draws back: she cannot destroy the son she loves and hates, and that weakness, if it is one, will cost her her life. Like Athalie again, Agrippine will perish not because of her crimes, but because of her love. After a long career of murders, through a sudden and, to herself, incomprehensible impulse of compassion and love ('Je serais sensible à la pitié?'), Athalie will spare the child Eliacin, and that one impulse is enough to cause her ruin. In the terrible world of Racine, perhaps the most cruel and implacable ever created by a poet, mercy is offered at the peril of one's life, men and women perish through their virtues as often as through their vices.

When Néron openly accuses his mother of plotting against him:

> Vous voulez présenter mon rival à l'armée.
> Déjà jusques au camp le bruit en a couru. (1256)

Agrippine indignantly denies the charge:

> Moi, le faire Empereur, ingrat? L'avez-vous cru?

We know she is lying. And yet she is not altogether lying: the plot was real, and Néron has every right to feel himself threatened, but at the same time Agrippine has so completely refused its implications, she has so passionately put it out of her mind, that she hardly believes she ever contemplated it. Racinian heroes have lucid,

28

powerful minds, which passion makes liable to astonishing fits of blindness and self-deception; they are logical, coherent personalities capable of the most unexpected *volte-faces* and contradictions, and it is on this point perhaps that Taine's analysis of Racine's psychology is at its most preposterous ('Ses personnages sont des êtres abstraits plutôt que des hommes réels; il esquisse un contour, il n'approfondit pas une physionomie; il développe une vertu, il ne construit pas un caractère. . . . Il saisit quelque passion simple, la fierté, l'emporte-ment . . . et il en fait une âme'). When Néron—no more 'le timide Néron'—sternly accuses her of putting him and the State in danger, Agrippine breaks down. There could be no greater mistake in the interpretation of the character than to doubt the sincerity of her grief. Her tears are real tears; her despair and sudden longing for death are genuine:

> Avec ma liberté, que vous m'avez ravie,
> Si vous le souhaitez, prenez encor ma vie;
> Pourvu que par ma mort tout le peuple irrité
> Ne vous ravisse pas ce qui m'a tant coûté.   (1283)

And at this late moment, when Narcisse is preparing the poison, and it seems that nothing Agrippine can say will alter the course of events, suddenly everything becomes possible again, and Agrippine is given a last chance. For Néron had strengthened himself against her violence, but he was not prepared for her tears. His hard-won determination weakens and dissolves: 'Hé bien donc! prononcez: que voulez-vous qu'on fasse?' For a brief moment victory is within her reach . . . or it would be if, for one moment, Agrippine could stop thinking in terms of defeat and victory. But her terrific will-power re-asserts itself almost in spite of herself: she pounces on her prey; the catalogue of her demands is ready; she makes no conces-sions; what she asks for is unconditional surrender: Néron will bow, and will be seen to bow, to his mother's will in all things, great and small. While Agrippine proudly dictates her terms, she does not see that Néron, just in time, has got out of her trap.

In the fourth Act it is still possible to wonder if, even though her grief is genuine, Agrippine does not make use of it once more to force her son into obedience. In the fifth Act no doubt is possible: in her son's arms Agrippine's hard, masculine spirit has mellowed, her suspicions have melted. She has forgotten her dark forebodings of the first Act, or rather she confesses having been mistaken in her judgment. On Néron's face she sees nothing but love and respect.

When he is about to burst into existence she does not discern any
more 'le fier Domitius'. There is, she says, no malice in Néron.
Néron is a faithful son, therefore Néron is a great Emperor: 'auguste'
she calls him. How good and kind is Néron!

> Ah! si vous aviez vu par combien de caresses
> Il m'a renouvelé la foi de ses promesses!
> Par quels embrassements il vient de m'arrêter!
> Ses bras dans nos adieux ne pouvaient me quitter.
> Sa facile bonté, sur son front répandue,
> Jusqu'aux moindres secrets est d'abord descendue.
> Il s'épanchait en fils, . . .   (1587)

Such accents are unmistakable. And why should Agrippine now
play a part for the sake of Junie, of whose presence she is hardly
aware? Like a mistress who knows herself to be loved after fearing
she was abandoned, 'délaissée', Agrippine is now becoming herself
again. Proudly she looks around for new enemies to bring down, new
victories to be won, new peaks of power to be reached. Like the
Shakespearian Caesar dreaming of cosmic omnipotence while the
conspirators are closing in upon him, Agrippine sings her song of
triumph, and never more fully realizes her dream of power and of
love than in that pathetic moment when the shattering blow is
about to fall.

Néron

Racine, always a master of polemics—Boileau said that he had a
more satirical mind even than himself—possessed to a high degree
the art of making his critics look foolish by knocking their heads
together. 'Some even sided with Néron against me', he disdainfully
wrote in his First Preface. 'They said I had made him too cruel. . . .
Others, on the contrary, said I had made him too kind.' The reader
is left to conclude that critics do not know what they are talking
about, but, clever as Racine may have been, both criticisms make
sense, and it is a fact that both were made, the first one, in a less
crude way, by Saint-Evremond (see p. 7), the second by Boursault
who complained that Néron was 'cruel sans malice', meaning
probably that, although Néron does finally kill Britannicus, his
scruples and hesitations do not illustrate the traditional idea of a
'malicious' Néron, exclusively bent on inflicting harm. Racine
countered by answering that Néron was 'un monstre naissant'.
'Naissant' is the important word, for it is not a monster Racine shows

us: classical art is not interested in the abnormal and the subnormal; it is the birth of a monster, and what should be understood by that is far more disquieting than the characters of horror films.

Néron then is a character in a fluid state; he is in the process of becoming what he will be, and we must be careful not to look for monstrous deeds where there are none. The arrest of Junie, for instance, is a rough, brutal answer to Agrippine's intrigues, and one that takes no account of the personal feelings of either Junie or Britannicus. But the political stakes are high: unwittingly perhaps the two lovers have allowed themselves to become, in Agrippine's hands, a weapon with which she is trying to undermine the Emperor's authority, and endangering the security of the State. Néron and the Emperor's party cannot remain passive, and their reaction, rough as it is, is not disproportionate to Agrippine's threat. (We may marvel, by the way, at Agrippine's self-righteous indignation: she did not shrink from taking Octavie away from Silanus, Junie's brother, and finally forced him to suicide. But Junie's arrest, which disturbs her plans, is 'un attentat', 'une ignominie'.) Let us therefore keep a sense of proportion: Néron is fighting Agrippine with her own weapons. It seems that Narcisse, not Burrhus, advised the move (cf. 286), but Burrhus, the 'honnête homme', as Racine calls him in his Preface, loyally defends his master against Agrippine's wild accusations:

> Vous savez que les droits qu'elle porte avec elle
> Peuvent de son époux faire un prince rebelle, . . .
> Et vous-même avoûrez qu'il ne serait pas juste
> Qu'on disposât sans lui de la nièce d'Auguste.   (239)

Junie's arrest is a purely political move, but soon passion appears. Just as it needed Victorian prudishness (or its French equivalent) to find Molière obscene and scurrilous, only the Romantic conception of love which obtained in the nineteenth century could find a monstrous perversion in Néron's falling in love. 'J'aimais jusqu'à ses pleurs que je faisais couler': but what boy has not been moved and secretly flattered by the tears a girl sheds for his sake? 'J'employais les soupirs, et même la menace': there is some roughness in the game of love, but *at this stage* it means nothing very precise. It is of course disturbing for Néron to find there is another boy around, but Narcisse has reassured him: to Junie Britannicus' calf-love cannot mean much, and it should be easy to get rid of a simpering youth. Néron can still have no idea of the deep injury he is about to inflict upon his victims. After Junie has stood up to his prayers and his threats, after she has quietly, movingly confessed her love, he can have no doubt about it, yet he persists and will not be denied; her very resistance hardens his purpose, and out of the turmoil of his emotions in the previous night arises the sombre violence common to Racine's unhappy lovers: if persuasion fails, they will use force, and the image of a rival moves them to wild, murderous threats. For among them we cannot single out Néron as an example of *monstrous* cruelty: if we wish to pass sentence upon him we must bring to the bar Oreste and Pyrrhus, to say nothing of Roxane, Mithridate, and Phèdre. Pyrrhus threatening death to Andromaque's son if she will not be his, Oreste dreaming of carrying away by force Hermione who rejects him, so that at least she will be as unhappy as himself, are no less cruel and pitiless than Néron, and Phèdre herself will passionately wish for the death of the innocent girl, her rival, whom she hardly knows. Among them Néron is not out of place; he is the victim of a passion which, in Racine's pessimistic conception, often—not always—drives men to madness, crime, and self-destruction, and is not a blessing but a curse.

Néron's position, of course, is peculiar, for Racine does not repeat himself. *Britannicus* is a political play as well as a tragedy of love, and Néron happens to be at the centre of both. The long struggle with Agrippine has been in process before the play started, and Néron's ministers, not suspecting the forces they are unloosing, strive to buttress the still fragile power of the young Emperor against her, for political as well as moral reasons. Burrhus, as a good tutor, knows he must teach Néron to do without a tutor, to stand on his own feet, to form his own opinions, to make his own decisions. This, as we saw, Agrippine cannot accept. She is unable to relinquish her control. With all her intelligence, knowledge of life, and experience of men, she cannot realize that Néron must some day live his own life. This conflict, centred on the abstract concept of supreme power, suddenly assumes a concrete form when it means for Néron the loss or possession of Junie. For the 'cornéliens', of course, the idea of Néron fighting for a woman when the fate of an empire is at stake, meant a sharp decline in dramatic tension. What they did not see was that Racine viewed his character from the inside, and that Néron's self-assertion as a lover was intimately bound up with his self-assertion as a ruler.

So far everything has been done for Néron. His accession to the

throne is no achievement of his, as Agrippine is never tired of
reminding him:

> Eussiez-vous pu prétendre
> Qu'un jour Claude à son fils dût préférer son gendre?   (1144)

His policies, in so far as he can free himself from his mother, are
fixed by his ministers. Narcisse jeeringly repeating Roman gossip is
not far from the truth:

> Il ne dit, il ne fait que ce qu'on lui prescrit.
> Burrhus conduit son cœur, Sénèque son esprit.   (1469)

His marriage itself has been settled by his mother: he is tied to a
woman for whom he has never felt anything but dislike. At eighteen
Néron awakening to life finds himself in a strait-jacket. The normal
ties, conventions, duties, and taboos which bind all adolescents are
in his case multiplied by his exalted position, and by the presence of
his formidable mother, his ministers offering only an alternative
obedience, and his normal adolescent rebelliousness is correspond-
ingly increased to the point of explosion. And then, in this marvellous
scene of the first meeting, comes Junie. Junie is his own find: no
overbearing mother pushed her into his arms, no minister gravely
advised him about her. His love for her is more than the dazzling
discovery of love: it is the discovery of himself, of his power of seeing
for himself, acting by himself, being himself. To conquer her would
not only be the visible sign of his liberation from his various task-
masters, it would be the conquest of his own manhood. Junie is not
only his own choice: she means to him his right to choose and to
exclude, she is the symbol of his freedom. For her he is ready to face
all obstacles, all the 'chagrins' and 'importunités' he must expect,
he is ready to defy 'l'implacable Agrippine'. In his case 'il faut que
j'aime' does not, as in *Phèdre*, refer to a compelling divinity—'Vénus
tout entière à sa proie attachée'—it is the irresistible attraction of
life itself, opening out in front of him, with all its intoxicating
possibilities.

And if Junie had responded! . . . If Hermione could have loved
Oreste, if Hippolyte could have been moved by Phèdre's suffering.
. . . But, alas! Hermione 'voudrait aimer' Oreste, but he soon understands that 'les vœux sont pour Oreste, et le cœur pour Pyrrhus'.
One does not love at will in Racine's plays, or rather his lovers,
like Mithridate, can never be satisfied by that kind of love. Hidden,
silent, behind his curtain, Néron catches a glimpse of that magic

world of love in which others live, before its gates are brutally slammed in his face: Junie will never love him, and such a searing experience, the sudden withdrawal of the happiness he thought was in his grasp, cannot remain without an outlet. His frustration, seeking a substitute, finds it in revenge: let Britannicus suffer what he has suffered, let him be deprived of that of which he, Néron, has just been cruelly deprived. Néron's fierce jealousy is no doubt understandable. Yet at the same time, by a subtle but ominous transfer, the eagerly expected joy of love is transmuted into the joy of inflicting pain upon the envied lover: 'Je me fais de sa peine une image charmante.' In the susceptible soul of an adolescent something inhuman and sinister is being born, something which—later—will grow and gather strength: for the first time a faint outline of the sadistic Néron of the future becomes perceptible. . . . The delicacy with which Racine suggests, under our very eyes, the mysterious birth of a human personality has seldom been equalled, even by himself.

Néron, however, is far from having reached a point of no return. Even after the end of the third Act, when he has imprisoned Britannicus and ordered the poison to be prepared, rebuffed Burrhus, defied Agrippine, nothing is settled. For one thing Néron is not Oreste or Pyrrhus: his love is still young, it has not had time yet to take possession of his whole being. With the flexibility of a poet who never applies a formula Racine knows that passion is an irrational thing, the ebb and tide of which is not predictable. Néron's great hope suddenly seems to sag, and he will for a while resign himself to the melancholy idea of giving up his love. In the political battle he similarly vacillates. With Agrippine first. For the last time, '*son génie étonné* tremble devant le sien', and he cannot bear the tears 'De ces yeux, où j'ai lu si longtemps mon devoir'. But this lasts only a moment: after Agrippine's exorbitant demands Néron's fury reaches a climax of violence in this violent play:

> J'embrasse mon rival, mais c'est pour l'étouffer.
> . . . Il faut que sa ruine
> Me délivre à jamais des fureurs d'Agrippine.
> Tant qu'il respirera, je ne vis qu'à demi. (1314)

This time, it seems, nothing can make Néron retrace his steps, and yet, so uncertain and divided against himself is the monolithic monster some have tried to see in him, that twice again he will change his mind, and a much more fundamental debate will start after Agrippine's departure.

Burrhus' arguments are put with great eloquence and great emotion. Into the balance he throws not only persuasive words but his own life. He openly defies the Emperor's express order and his declared decision, and the fulminating 'Burrhus!' that answers the daring 'Non!' of a subject (1325) is heavy with the outraged majesty of an absolute ruler—Roman or French. What Burrhus says, however, has less importance than the repercussions his words will have in Néron's mind in the following scene, in the final struggle of Néron against Narcisse.

For in spite of Néron's non-committal statement ('Dans mon appartement qu'il m'attende avec vous') it soon becomes clear that he was not lying, or trying to trick Burrhus. Alone with Narcisse he at once cancels the order for Britannicus' execution. During the whole scene, while Narcisse probes and needles him unmercifully, Néron puts up a desperate resistance. The appeal to his own safety ('. . . peut-être il fera ce que vous n'osez faire'), or to his love ('Et l'hymen de Junie . . . Seigneur, lui faites-vous encor ce sacri-fice?') cannot move him. When Narcisse plays what should be, and perhaps is, his winning card, Agrippine's arrogance, and her boast of victory, Néron is shaken, but not convinced: 'Narcisse, encore un coup, je ne puis l'entreprendre.' Even when in a passage as daring perhaps as Burrhus' offer of his own life Narcisse heaps insult and ridicule upon Néron, the Emperor leaves in shocked silence but still unyielding. What is it Néron is defending against Narcisse? What supports him in his struggle against the representative of *Realpolitik*? His arguments are most unexpected: Rome, he says, will accuse him of parricide. He will go down in history as a poisoner. He has given his word. If he breaks the promise he gave to Burrhus, he will never dare look him in the face again. The debate is in fact about right and wrong, but it is not a struggle between the good Burrhus and the bad Narcisse, a transposition of the fight between the good and the bad angel for the possession of a soul: the time of medieval moralities is gone. What Néron, on the threshold of manhood and absolute power, dares not let go is the very notion of right and wrong, the notion of *value*.

This is not a notion that is called for as often as it seems; in every-day life a number of props contrive to keep us on the right track: the influence of parents, the authority of teachers, later the power of the

State with its police, its judges, and its gaols considerably limit our possibilities of evil doing. Néron is free now from the authority of parent and tutor, and there is no law to control him; Racine's heroes are, significantly, above the laws: the absolute ruler is the source of the law, he does not obey it. What is there to guide him then? Religion has traditionally given a supernatural sanction to moral values, but religion plays no part in Néron's motivation, or in any other character in *Britannicus*. A kind of dizziness seems to seize Néron when confronted with his own omnipotence. If there is no law, is everything allowed and nothing forbidden? The duel between Narcisse and Néron is, for Néron, a terrified recoil from the awesome freedom that is within his grasp, a frantic search for standards and values every one of which is inexorably dismissed by Narcisse. Public opinion? What is public opinion in the universal servility of the Roman State? 'Leur prompte servitude a fatigué Tibère'; they praise only success, worship only power. The judgment of History? But History is made by the victors:

> Faites périr le frère, abandonnez la sœur: . . .
> Vous verrez mettre au rang des jours infortunés
> Ceux où jadis la sœur et le frère sont nés.   (1450)

Honour, and the keeping of one's word? Significantly, in the aristocratic world in which French tragedy was born, this is Néron's last line of defence: honour, the need for the esteem of other men, or at least of those we admire, or at least of one man, whose approval or disapproval means something to us. But no man, not even Burrhus, is the incarnation of good and the soul of honour; Burrhus is 'un honnête homme', who often speaks what is right; but Burrhus is also a politician, who sometimes says and does what is expedient. How can we be sure?

> Burrhus ne pense pas, Seigneur, tout ce qu'il dit.
> Son adroite vertu ménage son crédit.   (1461)

Is nothing left then but naked power, the free play of force against force, and the stark need for survival? From a man who possesses absolute power can we not hope for a free act of generosity? If Néron can choose to be what he likes, could he not choose to be magnanimous? And if there is no absolute value, cannot man create his own? We shall see later why this does not happen in *Britannicus*. What must strike us at this stage is the direct result of Néron's absolute power: his loneliness. Raised above all men, above their conventions, their obligations, their duties, he no longer belongs to the community of men; we cannot expect a feeling of fellowship from one who has no fellow-man: is he still a man?

The final step in Néron's dehumanization is of course the murder. Not just because he uses violence: man is a fierce animal, and violence has—so far—been part of his life as an individual and as a species. But so is empathy, compassion, and love. Men wound, and murder, and torture—but they faint at the sight of blood; they fight and scheme against each other, but they give a hand to a friend, or even to an enemy. When Britannicus collapses and writhes in agony, Néron remains impassive. A youth is dying under his eyes, a rival, it is true, but the companion of his childhood, and his 'brother'— and his eyes remain expressionless, his face shows not a flicker of emotion, his voice is steady, his pulse has not quickened. Burrhus himself makes the distinction:

> Son crime seul n'est pas ce qui me désespère;
> Sa jalousie a pu l'armer contre son frère.
> Mais, . . .
> Néron l'a vu mourir sans changer de couleur.
> Ses yeux indifférents . . .   (1707)

Something withers in Néron at that moment; part of his humanity shrivels and dies; he will never more be a complete man: the monster is born. Not a melodramatic monster, with obscene threats, or insane laughter, but a frozen one with in his eyes the glazed look of a murderer at peace with himself. Not a Romantic monster either: nothing so reassuringly remote as Han d'Islande or Frankenstein. A more disturbing kind of monster, because much closer to our personal reality, to the reality of our time, in which ordinary men and normal youths in their thousands have quickly learnt to forsake compassion, and to settle down, comfortably, in inhumanity.

Junie and Britannicus

From the very beginning people looked askance at Britannicus. Racine already tells us that many were 'scandalized' that he had chosen a youngster as the title-hero of a tragedy, and he artfully, if not very convincingly, argues that Britannicus' youth and in- experience are in fact that imperfection which Aristotle demands from the tragic hero. In his Second Preface, trying as usual to placate his critics after claiming they were wrong, he himself seems anxious to tone down the importance of Britannicus: 'My tragedy', he assures us, 'is as much about Agrippine's disgrace as Britannicus' death', which is true, but sounds faintly apologetic. Half-heartedly defended by his creator, Britannicus fared even worse when the time came when all Racinian characters who were not murderous were dismissed as insipid. A. Adam was the first perhaps to point out the fallacy and the dangers of such oversimplifications: just as much as 'les grandes figures ténébreuses', 'les êtres jeunes, fragiles et touchants' have a peculiar attraction for Racine. He has drawn his two lovers with loving care, and, in the case of Britannicus, with a gentle, melancholy irony, almost with a kind of nostalgia that gives him a poignant charm, unique in his theatre.

His youth, even if Racine ever really meant what he said, no longer strikes us an an imperfection, but it is true that even to Racine's youngest readers, Britannicus must at times appear very young. In this drama of violent teenagers—for Néron himself is eighteen or nineteen—Britannicus and Junie, serious children whom grief and tragedy have made older than their years, have the pathos of extreme youth. Racine himself has drawn a brief, but accurate portrait of his hero, 'a young prince full of spirit, full of love, open-hearted, overtrustful. . . . He was fifteen, and it was said that he was exceptionally gifted, whether it was a fact, or whether the trials he went through gave him such a reputation, although this reputation was never put to the test.' Untested, incautious, and often naïve, Britannicus at least never wavers over one thing, his love for Junie: 'L'amour toujours n'attend pas la raison', Narcisse ironically comments. His love is to Britannicus the most important thing in the world, and his main anchor in life. Love makes him rush into Néron's palace, unaware of his own danger. His joy at meeting Junie makes him deaf to her warnings. His stubborn refusal to give her up in the face of apparent betrayal is a decisive element in the progress of the drama, and whatever he may say, his determination to keep her out of Néron's hands is obviously a more potent motive than the honour of his sister Octavie, Néron's wife. It is first of all to recover Junie that he bravely links hands with the dangerous Agrippine, an unnatural association with his father's murderess. It is Junie's presence that gives him the strength to stand up to Néron's formidable presence, and to get the better of him, and it is love that finally makes him forget his ambition in the joy of her possession.

Britannicus' love is not the fierce love of Néron, Pyrrhus, or Mithridate. He and Junie were promised to each other years before by his father's wish. Their love was born in 'le vert paradis des amours enfantines', and it has imperceptibly grown into a deeper attachment. To the lonely princeling it has been a source not of bitterness but of strength and peace:

> Je l'ai vu quelquefois s'arracher de ces lieux,
> Le cœur plein d'un courroux qu'il cachait à vos yeux,
> D'une cour qui le fuit pleurant l'ingratitude,
> Las de votre grandeur et de sa servitude,
> Entre l'impatience et la crainte flottant;
> Il allait voir Junie, et revenait content. (437)

However profound and genuine, Britannicus' love has also the thoughtless, self-centred, and somewhat theatrical quality of a very young lover's love. With what fine forgetfulness of common sense he runs alone to Junie's rescue, when she is the Emperor's prisoner, guarded by the praetorians! How he wishes he could have died in her defence, 'mourir à vos yeux'! And even though he loves her dearly, how concerned he is with his own feelings, how important are to him *his* unhappiness, *his* grief: in front of Junie's tragic, terrified face, he is at first annoyed at her not giving them enough attention:

> Songiez-vous aux douleurs que vous m'alliez coûter? ... (706)
> Est-ce ainsi que vos yeux consolent ma disgrâce? ... (708)
> ... la douleur qui m'accable. ... (731)

With this demanding attitude, which makes him sulk whenever he fears he is no longer in the centre of Junie's preoccupations, there goes a pathetic humility which makes it hardly credible to him that Junie has actually refused the Empire for his sake. Now at the height of bliss, now in the depths of gloom, humble and demanding, expecting everything, and overcome with amazement when he gets it, he has the freshness, mobility, and capacity for ravishment of a child. Yet, under the shock of disappointment and betrayal, dark shadows at times pass over the fresh face of Britannicus: he cannot hate Junie, but he wishes he could, and, in a line of astonishing harshness, he dreams of a steady, quiet hatred: 'Je la voudrais haïr avec tranquillité.' How wounding he can be when he throws in her face the scornful *Così fan tutte*, and how well he knows already how to humiliate and to hurt! If only for a few moments, the violence and cruelty of Racinian love loom in the gentle soul of Britannicus.

And, although in a different way from that of Néron, Britannicus too is in the process of becoming a man; he would otherwise lack too completely the dignity required of a character in a tragedy. Princely born, the son of a reigning Emperor, the descendant of Tiberius and Livia, he has only recently become aware of the exalted rank which is his birthright:

> Pour moi depuis un an qu'un peu d'expérience
> M'a donné de mon sort la triste connaissance, . . .   (327)

His ambition, his determination not to submit for ever to the usurper, is of course an important element in the drama. It also gives the character the additional firmness it needs. It is true that Britannicus is at every stage deceived and outmanœuvred. But we should perhaps dwell less on his naïveté and more on his precocious lack of illusions: Britannicus knows that he is surrounded by traitors and informers, that in his bitter words 'on *le* vend tous les jours', that people are careful not to be friendly to him so as not to compromise themselves. He is surprisingly quick at seeing his chance, and at making use—better use than she wanted him to—of Agrippine's false move: in a few hours he has become head of a powerful faction. That the lonely youth, without a father, a mother, or a friend, should have put his trust in the treacherous Narcisse is no more than a tribute to Narcisse's cleverness and power—but Narcisse will deceive even Agrippine, bend even Néron to his will, and only Junie will see through him. Because trust and magnanimity are deadly weaknesses in the jungle of *Britannicus*, we should not forget that they were usually held as virtues characteristic of a generous nature: 'Soyons amis, Cinna, c'est moi qui t'en convie. . . .' In Racine nothing answers the proffered hand, and Britannicus' trust will be the immediate cause of his downfall. Yet it would be a gross misreading of the text to think Racine intended Britannicus to arouse contempt and derision. When the time comes for the decisive battle with Néron, the premature battle which all his well-wishers have done everything to prevent, Britannicus fights it as if he had legions at his call, and it is enough for our sympathy that he should show pride, courage, and wit. We can hardly expect wisdom as well, and perhaps he is at an age when it is better that he should not think discretion the better part of valour. And when the time comes for him to die, death will take him gently, happy in the knowledge of Junie's love, without jealousy, without rancour, without the bitterness and the self-hatred that are the lot of so many Racinian heroes; a smile will still hover on his lips while Néron watches him lift the fateful cup, and he will die a quick, merciful death: 'Le fer ne produit pas de si puissants efforts.' None of his heroes has Racine treated with such tenderness.

If Britannicus never really understands the world in which he dies, Junie has no illusions about it. Of all the characters she is the most lucid and clear-sighted. In spite of some initial, pardonable errors, she correctly assesses the true violence of Néron's passion, and gives Britannicus a supreme warning he does not heed; she refuses to believe in the reality of their reconciliation, distrusts Narcisse, and throws doubt upon Agrippine's proud assurance. In spite of her youth and total inexperience of the Court, she holds her own, when suddenly confronted with the Emperor, with the dignity one expects from a descendant of Augustus, and she proudly asks to know her crime. When Néron's intentions become clear, she first cautiously manœuvres and retreats, and, when he has her cornered, daringly faces up to him, and confesses to her love without coyness and without fear. L. Goldmann is not mistaken in noticing that Racine seems here to renounce the Aristotelian principle according to which tragic characters must not be wholly good or wholly bad: there seems to be no flaw in Junie's steadfastness, understanding, and generosity.
Her devotion to Britannicus is the more remarkable because according to the proprieties and conventions of seventeenth-century tragedy (and of seventeenth-century society) a lady of high rank owed it to herself and to her honour only to marry a ruling prince: Junie refuses to abandon Britannicus *because* he is lonely, dispossessed, and slighted. To Bérénice too, only Titus, not the Caesars' purple, will matter, but even Bérénice's pride at times revolts. To Britannicus' elaborate insults, made the more cutting by the formal politeness with which they are delivered, Junie declines to answer in kind; she will not be drawn into a cruel and futile quarrel; she accepts being hurt without trying to hurt him in return. She is of course immensely more mature than he is, and whereas Britannicus gets himself into serious difficulties in rushing to the rescue of 'his Princess', it is she who tries to keep him out of trouble. Her relationship to Britannicus, which must be unique in seventeenth-century tragedy, and brings to mind Rimbaud's 'sœur de charité', has a strangely protective, almost maternal quality.

Admirable Junie! Not even Monique, embarrassed in her Cornelian ideas of duty, not even Bérénice, reach the height of her simple, unaffected selflessness. But even Junie is human. Junie cannot escape that 'tragic error', the Aristotelian *hamartía*, for which the tragic hero pays so dearly, and so disproportionately. Already, when ordered by Néron to dismiss Britannicus, she almost breaks under the strain, and it can hardly be said that she carries out the Emperor's orders. As the hours go by, the thought of Britannicus' misery becomes intolerable to her: she must seek him out and let him know. Two words only, which ought to reassure him. But Britannicus will not be reassured; Junie explains, soothes him at last. Ineffably sweet moments, rare moments in Racine, when lovers' hands are briefly joined. But it is the sweetness of death. Junie's words have made her prince happy again, but they are the immediate occasion of the violent encounter of the two rivals, which will consummate the ruin of Britannicus.

6. *The political drama in 'Britannicus'*

Et peut-être ta plume aux censeurs de Pyrrhus
Doit les plus nobles traits dont tu peignis Burrhus.

Thus Boileau in the *Epître VII*, in which he tried to console Racine for the unfair criticism to which his *Phèdre* was subjected. Criticism, Boileau argued, is a help to a poet; it spurs him on to higher achievement, and *Britannicus* surpassed *Andromaque* partly because Burrhus is a greater creation than Pyrrhus, whom Boileau was reported to have dubbed 'un héros à la Scudéry', an insipid lover such as are to be found in the *précieux* novels of Madeleine de Scudéry. Such an incredible error in perspective well illustrates how little Boileau understood Racine's tragedy, even though he had, or thought he had, taken Racine as his model in the definition of tragedy he was to present to the public in his *Art Poétique*, five years after *Britannicus*. For Pyrrhus is, like Néron and Agrippine, one of the protagonists of the play, while Burrhus is outside the fateful circle of tragedy. It is true that his part is considerably longer than that of Britannicus, and almost twice that of Junie; he appears in every act, he is always seen attempting to stop or guide Néron or Agrippine, and it is through him we are given a glimpse of Néron's final mutation. What Burrhus says, he says with great conviction, and above all with great eloquence. After thirty years of Cornelian eloquence and a century of baroque rhetoric, Burrhus was bound to attract an undue amount of attention; he also provided a ready-made interpretation of the play, and, with his counterpart Narcisse, a facile antithesis of Good and Evil. Time and again Molière's 'raisonneurs' have been mistaken for Molière: Burrhus is the 'raisonneur' of *Britannicus*.

Burrhus, as well as Narcisse, is of course far more elaborate and characterized than the average confidant. His public-spirited loyalty towards Néron, his efforts at preserving peace between the rival factions in Rome entitle him to the sympathy he usually arouses. In various ways, however, there are flaws in the character. He apologizes for the brusque 'franchise' of a soldier at the beginning of a speech of fifty lines, which is a political manifesto. The incorruptible moralist was also the man who took Néron to the praetorians and had him proclaimed on Agrippine's orders after the murder of Claudius. Perhaps he was a subordinate who knew nothing: has he still discovered nothing? Is he such a simpleton that he can believe that Rome has freely elected Néron as its Emperor? We could shrug off the theorizing of a good man who knows so little of the world in which he is living. On the other hand a clear knowledge of the evil intrigues in which he has been involved would sorely tarnish the image of the 'honnête homme'. Perhaps the dilemma is too brutal; perhaps Burrhus is as honest as he humanly can be in the dangerous times in which he is living; he makes compromises, states principles to which he keeps as far as is possible. He is no incarnation of Good (how could a Racinian character ever be reduced to an abstraction?), and Narcisse may be nearer to the mark when he pungently remarks: 'Burrhus ne pense pas, Seigneur, tout ce qu'il dit.' But Racine did not have time to make the character more explicit, or dwell on him for his own sake, because he needed him, as well as Narcisse, for other purposes.

Narcisse does not, any more than Burrhus, so much admired by Boileau, attain complete, organic coherence. Again the character is fully alive: if Burrhus attracts immediate sympathy, Narcisse arouses instant odium. His treachery, his cynical amusement at the trust his ward shows him, and, when Néron is prepared to spare his brother, the formidable pressure he exerts upon the Emperor to bring about the murder of his victim, all this more than explains the exclusively moral view critics have taken of Narcisse as a mere evil-doer and another example of that traditional character in seventeenth-century theatre, the 'mauvais conseiller'. Partly because of the twist Racine gave here to history, the background of the character remains weak (see Chapter 4). His motives, although only outlined, are readily understandable: ambition, not revenge as in Iago, is his driving force; if his advice prevails against Agrippine and Burrhus, his position at Court will be a dominant one. But again, Narcisse, as well as Burrhus, is subordinated to Néron. Neither character merely externalizes Néron's alternative policies, but Racine wishes first of all to concentrate the light upon Néron, not to lead us into the exploration of a secondary character. This partly explains perhaps why he cancelled the last scene of Act III at the representation (Louis Racine tells us it was because it shocked and upset the spectators too much, which is hard to swallow). Also Racine's tact felt that this self-confession of undiluted villainy gave the character a melo-dramatic blackness which was neither credible nor in tune with the play. But he allowed the scene to remain in the printed text. Blackening Narcisse and making him into a conventional villain was a way of taking the sting out of Narcisse's disturbing message, although it is an integral and necessary part of the tragedy. Racine's polite, unmodern way of veiling, rather than emphasizing, the daring of his plays is one of our difficulties in fully appreciating him. Also Racine, overpreoccupied with critics' reactions and public conventions, was, sometimes, too clever.

Narcisse and Burrhus, then, are primarily political characters, relatively undisturbed by the emotional pulls to which Néron, Agrippine, Britannicus are subjected. What policies do they stand for? Burrhus' policy, considered in its most practical aspects, is one of return to the customs and institutions of the past. Whereas Agrippine thinks in terms of pure despotism and personal power, he rejoices in seeing the people electing his magistrates, and the Senate, who for so many centuries guided the destinies of the Roman Republic, regaining its influence and prestige, and this is what, like Cicero, he calls 'freedom'. Respect for the past means respect for the law, which must contain the caprices of the great, the violence of the mob, and the arbitrary actions of the ruler. For Burrhus, following the Augustan line, sees, or pretends to see, no contradiction between the Republican institutions and the presence of a monarch, who is no doubt to act as guardian of the law, and, if necessary, to enforce 'freedom' from above. Do not let us be too hard upon Burrhus: politicians have to compromise. The notion of freedom is essential to Burrhus, because it is a clear, established value, the objective character of which is guaranteed by centuries of acceptance; and Néron correctly understands the gist of his appeal when he perceives that it rests upon the notion of value. Indeed Burrhus' approach to the whole tangle of passions and political rivalries in *Britannicus* is dominated by the concept of indisputable values. Political values, reinforced by family values. That Agrippine might side with Britannicus against her own son, or that she might imagine Néron to suspect her of such behaviour, is to him ludicrous: 'L'Empereur vous croit-il du parti de Junie?' That anybody might believe Agrippine's self-accusation of her husband's murder is unthinkable: 'Madame, ils ne vous croiront pas.' That Néron should arrest his mother leaves Burrhus gasping: 'Quoi, Seigneur? . . . Une mère?' Néron's avowed intention of doing away with his brother strikes him like a thunderbolt: 'Songez-vous dans quel sang vous allez vous baigner?' *Une mère, un fils, un frère,* a world in which the self-obvious implications of such words are not acknowledged is a world in which Burrhus literally cannot live: the death-wish which is a recurrent theme in the rest of his part is a strictly logical and predictable development of the character. Remembering Burrhus' dubious background but ignoring its psychological aspect, we may say that Burrhus' politics allow of compromise, justify infringements, take into account special cases (Junie's kidnapping), but can never in his mind be deliberately dissociated from morals, can never be considered a privileged field in which the moral imperatives do not occur, in which moral obligation and moral restraint are invalid. To concede it would be to admit that morality is subordinated to politics, is in fact justified only by its political usefulness; that subjects must obey the moral law so that the ruler should the more easily follow the non-moral dictates of politics.

Such a view Burrhus utterly rejects. Britannicus' exclusion, although regrettable, is wholly legal: he has no right to try and reconquer a crown at the price of a civil war which he cannot morally desire. On the other hand let his resentment be smoothed and his feelings spared (see Variants, p. 143); let Néron forget his absurd infatuation, let Britannicus find happiness in love, and the worst consequences of the wrong he has suffered will be avoided. As for Agrippine, let her accept Néron's primacy, and she will be rewarded by being the first and greatest person in the State, after the Emperor. Some concessions and a little good-will, surely, can be expected from all concerned. Only those could refuse them who are blind to the indisputable fact that there are such things as duties, obligations, values. Burrhus' various pleas are made with great reasonableness; he is convinced that he is not asking for impossible sacrifices; he only asks that some regard should be paid to the claims of the common good, and the touchstone for such concern is the willingness to compromise. Burrhus' moderation makes it perfectly understandable that he should have appeared to provide the moral and political frame in which Racine wished his tragedy to be read and understood, a system of references general enough to be acceptable to all, and one according to which Racine would not refuse his characters themselves to be judged. *Britannicus* is, I believe, the only one among his tragedies, with the exception of *Esther*, if *Esther* can be considered a tragedy, in which critics have so easily and so peremptorily bandied the words of Good and Evil, Good being represented by Burrhus' attempts at a general reconciliation, Evil in its most unadulterated form by Narcisse the Tempter and the Seducer. Between them, like Heracles poised between Vice and Virtue, Néron is pictured as a free agent (whatever has been said before about his tainted heredity), inclining now to his 'bon conseiller', now to his 'mauvais conseiller', but finally choosing the path of the bloodthirsty tyrant, when he could perfectly well have chosen that of the virtuous ruler. At the *dénouement* terror and pity are, if one may so express it, polarized. Pity is all for the unfortunate victim, the innocent and therefore purely pathetic Britannicus; terror is aroused by the inhuman monster Néron has finally become. We are in fact left with impotent indignation at the total victory of Evil, an indignation only tempered by the anticipated satisfaction of the coming punishment of the evil-doer (punishment by remorse and later by enforced suicide), with an immediate instalment in the quick demise of Narcisse manhandled by an indignant mob. This is a possible interpretation of *Britannicus*. As a political drama (and as a tragedy) it would make it a very shallow piece of work.

There is, however, an alternative interpretation of the political drama, and of *Britannicus* as a whole. It has the advantage of taking into account a number of elements to which we have otherwise deliberately to close our eyes. For one thing is clear in Burrhus' moving plea for Néron to spare his brother's life: it is that it rests upon assertions we know to be untrue. Just as it is not true to pretend that Rome has 'chosen' Néron, as Burrhus candidly says in Act I, or that he has not reached the throne through incest and murder, as Burrhus refuses to acknowledge, it is simply not true to present Britannicus as the innocent victim of calumny. The fact is that ever since he has been of an age to understand his situation, he has refused to accept it. The fact is that he weeps with rage and humiliation at the sight of the hated Domitius, the intruder, the enemy, occupying the throne that belongs to him. We may of course, as Racine no doubt means us to, sympathize with the young pretender and wish him well, but the fact remains that he is now conspiring against the legitimate ruler of Rome with the help of the most powerful person in the Empire, the very mother of the Emperor, that Néron's fall must result in his death, that Néron's power and his life are threatened. These are the facts that, in his passionate appeal, Burrhus chooses to ignore, or forgets, or does not know. It is true that at the beginning of Act v a peaceful solution seems possible, and Burrhus' policy seems justified: at the cost of sacrificing his love, Néron may keep his crown, spare his brother, and preserve law and order in Rome. But things have gone too far for such a solution to be a convincing or a lasting one. Agrippine has been pacified at the price of total, unconditional surrender. Néron once more has, or seems to have, yielded. Will he for ever retreat and retreat? Can Agrippine ever be satisfied? Will she never be tempted to use the weapons Néron leaves in her hands? In the joy of recovering Junie, Britannicus has, for the time being, forgotten his ambition, but for how long will he be content to live quietly by her side? Can we imagine him shorn of the youthful pride which makes him worthy of our respect, which is part of his charm too? He hated the usurper long before Néron tried to take Junie away from him: will gratitude now replace jealousy? If he escapes with his life, how long will it be, as Narcisse shrewdly points out, before he knows how near he was to total disaster? However trusting he may be, will he not wonder whether Néron may not be tempted to try again what he nearly did once? Even with the best intentions in the world Britannicus cannot cease to be the son of Claudius, and if he prefers to forget that Agrippine murdered his father to make room for Néron, he is still, willy-nilly, the potential leader of every faction of malcontents which may wish for Néron's downfall: one sprang into being at his call within hours. We are therefore compelled either to believe that none of the characters in *Britannicus* means what he says or is what he seems, or else dismiss Burrhus' 'solution' as totally unreal. Unless we are ready to consider the formidable storm of passions Racine has conjured up as sheer make-believe, Burrhus' well-meaning efforts are but a smokescreen of illusions spread before the hard reality of facts.

Those facts are scattered everywhere in the play; stated, implicitly or explicitly, not only by Néron or Agrippine, but by Britannicus, or Burrhus himself. But it is Narcisse who expresses them in their stark, sombre truth, and draws from them the logical, inescapable consequences. For Narcisse's personal stake in the matter and his consummate address do not detract at all from his powerful case. Néron cannot afford to yield once more to Agrippine without conceding to her the very substance of Imperial power; already she is boasting of it. Narcisse is not lying; what else is Agrippine doing when she says to Junie: 'Il suffit, j'ai parlé, tout a changé de face?' It is not only Narcisse who suggests it, or Néron: 'Mais si vous ne régnez, vous vous plaignez toujours'; it is Burrhus himself: 'Toujours humble, toujours le timide Néron/N'ose-t-il être Auguste et César que de nom? ... Serez-vous toujours prête à partager l'Empire?'; and even Agrippine: 'Je le craindrais bientôt, s'il ne me craignait plus.' Absolute power cannot be divided; Néron must conquer or be conquered. Nor can Néron afford, without imperilling his own life and the security of the State, to allow a shadow Emperor to lurk for ever in the dark, or to trust for ever in the gratitude or the generosity of a rival convinced of his right to rule. ('Ah, Narcisse! tu sais si de la servitude/Je prétends faire encore une longue habitude./Tu sais si pour jamais de ma chute étonné,/Je renonce à l'Empire, où j'étais destiné.') The choice for Néron is between the probability, in a not too distant future, of his own fall, and the decision to fell Britannicus now that he has the chance. The throne, where his mother has placed him, is like an embattled fortress to which he must now hold on as to his own life. His choice is not the facile one between good and evil; it is between killing and being killed. As in Corneille's *Othon*, his dilemma is 'ou périr ou régner'.

Shall we then whitewash Néron's deed, and absolve him on grounds of legitimate defence? No, for the preventive murder of a trusting youth is still murder. And if it is forced upon Néron by the fierce political conjuncture in which he is placed, if he cannot indeed afford to allow Britannicus to live, the self-destructive effect of a deliberate, cold-blooded murder—from which even Agrippine shrinks—recoils upon Néron with devastating effect. Néron must kill or perish, but he cannot kill without impairing his own humanity.

'On ne peut régner innocemment' the revolutionary Saint-Just was later to say. Now perhaps we can appreciate the full significance of the political dilemmas in *Britannicus*. For Agrippine it is whether to destroy her own son, whom she herself has spent a lifetime to set upon the throne, or to renounce all power, with the ultimate prospect of total ruin. For Britannicus it is to risk all, eventually to lose all, in open defiance of the ruling Emperor, or to abdicate, with his claims, his princely, even his human, dignity. For Néron it is whether to accept the permanence of a deadly blackmail, thus giving up real power, or to resort to a preventive execution which, on the moral plane, is nothing but murder. None of the characters can back out of their own dilemma; but Néron, alone, driven by Narcisse, goes to the bitter end, and there is no doubt that, on the political plane, he emerges triumphant from the trial of strength in *Britannicus*. Yet the penalty he pays, and will have to pay, is hardly less than the one he inflicts upon the others. The frightening trap in which Racine's characters are caught now appears with blinding clarity, and so does the importance of the political drama in its relationship with the human tragedy.

But it would be a mistake to imagine that the politics are nothing but an aside, part of the scaffolding used by Racine to give his play its full tragic effect. There may well be a hierarchy in the various aspects of the play, and the political one may not be the most important, but Racine has worked out every one of them with the same thorough craftsmanship. Like Corneille in *Cinna*, he wished to oppose and to illustrate two entirely different systems of government, two different conceptions of the relationship between the ruler and the ruled. The first one, eloquently defended by Burrhus, goes back to Seneca: it has been examined in some detail in the chapter on the sources of *Britannicus*. The second one, Narcisse's, comes straight from Machiavelli. Machiavelli was not an evil spirit intent on destroying every generous impulse in the soul of man. He was, first of all, an Italian patriot dismayed at the sight of his country devastated by foreign invaders and torn by civil war; and, often drawing inspiration from Tacitus, he tried to discover, by careful observation and scientific reasoning, the methods and techniques by which Italy could give herself peace and order, and a strong government which would rid her of her brutal conquerors. In so doing he founded modern political science. In the seventeenth century many of his ideas were re-stated, in a different context and with a different approach, by Hobbes in his *Leviathan* or his *Behemoth*. Racine certainly had read Machiavelli, whose *Ruler* was to be found in his library. It is doubtful that he had heard of Hobbes, but his Narcisse is the spiritual descendant of Tacitus, of Machiavelli, and of Hobbes. His creed, like theirs, is based on the twin principles of the contempt of the crowd and the exaltation of personal rule. The crowd is unable or unwilling to overcome its natural anarchy, and at the same time resentful of the master who enforces upon it the order it needs and obscurely craves. The Ruler must never pay attention to, or in any way be swayed by, its wishes and its whims; his duty as well as his right is to be strong and to impose his will, for 'though of so unlimited a Power men may fancy evil consequences, yet the consequences of the want of it, which is perpetuall warre of every man against his neighbour, are much worse' (Hobbes).

> Et prenez-vous, Seigneur, leurs caprices pour guides? . . .
> Est-ce à vous de prêter l'oreille à leurs discours? . . .
> Mais, Seigneur, les Romains ne vous sont point connus. . . .
> Tant de précaution affaiblit votre règne.
> Ils croiront en effet mériter qu'on les craigne.
> Au joug depuis longtemps ils se sont façonnés.
> Ils adorent la main qui les tient enchaînés.   (1432)

Agrippine's intrigues must be put down because they are a cause of political and military weakness for which the Emperor angrily, and not unjustifiably, reproaches his mother (1240 *et seq.*). The safety of the Prince is the safety of the State. And that too is why Néron cannot and must not for a moment tolerate a rival:

> Tant qu'il respirera je ne vis qu'à demi . . .
> Et je ne prétends pas que sa coupable audace
> Une seconde fois lui promette ma place.   (1317)

The Ruler must not wait for his enemy to strike the first blow; 'he must destroy those who are in a position to do him harm, and are likely to do so' (Machiavelli). What in any case is Néron worrying about? The ignorant, servile populace is always impressed by bold deeds and bold lies, and it is quite incapable of pronouncing fair and sensible judgment:

> Faites périr le frère, abandonnez la sœur:
> Rome, sur ses autels prodiguant les victimes,
> Fussent-ils innocents, leur trouvera des crimes.   (1450)

It might be said that such a totally amoral philosophy is only of historical interest. But Racine certainly did not mean it to have a purely local relevance: he was not writing an historical drama, or a painstaking reconstruction of ancient Rome. He undoubtedly believed it to have a universal application, and therefore to be relevant as well to the France of the Bourbons and to the England of the Stuarts, and Racine boasted of Colbert's interest in the play. The whole impact of the play makes it clear that Narcisse, not Burrhus, draws the correct lesson from the facts. Agrippine goes under when, under the stress of passion and jealousy, she forgets her old skill and ruthlessness, her caution and her foresight: she is beaten at her own game. If Britannicus is at no time a match for Néron, it is because he never suspects that distrust and ruthlessness are necessary in a ruler, because after threatening the power and the very life of the Emperor, he naïvely believes that Néron cannot possibly think of murder. And if we are tempted to dismiss Narcisse's politics as irrelevant to our times, we should remember that the Narcisses soon reassert themselves whenever men and women are not willing or not able to think and act for themselves, whenever the people becomes a mob.

After dismissing Burrhus as Racine's mouthpiece we should be careful, however, not to fall into an even more preposterous error, and choose Narcisse, as if Racine cynically urged us to forget compassion and humanity. In the deadly struggle of *Britannicus* Narcisse sees through Burrhus' illusions and states the truth. But it is a harsh and a hateful truth, and the world in which it holds sway is a cruel and a sombre world—a tragic world. That Racine shows us his characters labouring under an iron law which will finally destroy them all does not mean that he does not feel, and does not wish us to feel, compassion for the victims of a necessity as implacable as the ancient *Fatum*.

7. Drama, poetry and tragedy in 'Britannicus'

A tragic vision of man and man's world is not an outstanding characteristic of seventeenth-century theatre in France, as it is in the Greek, or the Elizabethan, theatre. Racine here stands apart, if not alone. What his contemporaries cared for above all was drama. The contriving of an ingenious situation full of potential conflicts and developments, the working out of incidents deriving from such a situation, stemming from the hero's character but in accordance with the recognized social code of an aristocratic society, and finally the solution of the conflict, credible and *vraisemblable*, yet unexpected and striking, like the elegant solution of a difficult mathematical problem, such was the ideal, not often achieved, but more or less consciously present in the minds of the authors, the critics, and the public. Corneille, who gave it its supreme embodiment, was rudely criticized when he occasionally fell from the high standards he himself had established.

Racine was too keen to achieve success, too much a writer of his own age, not to pay particular attention to an aspect of his play which he knew would be his spectators' first criterion. His dramatic technique, less varied as a whole, less experimental than Corneille's, is impeccable. His *exposition* is masterful, and from the second act onwards the whole of *Britannicus* could be described as a deadly game of chess, in which every move is followed at once by a countermove, until Agrippine is finally check-mated. It has been said that Néron holds the initiative in the whole play, and is therefore the one and only *agent* in the drama. This seems an artificial simplification. True, it was Néron who, artfully deflecting Agrippine from the throne she prepared to share with him, first aroused the Empress's anger. But this protocol incident seems trivial enough when set against Agrippine's disproportionate reaction, and the vast machination which must, by means of a political marriage, make the power-less Britannicus the rallying point of a potential opposition, and provide Agrippine with a counterweight against Néron's growing independence. Indeed Agrippine must be said really to set the drama in motion: she it is who openly declares war on Caesar. But from now on action and reaction will quickly follow upon each other, and so obvious is Racine's competence in presenting a closely knit succession of events, each one clearly motivated by the characters' passions, that in the neo-classical reaction of the 1840s, when the dramatic incoherence and the psychological indigence of many French Romantic dramas had become all too apparent, Racine's psychology, Racine's naturalism, Racine's dramatic power were the first aspects of his art to emerge clearly. And the nineteenth century seems to have seen little else. Lanson's conception of Racinian tragedy as a *fait-divers* is the extreme form of such an interpretation, but Sainte-Beuve's incomprehension of *Bérénice* has similar causes.

It would be a mistake then to deny or to underestimate the power-ful impact of Racinian drama. There are no battles and no duels on the stage, yet the whole play is a battle, in which blow follows blow in rapid succession, in which every character stakes his life, and knows it. In every scene the relative position of the adversaries alters and shifts, and the action now slows down, now gathers momentum, and rushes towards the looming catastrophe; then every cue, every line, or half-line is like a thrust or a counter-thrust. In the more detailed study of the *Notes*, we shall see how, in the scenes that confront Junie and Néron (II, 3), Britannicus and Junie (II, 6), Néron and Britannicus (III, 7), Burrhus and Néron (IV, 3), Narcisse and Néron (IV, 4) . . . each character in turn steps forward and backward, feints, parries, or lunges. Even in the ever-moving pattern of conflicting motives inside one particular character, emotions increasingly fluctuate, and passion fights passion for the possession of his soul: in the course of the second scene of Act IV, with the lengthy speech Agrippine addresses to a sullen, silent Néron, the dramatic nature of her revelations—for we must under-stand that Néron was not aware of the full story of his own accession —Agrippine's reproaches, her grief and despair, her short-lived triumph, Néron's grim determination to withstand his mother's onslaught, his sudden collapse, followed by his gasp of fury and rebellion, all this gives to a scene which might at first sight appear static a hidden, quivering drama.

And yet, we soon realize that, in describing Racine's plays as psychological dramas, we are closing our eyes to large areas of his art, pretending they are not there. The verse, for instance. If it is psychological realism and rapid action we are after, the verse becomes an irrelevance and an encumbrance. In fact we have seen that it has, in Racine, great power of expression, but it serves not an analytical, but an emotional, purpose; it is one of Racine's ways of drawing the spectators in, to enhance, not only comprehension, but sympathy or identification: this has nothing to do with realism and everything with poetry.

Racine's poetry is an elusive and a difficult subject, partly because we are still inclined to think of poetry in terms of Romantic poetry: splendid similes, original metaphors, a rich and rare vocabulary, a powerful, evocative imagery. Racine's imagery is at times superb: it is enough to think of the nocturnal scene of Junie's arrival at the Imperial palace (see *Notes*), and it would not be difficult to discover a number of similar examples in his plays: Andromaque's eyes again stare at Troy, blazing in the night; Hippolyte's chariot once more, in Phèdre's hallucination, flies past in a glory of dust. Even when they are very brief, such images have an incisive, unforgettable quality: Néron, sitting on his throne, hastily rises to embrace Agrippine—and lead her away; the seasoned courtiers' eyes remain glued to the face of the master, while Britannicus is dying. But the point is that Racine seems intent on keeping them brief and few. It would be possible to gather quite a number of them, but the resulting impression would be misleading: is Racine a poet intermittently? As for his metaphors they seldom reveal a hidden relationship or a metaphysical 'correspondance': they are not those of a *voyant*; they are often the ordinary metaphors of the language of *galanterie* (not particularly *précieux* in the strict sense of the word[1]). *Fers, feux* and *flamme, vœux, soupirs* and *yeux,* are found in all contemporary writers. Sometimes (but only sometimes) Racine gives them a new, even a striking value. In *Phèdre,* it is impossible that such a self-conscious writer as he was, should have been unaware of the strange, almost unearthly, effect he was achieving when he called Phèdre's love a *dark flame* ('une flamme si noire'), and there are similar daring combinations of words in *Britannicus* (see *Notes*). When Néron offers to Junie the crown that is 'digne de *ses* beaux yeux', the metaphor is as banal as in Quinault, or in Thomas Corneille. When urged by the Emperor to send away Britannicus, Junie answers with indignation: 'Mes yeux lui défendront, Seigneur, de m'obéir', the word is used in its literal meaning, but it retains all its emotional associations, and finds a new strength in its new context. It is not only 'les yeux de César' (Brody) which are ever present in the play ('J'entendrai des regards que vous croirez muets'); it is Junie's eyes, 'ses yeux mouillés de larmes,/Qui brillaient au milieu des flambeaux et des armes', and Britannicus' eyes anxiously seeking her averted look; Agrippine's eyes ('ces yeux, où j'ai lu si longtemps mon devoir'), and her 'œil enflammé', which Néron fears; Claudius' eyes, 'longtemps fermés' and soon to close for ever, at last open to his, and his son's, mortal peril; and finally, after the murder, Néron's deadly, icy eyes. In those haunted eyes all the passions in *Britannicus* seem to pass as in a stormy, changing sky. The very word assumes a power of suggestion which the whole

---

[1] The term should be reserved for the fashionable set of people who *called* themselves so in the 1650s.

play combines to give it; it acquires a new, obsessive significance. It is not Romantic *chiaroscuro* which Racinian poetry suggests here, but rather the Mallarméan dream of 'donner un sens plus pur aux mots de la tribu'.

Rhythm and sound—one always comes back to them in Racine— are of course his main device to give words their evocative, magic power: the subtle use of *enjambement,* the constant shift in the *coupes* and the stresses, the line that now slows down and ponders heavily, now rushes to its end, the internal echoes, the mysterious chord Racine strikes between sense and sound, and the sinuous melody of his line that now vibrates and now whispers, or rasps, or urges, or lashes, or sings. Yet the expressive rhythm can only have its full value if it is set against a regular pattern. Racine, who can, when he chooses—in *Les Plaideurs*—dislocate the alexandrine with as much daring as Hugo, here often prefers to subdue it into a severer frame. Only to an untrained, or an inattentive, ear can this appear monoto- nous or stilted: the subtle, but constant, variety inside the *hémistiches* gives it the regularity not of a machine, but of breathing, and of life. And the same could be said of Racine's sentences, which he more usually groups in *quatrains,* but the *quatrains* are often subdivided into clauses and sentences which do not coincide with the lines, and when- ever emotion swells the breast of the speaker, the *quatrain* expands to 5, 6, 8, even 10 lines, before contracting again to its basic length. Here perhaps is one of Racine's major, if less obvious, achievements, for it is this rhythmic quality of the line and the speech that raises the play above the level of a 'drame réaliste'. In Britannicus' and Néron's decisive encounter, the use of stychomythia, the shifting opposition of lines, half-lines, and couplets create the impression of a *stylized* duel. As well as rousing the spectator's emotion and drawing him in, the effect of Racine's poetry is to *distance* the drama from the world of everyday reality. His heroes live in a brighter light, breathe a purer air than ours; they are akin to us, yet out of our world; they labour under human passions, yet they belong to a more radiant, more exemplary humanity. They live and die in a poignant yet remote universe, which can never, without absurdity, be identified with the disorderly world of the particular, the anecdote, or the *fait-divers.*

If then we attempt, imperfectly, to describe Racine's poetry, it is not so much of the painter, or the sculptor we are reminded, not of shades, and colours, and plastic shapes, as of rhythm, and sound,

and pattern—of music and ballet. 'Elle commence', Valéry said
(*L'Ame et la Danse*) of the dancing girl, 'par une marche toute
divine: c'est une simple marche circulaire. . . . Elle commence par
le suprême de son art; elle marche avec naturel sur le sommet
qu'elle a atteint. Cette seconde nature est ce qu'il y a de plus
éloigné de la première, mais il faut qu'elle lui ressemble à s'y
méprendre. . . . Une simple marche, et déesse la voici. . . .'
Racine's utterly un-Romantic poetry is an intangible, almost an
abstract, poetry. Un-Romantic too, because it springs from different
impulses and aims at different achievements. When it soars above
reality Romantic poetry more often wishes to escape through
imagination from a world too sordid and too vile to be endured; it
echoes all through with Gide's desperate cry: 'J'aime mieux mes
rêves!' What Racine reaches for, beyond the confusing world of
reality, is truth—*his* truth no doubt, but the truth of the world as he
believes it to be, not as he wishes it to be—the vision of a tragic
universe. It is, to some extent, an intellectual poetry, not less deeply
felt for that, but which, to be felt, must first be lucidly understood.
For Racine's poetry blossoms out not in the mysterious shadows of
dream, but in the blinding light of truth; and his poetry is, essentially
perhaps, his tragic poetry. Here perhaps lies the most original aspect
of his genius; here is perhaps the commanding factor of his art. In this
particular field, no poet, not even Euripides, whom Aristotle called
the most tragic of poets, not even Shakespeare have surpassed Racine.

We must guard, however, against giving too exclusive or too
rigorous a definition of tragedy. If the only tragic character is the one
who, without ever considering the possibility of compromise, freely
refuses a life that is not possible without compromise and chooses
death (Goldmann)—an admirable definition, but that of a limit
towards which the hero may tend without ever reaching it—then
most of Racine's heroes are unauthentic, non-tragic heroes, blindly
groping in, never emerging from, the vain agitation of drama; then
the only tragic character in *Britannicus* might be Junie, who never
lies or compromises, who, even if she does not die a physical death
at the end, finally and totally withdraws from life. But this interpretation, whatever its sociological and philosophical value, which is
great when Racine is considered in a vast historical context, is too
philosophical to do justice to a literary creation, and by dissociating
the tragic from the dramatic element in Racine's theatre, it risks
misrepresenting both.

The spirit of compromise, in so far as it is embodied in Burrhus, is not necessarily unethical in *Britannicus*, but it is of course incompatible with tragedy. It is everywhere in the play, and all the characters give it at some time qualified or temporary acceptance, Britannicus when he forgets his ambition and his revenge, Agrippine when she backs out of the plot, Néron when he fights desperately against Narcisse's ruthless solution. It is true that at no time do we find it convincing that Néron might go back to the pale embraces of the 'triste Octavie', or resign himself to being a cardboard Emperor, or that Agrippine's violence might not carry her beyond the point of no return. At the same time that growing, looming sense of the inevitable which Racine knows so well how to create must not be transformed into a banal *maktûb*, the shallow notion that 'it was written' all in advance. This is not only contrary to the poet's intention; it also robs the play of much of its interest. It irreparably splits the drama from the tragedy, with sad consequences for both: the drama becomes irrelevant to the tragedy; the tragedy reverts to the static type of the Renaissance, whereas in Racine's dynamic play drama and tragedy are interdependent: drama culminates in tragedy, it is the discovery of tragedy, the gradual closing in, as well as the sometimes imperfectly realized recognition by each character, of the *impasse*. Against that final vision all characters, because they are human, not ideal, characters, struggle and rebel; all try to delude themselves, or to escape through retreat or compromise. All, finally, in varying degrees of freedom and awareness, choose death, not only Junie, but Britannicus when he openly defies Domitius, Agrippine when in her final imprecation she refuses to accept Néron's denials and Narcisse's excuses, and Néron himself, not only when he makes the first fateful step into the darkening road Burrhus outlines for him as his future, but more immediately when, at the same time as Britannicus, he murders in himself the yearning, rebellious, ambiguous, but not vicious, adolescent we first met. But their desperate attempts to get out of the trap do not in themselves constitute a fall from the true spirit of tragedy, nor is it Racine's way of keeping his spectators occupied, or amused, before tragedy stalks upon the stage: those vain efforts to escape are in some way part of the tragedy. The drama as well as the verse are Racine's essential instruments in the final accomplishment of the tragic ritual.

Tragedy must not of course be thought of as an attribute of any particular character; it belongs to the play as a whole. In *Britannicus*, as we saw, the *impasse*, the insoluble dilemma, the impossible choice first springs from the political drama: Agrippine cannot abdicate her power, and she cannot destroy her son. Britannicus must fight a battle he cannot win. Néron must become a doomed tyrant or allow a rival to destroy him in time. The iron law of the Reason of State is here the sophisticated form of the law of the jungle, the only one valid among characters who, being above the law, live by definition in a state of lawlessness, whose relationships are exclusively ruled by force and by ruse. But the Reason of State also plays the part of Fate or Destiny. Every character walks in peril of his life, every one of them, whether he wishes or not, is a mortal peril to the other. All of them can arouse that terror which Aristotle saw as one of the fundamental emotions of tragedy, and those that survive have no prospect but that of coming destruction: Agrippine, Burrhus, Néron can all discern the abyss that will engulf them. But pity as well as fear, compassion as well as terror were for Aristotle tragic emotions of equal importance. And so did Racine believe. In a century in which tragedy, when it aimed above the interest of curiosity, suspense, and surprise, dealt mainly in the conflicts or the triumphs of will, Racine re-introduced emotion and tears: 'le pathétique retrouvé' (Vinaver) is a novel and a major element in his theatre. Critics, inexplicably anxious to emphasize some aspects of Racine's complex genius and to play down or ignore the others, have often underrated it, and this is particularly visible in the short shrift Britannicus has received from so many of them. For he does not fit in the dramatic scheme of the nineteenth-century Racine, being a largely powerless character, *agi* rather than *agent*; and he is of little relevance to the image of a 'tigerish' Racine; nor does he satisfy those who demand from the tragic hero a free, lucid acceptance of death: Britannicus goes to the banquet happy and peaceful; he will die without having understood. Yet if Racine has not succeeded in arousing a feeling of protective sympathy for his youthful, charming, wrong-headed hero, if the heart-rending, protracted separation of the two lovers, and the thrice-repeated farewell, which is to be the final one between them, fail to move his spectators or his critics, it must be their fault rather than his: Britannicus is not his most arresting creation, but an exceedingly condescending, or sarcastic, treatment of the character is a sure sign of a lop-sided approach to the play.

For we must not forget of course that if *Britannicus* is a tragedy of the Reason of State, it is also a tragedy of love, in a way not always dissimilar from *Andromaque*. It is not only in Junie and Britannicus that love is a powerful motive: Néron's tragedy, like Oreste's, is that he is in vital need of something which Junie alone could give him, and which she cannot possibly give him; and it is Agrippine's jealous, possessive love, as well as her ambition, that drives her into the ill-conceived plot that will, as in the case of Oreste, precipitate what she wishes to avoid. For in *Britannicus*, as in other Racinian plays, one of the main springs of tragedy is the self-destructive impulse, conscious or unconscious, that is one cause of the character's ultimate ruin: Junie herself prepares the ground for Néron's and Britannicus' duel, and Agrippine's premonitions are less a prophecy than a preconception of her mind, a prepared frame into which she, to a large extent, will force Néron.

And this is one reason why Britannicus and Junie have no monopoly of the pathos in the tragedy. Agrippine, as criminal as Athalie, is no less tragic and no less pathetic than the dying Queen of Judah: the brutal collapse of her hopes in the fifth act has an almost Shakespearian violence and irony. Agrippine has recoiled from sacrificing her son to her power; she now loses her son *and* her power, and the depth of her illusion brings proof, if it was required, of the depth of her love. And Néron, Néron himself. . . . If Racine's purpose was only, as he tells us in his Preface, to show the first stirring, then the birth, of a monster, why then has he not left us with the terrifying impact of Burrhus' message? Why has he preferred to superimpose, over that of the triumphant tyrant, a different image, a Néron in despair, in whose mind the spectre of suicide rises for the first, but, as Agrippine has reminded us, not for the last time, a Néron crushed and maddened by grief—an object of compassion as much as of horror? With Junie, Néron has lost his dream of happiness and tenderness, even his dream of fulfilment and manhood: Néron is maimed, for life. All that remains now is loneliness, and the fatality of future crimes, and death. Racine is a poet, not a moralist: he would have scorned to leave us with a self-complacent, self-conceited, feeling of righteous indignation that is alien to the spirit of tragedy. His art illuminates, it does not pass sentence, and the fierceness of Racinian tragedy must not make us blind to the compassion of its creator.

London, May 1966   P.F.B.

SELECT BIBLIOGRAPHY

I. FIRST READINGS

G. LYTTON STRACHEY, *Landmarks in French Literature*, 1911 (pp. 89–110).
— *Books and characters*, 1922 (pp. 3–27).
W. G. MOORE, *Racine: Britannicus*, London, Arnold, 1960 (a critical study, not an edition; in English).
— *French Classical Literature*, Oxford University Press, 1961 (pp. 60–82).
P. MOREAU, *Racine, l'homme et l'œuvre*, Paris, Boivin, 1943.
J. LEMAÎTRE, *Racine*, 1908 (*Britannicus:* pp. 169–189).

II. NINETEENTH CENTURY

Now largely of historical importance, but still useful to readers equipped to make the necessary adjustments.

J.-F. DE LA HARPE, *Lycée, ou Cours de littérature ancienne et moderne*, 1799–1805.
STENDHAL, *Racine et Shakespeare*, 1823–1825.
C. A. SAINTE-BEUVE, *Portraits littéraires*, vol. I (1829).
— *Nouveaux Lundis*, vol. III (1862).
— *Port-Royal*, vol. VI (1871).
H. TAINE, *Nouveaux Essais de critique et d'histoire*, 1865.
F. BRUNETIÈRE, *Manuel de l'histoire de la littérature française*, 1898.
G. LANSON, *Histoire de la littérature française* (First edition, 1894).

III. BEFORE 1940

G. LE BIDOIS, *La vie dans la tragédie de Racine*, 1922.
L. DUBECH, *Jean Racine politique*, 1926.
H. GAILLARD DE CHAMPRIS, *Les écrivains classiques* (in: ABBÉ CALVET, *Histoire de la littérature française*, V, 4), 1934.
H. CARRINGTON LANCASTER, *A history of French dramatic literature in the seventeenth century*, 1929–1942, 9 vols. *The period of Racine*, vol. IV, pt. 2.
T. MAULNIER, *Racine*, 1935.
D. MORNET, *Andromaque, Les Plaideurs, Britannicus*, Chefs-d'œuvre expliqués, Mellottée, s.d., with *Introduction, Lexique, Grammaire*, and extracts from contemporary authors.

IV. CONTEMPORARY

After the old concepts about *l'Ecole classique*, and about Boileau's influence as the master and adviser of Racine and Molière have been abandoned, the approach to seventeenth-century studies has been radically altered.

SELECT BIBLIOGRAPHY

A. ADAM, *Histoire de la littérature française au XVIIe siècle*, Paris, Domat, 1948–1956, 5 vols. (Racine in vol. IV).

J. BÉDIER et P. HAZARD, *Littérature française*, Paris, Larousse, 1948–1949, vol. I. (First edition of 1923–1924 brought up to date under the direction of P. Martino. Superbly illustrated.)

G. BRERETON, *Jean Racine, a critical biography*, London, Cassell, 1951.

P. GUÉGUEN, *Poésie de Racine*, Paris, Ed. du Rond-Point, 1946.

J. D. HUBERT, *Essai d'exégèse racinienne. Les secrets témoins*, Paris, Nizet, 1956.

J. C. LAPP, *Aspects of Racinian tragedy*, University of Toronto Press, 1955.

D. MORNET, *Histoire de la littérature française classique, 1660–1700*, Paris, Colin, 1947.

V. ADVANCED STUDY

Books suitable for advanced study of Racine, and particularly for students whose reading will extend beyond *Britannicus*.

(a) Editions

Œuvres complètes, ed. R. PICARD, Paris, La Pléiade, 1951, 2 vols. (The plays are in vol. I).

Œuvres de Racine, ed. L. MESNARD, Collection des Grands Ecrivains de la France, 1923. 8 vols. (*Britannicus* in vol. II).

(b) Biographical, historical

L. RACINE, *Mémoires sur la vie de Jean Racine*, 1747. (By Racine's son; reproduced in Picard's and Mesnard's editions.)

A. MASSON-FORESTIER, *Autour d'un Racine ignoré*, 1910.

C. MAURON, *L'inconscient dans l'œuvre et la vie de Racine*, Publications des Annales de la Faculté des Lettres, Aix-en-Provence, 1957.

R. PICARD, *La carrière de Jean Racine*, Paris, Gallimard, 1956.

— *Corpus Racinianum*, Paris, Belles-Lettres, 1956, followed by a *Supplément*, 1961.

J. DUBU, *Racine. Lettres d'Uzès*, Péladan, 1963. (Introduction, and text of Racine's letters from Uzès.)

(c) Critical

R. BARTHES, *Sur Racine*, Paris Seuil, 1963.

P. BÉNICHOU, *Morales du grand siècle*, Paris, Gallimard, 1948.

J. BRODY, ' "Les yeux de César": the Language of Vision in *Britannicus*' (in: *Studies in Seventeenth Century French Literature*, Ithaca, 1962.)

P. BUTLER, *Classicisme et baroque dans l'œuvre de Racine*, Paris, Nizet, 1959. (On *Britannicus* see chapters VI and VII.)

J. CAIRNCROSS, *Andromache and other plays*, Penguin Classics, 1967 (Critic. essays and transl.).

L. GOLDMANN, *Le dieu caché. Etude sur la vision tragique dans les Pensées de Pascal et dans le théâtre de Racine*, Paris, Gallimard, 1955. (*Britannicus*, p. 363.)

R. C. KNIGHT, *Racine et la Grèce*, Paris, Boivin, 1950.

R. JASINSKI, *Vers le vrai Racine*, Paris, Colin, 1958, 2 vols.

G. MAY, *Tragédie cornélienne, tragédie racinienne. Etudes sur les sources de l'intérêt dramatique*, Urbana, The University of Illinois Press, 1948.

BRITANNICUS

J. POMMIER, *Aspects de Racine*, Paris, Nizet, 1954.
I. SICILIANO, *Racine e il classicismo francese*, Milano, Montuoro, 1943.
E. VINAVER, *Racine et la poésie tragique*, Paris, Nizet, 1951 (Transl. Mansell Jones, Manchester University Press, 1955). Revised edition, 1963.
C. VOSSLER, *Jean Racine*, München, 1926 (in German).

(d) History of criticism

E. BOURSAULT, *Artemise et Poliante, Nouvelle*, 1670. (The *première* of *Britannicus*. Relevant pages in Coll. des Gr. Ecr. de Fr. and in La Pléiade.)
F. Y. ECCLES, *Racine in England*, 1922.
M. FUBINI, *Jean Racine e la critica delle sue tragedie*, 1925.
W. MCSTEWART, 'Racine vu par les Anglais de 1800 à nos jours', *Rev. de Litt. Comp.*, XIX, 1939.

(e) Dramatic technique

R. BRAY, *La formation de la doctrine classique*, 1927.
E. VINAVER, *Racine. Principes de la tragédie en marge de la Poétique d'Aristote*, Editions de l'Université de Manchester, 1944.
J. SCHÉRER, *La dramaturgie classique*, Paris, Nizet, 1954.

(f) Stagecraft

Mémoire de Mahelot, Laurent et d'autres décorateurs, publ. by H. C. Lancaster, 1920.
S. W. DEIERKAUF-HOLSBOER, *Histoire de la mise en scène dans le théâtre français de 1600 à 1657*, Paris, Droz, 1933 (Revised edition 1960).
P. MÉLÈSE, *Le théâtre et le public à Paris sous Louis XIV*, 1934.
T. E. LAWRENSON, *The French stage in the seventeenth century. A study in the advent of the Italian order*, Manchester University Press, 1957.
J. LOUGH, *Paris theatre audiences in the seventeenth and eighteenth centuries*, Oxford University Press, 1957.
J. HEUZEY, 'Costume et décoration tragique', *Rev. d'Hist. du théâtre*, XII, 1, 1960.
D. ROY, 'La scène de l'Hôtel de Bourgogne', *Rev. d'Hist. du théâtre*, XIV, 3, 1962.

(g) Lexicography

C. MARTY-LAVEAUX, *Lexique de la langue de Racine*, Coll. des Gr. Ecr. de Fr., vol. VIII.
J. CAHEN, *Le vocabulaire de Racine*, Paris, Droz, 1946.
F. CAYROU, *Le français classique*, Paris, Didier, 1930.
R. HARTLE, *Index des mots de 'Britannicus'*, Klinsieck, 1956.

(h) Bibliography

G. LANSON, *Manuel bibliographique de la littérature française*, 1931. (Mainly for seventeenth, eighteenth, and nineteenth centuries.)
J. GIRAUD, *Manuel de bibliographie littéraire, 1921–1935*.
— *Manuel de Bibliographie littéraire, 1936–1945*.
E. E. WILLIAMS, *Racine depuis 1885*, Baltimore, Johns Hopkins Press, 1940.
C. CORDIÉ, *Raciniana, studi, testi e traduzioni, 1940–1950*, Milano, Malfasi, s.d.
D. C. CABEEN and J. BRODY, *A critical Bibliography of French Literature*, vol. III: *The seventeenth century*. Syracuse University Press, 1961.

62

SELECT BIBLIOGRAPHY

(i) *Current bibliography*

Revue d'histoire littéraire de la France.

Dix-septième siècle.

The Year's Work in Modern Language Studies. (Selective and critical.)

Bibliographie der Französischen Literaturwissenschaft, ed. OTTO PLATT. Kloster-
mann, Frankfurt-am-Main. (Exhaustive.)

BRITANNICUS

A MONSEIGNEUR
LE DUC DE CHEVREUSE

MONSEIGNEUR

Vous serez peut-être étonné de voir votre nom à la tête de cet ouvrage. Et si je vous avais demandé la permission de vous l'offrir, je doute si je l'aurais obtenue. Mais ce serait en quelque sorte ingrat que de cacher plus longtemps au monde les bontés* dont vous m'avez toujours honoré. Quelle apparence* qu'un homme qui ne travaille que pour la gloire se puisse taire d'une protection aussi glorieuse que la vôtre? Non, MONSEIGNEUR, il m'est trop avantageux que l'on sache que mes amis mêmes ne vous sont pas indifférents, que vous prenez part* à tous mes ouvrages, et que vous m'avez procuré l'honneur de lire celui-ci devant un homme dont toutes les heures sont précieuses. Vous fûtes témoin avec quelle pénétration d'esprit il jugea de l'économie* de la pièce, et combien l'idée qu'il s'est formée d'une excellente tragédie est au delà de tout ce que j'en ai pu concevoir. Ne craignez pas, MONSEIGNEUR, que je m'engage plus avant, et que n'osant le louer en face, je m'adresse à vous pour le louer avec plus de liberté. Je sais qu'il serait dangereux de le fatiguer de ses louanges. Et j'ose dire que cette même modestie qui vous est commune avec lui n'est pas un des moindres liens qui vous attachent l'un à l'autre. La modération n'est qu'une vertu ordinaire quand elle ne se rencontre qu'avec des qualités ordinaires. Mais qu'avec toutes les qualités et du cœur et de l'esprit, qu'avec un jugement qui, ce semble, ne devrait être le fruit que de l'expérience de plusieurs* années, qu'avec mille belles connaissances que vous ne sauriez cacher à vos amis particuliers, vous ayez encore cette sage retenue que tout le monde admire en vous, c'est sans doute une vertu rare en un siècle où l'on fait vanité des moindres choses. Mais je me laisse emporter insensiblement à la tentation de parler de vous. Il faut qu'elle soit bien violente, puisque je n'ai pu y résister dans une lettre

* Words marked with an asterisk are explained in the *Glossary*.

67

où je n'avais autre dessein que de vous témoigner avec combien de respect je suis,

MONSEIGNEUR,

Votre très humble et très obéissant serviteur,

RACINE

PREMIÈRE PRÉFACE

(1670)

De tous les ouvrages que j'ai donnés au public, il n'y en a point qui m'ait attiré plus d'applaudissements ni plus de censeurs que celui-ci. Quelque soin que j'aie pris pour travailler cette tragédie, il semble qu'autant* que je me suis efforcé de la rendre bonne, autant de certaines gens se sont efforcés de la décrier. Il n'y a 5
point de cabale qu'ils n'aient faite, point de critique dont ils ne se soient avisés. Il y en a qui ont pris même le parti de Néron contre moi. Ils ont dit que je le faisais trop cruel. Pour moi, je croyais que le nom seul de Néron faisait entendre quelque chose de plus que cruel. Mais peut-être qu'ils raffinent sur son histoire, 10
et veulent dire qu'il était honnête homme dans ses premières années. Il ne faut qu'avoir lu Tacite pour savoir que s'il a été quelque temps un bon Empereur, il a toujours été un très méchant homme. Il ne s'agit point dans ma tragédie des affaires du dehors. Néron est ici dans son particulier et dans sa famille. 15
Et ils me dispenseront de leur rapporter tous les passages qui pourraient bien aisément leur prouver que je n'ai point de réparation à lui faire.

D'autres ont dit au contraire que je l'avais fait trop bon. J'avoue que je ne m'étais pas formé l'idée d'un bon* homme en 20
la personne de Néron. Je l'ai toujours regardé comme un monstre. Mais c'est ici un monstre naissant. Il n'a pas encore mis le feu à Rome. Il n'a pas tué sa mère, sa femme, ses gouverneurs.* A cela près il me semble qu'il lui échappe assez de cruautés pour empêcher que personne ne le méconnaisse.* 25

Quelques-uns ont pris l'intérêt de Narcisse, et se sont plaints que j'en eusse fait un très méchant homme et le confident de Néron. Il suffit d'un passage pour leur répondre. Néron, dit Tacite, porta* impatiemment* la mort de Narcisse, parce que cet affranchi avait une conformité merveilleuse avec les vices du 30
Prince encore cachés. *Cujus abditis adhuc vitiis mire congruebat.*

Les autres se sont scandalisés que j'eusse choisi un homme aussi jeune que Britannicus pour le héros d'une tragédie. Je leur

ai déclaré* dans la préface d'*Andromaque* les sentiments d'Aristote sur le héros de la tragédie, et que bien loin d'être parfait, il   35
faut toujours qu'il ait quelque imperfection. Mais je leur dirai
encore ici qu'un jeune Prince de dix-sept ans, qui a beaucoup
de cœur,* beaucoup d'amour, beaucoup de franchise et beaucoup de crédulité, qualités ordinaires d'un jeune homme, m'a
semblé très capable d'exciter la compassion. Je n'en veux pas   40
davantage.

Mais, disent-ils, ce Prince n'entrait que dans sa quinzième
année lorsqu'il mourut. On le fait vivre, lui et Narcisse, deux
ans plus* qu'ils n'ont vécu. Je n'aurais point parlé de cette
objection, si elle n'avait été faite avec chaleur par un homme   45
qui s'est donné la liberté de faire régner vingt ans un Empereur
qui n'en a régné que huit, quoique ce changement soit bien plus
considérable dans la chronologie, où l'on suppute les temps par
les années des Empereurs.

Junie ne manque pas non plus de censeurs. Ils disent que   50
d'une vieille coquette nommée Junia Silana, j'en* ai fait une
jeune fille très sage. Qu'auraient-ils à me répondre, si je leur
disais que cette Junie est un personnage inventé, comme
l'Emilie de *Cinna*, comme la Sabine d'*Horace*? Mais j'ai à leur
dire que s'ils avaient bien lu l'histoire, ils y auraient trouvé   55
une Junia Calvina, de la famille d'Auguste, sœur de Silanus, à
qui Claudius avait promis Octavie. Cette Junie était jeune,
belle, et comme dit Sénèque, *festivissima omnium puellarum.* Elle
aimait tendrement son frère, *et leurs ennemis,* dit Tacite, *les
accusèrent tous deux d'inceste, quoiqu'ils ne fussent coupables que*   60
*d'un peu d'indiscrétion.** Si je la représente plus retenue qu'elle
n'était, je n'ai pas ouï dire qu'il nous fût défendu de rectifier les
mœurs d'un personnage, surtout lorsqu'il n'est pas connu.

L'on trouve étrange qu'elle paraisse sur le théâtre après la
mort de Britannicus. Certainement la délicatesse* est grande de   65
ne pas vouloir qu'elle dise en quatre vers assez touchants qu'elle
passe chez Octavie. Mais, disent-ils, cela ne valait pas la peine
de la faire revenir. Un autre l'aurait pu raconter pour elle.
Ils ne savent pas qu'une des règles du théâtre est de ne mettre
en récit que les choses qui ne se peuvent passer en action; et que   70
tous les anciens font venir souvent sur la scène des acteurs qui
n'ont autre chose à dire, sinon qu'ils viennent d'un endroit et
qu'ils s'en retournent en un autre.

Tout cela est inutile, disent mes censeurs. La pièce est finie au
récit de la mort de Britannicus, et l'on ne devrait point écouter   75
le reste. On l'écoute pourtant, et même avec autant d'attention
qu'aucune fin de tragédie. Pour moi j'ai toujours compris que
la tragédie étant l'imitation d'une action complète, où*
plusieurs personnes concourent, cette action n'est point finie
que* l'on ne sache en quelle situation elle laisse ces mêmes   80
personnes. C'est ainsi que Sophocle en use* presque partout.
C'est ainsi que dans l'*Antigone* il emploie autant de vers à
représenter la fureur d'Hémon et la punition de Créon après la
mort de cette Princesse que j'en ai employé aux imprécations
d'Agrippine, à la retraite de Junie, à la punition de Narcisse,   85
et au désespoir de Néron, après la mort de Britannicus.

Que faudrait-il faire pour contenter des juges si difficiles? La
chose serait aisée pour peu qu'on voulût trahir le bon sens. Il ne
faudrait que s'écarter du naturel pour se jeter dans l'extraordinaire. Au lieu d'une action simple, chargée de peu de   90
matière, telle que doit être une action qui se passe en seul jour,
et qui s'avançant par degrés vers sa fin, n'est soutenue que par
les intérêts, les sentiments, et les passions des personnages, il
faudrait remplir cette même action de quantité d'incidents qui
ne se pourraient passer qu'en un mois, d'un grand nombre de   95
jeux de théâtre d'autant plus surprenants qu'ils seraient moins
vraisemblables, d'une infinité de déclamations où l'on ferait
dire aux acteurs tout le contraire de ce qu'ils devraient dire.
Il faudrait par exemple représenter quelque héros ivre, qui se
voudrait faire haïr de sa maîtresse de gaieté de cœur, un   100
Lacédémonien grand parleur, un conquérant qui ne débiterait
que des maximes d'amour, une femme qui donnerait des leçons
de fierté à des conquérants. Voilà sans doute de quoi faire
récrier* tous ces Messieurs. Mais que dirait cependant le petit
nombre de gens sages auxquels je m'efforce de plaire? De quel   105
front* oserais-je me montrer, pour ainsi dire, aux yeux de ces
grands hommes de l'antiquité que j'ai choisis pour modèles?
Car, pour me servir de la pensée d'un ancien, voilà les véritables
spectateurs que nous devons nous proposer, et nous devons sans
cesse nous demander: Que diraient Homère et Virgile s'ils   110
lisaient ces vers? Que dirait Sophocle s'il voyait représenter cette
scène? Quoi qu'il en soit, je n'ai point prétendu empêcher qu'on
ne parlât contre mes ouvrages. Je l'aurais prétendu inutilement.

BRITANNICUS

Quid de te alii loquantur ipsi videant, dit Cicéron, *sed loquentur tamem.* 115

Je prie seulement le lecteur de me pardonner cette petite préface que j'ai faite pour lui rendre raison de ma tragédie. Il n'y a rien de plus naturel que de se défendre quand on se croit injustement attaqué. Je vois que Térence même semble n'avoir fait des prologues que pour se justifier contre les 120 critiques d'un vieux poète malintentionné, *malevoli veteris poetae,* et qui venait briguer des voix contre lui jusqu'aux heures où l'on représentait ses comédies.

> *Occæpta est agi:*
> *Exclamat,* etc. 125

On me pouvait faire une difficulté qu'on ne m'a point faite. Mais ce qui est échappé aux spectateurs pourra être remarqué par les lecteurs. C'est que je fais entrer Junie dans* les Vestales, où,* selon Aulu-Gelle, on ne recevait personne au-dessous de six ans, ni au-dessus de dix. Mais le peuple prend ici Junie sous 130 sa protection, et j'ai cru qu'en considération de sa naissance, de sa vertu, et de son malheur, il pouvait la dispenser de l'âge prescrit par les lois, comme il a dispensé de l'âge pour le consulat tant de grands hommes qui avaient mérité ce privilège.

Enfin je suis très persuadé qu'on me peut faire bien d'autres 135 critiques, sur lesquelles je n'aurais d'autre parti à prendre que celui d'en profiter à l'avenir. Mais je plains fort le malheur d'un homme qui travaille pour le public. Ceux qui voient le mieux nos défauts sont ceux qui les dissimulent le plus volontiers. Ils nous pardonnent les endroits qui leur ont déplu, en faveur de 140 ceux qui leur ont donné du plaisir. Il n'y a rien au contraire de plus injuste qu'un ignorant. Il croit toujours que l'admiration est le partage des gens qui ne savent rien. Il condamne toute une pièce pour une scène qu'il n'approuve pas. Il s'attaque même aux endroits les plus éclatants pour faire croire qu'il a de 145 l'esprit. Et pour peu que nous résistions à ses sentiments, il nous traite de présomptueux qui ne veulent croire personne, et ne songe pas qu'il tire quelquefois plus de vanité d'une critique fort mauvaise que nous n'en tirons d'une assez bonne pièce de théâtre. 150

Homine imperito numquam quidquam injustius.

72

SECONDE PRÉFACE

(1676)

Voici celle de mes tragédies que je puis dire que j'ai le plus
travaillée. Cependant j'avoue que le succès* ne répondit pas
d'abord à mes espérances. A peine elle parut sur le théâtre,
qu'il s'éleva quantité de critiques qui semblaient la devoir
détruire. Je crus moi-même que sa destinée serait à l'avenir   5
moins heureuse que celle de mes autres tragédies. Mais enfin il
est arrivé de cette pièce ce qui arrivera toujours des ouvrages
qui auront quelque bonté.* Les critiques se sont évanouies. La
pièce est demeurée.* C'est maintenant celle des miennes que
la cour et le public revoient le plus volontiers. Et si j'ai fait   10
quelque chose de solide* et qui mérite quelque louange, la plu-
part des connaisseurs demeurent d'accord que c'est ce même
Britannicus.

A la vérité j'avais travaillé sur des modèles qui m'avaient
extrêmement soutenu dans la peinture que je voulais faire de la   15
cour d'Agrippine et de Néron. J'avais copié mes personnages
d'après le plus grand peintre de l'antiquité, je veux dire d'après
Tacite. Et j'étais alors si rempli de la lecture de cet excellent
historien qu'il n'y a presque pas un trait éclatant dans ma
tragédie dont il ne m'ait donné l'idée. J'avais voulu mettre dans   20
ce recueil un extrait des plus beaux endroits que j'ai tâché
d'imiter. Mais j'ai trouvé que cet extrait tiendrait presque
autant de place que la tragédie. Ainsi le lecteur trouvera bon
que je le renvoie à cet auteur, qui aussi bien est entre les mains
de tout le monde. Et je me contenterai de rapporter ici quelques-   25
uns de ses passages sur chacun des personnages que j'introduis
sur la scène.

Pour commencer par Néron, il faut se souvenir qu'il est ici
dans les premières années de son règne, qui ont été heureuses,
comme l'on sait. Ainsi il ne m'a pas été permis de le représenter   30
aussi méchant qu'il a été depuis. Je ne le représente pas non plus
comme un homme vertueux, car il ne l'a jamais été. Il n'a pas
encore tué sa mère, sa femme, ses gouverneurs, mais il a en lui
les semences de tous ces crimes. Il commence à vouloir secouer

le joug. Il les hait les uns et les autres, et il leur cache sa haine   35
sous de fausses caresses,* *factus natura velare odium fallacibus
blanditiis.* En un mot c'est ici un monstre naissant, mais qui n'ose
encore se déclarer, et qui 'cherche des couleurs* à ses méchantes
actions', *hactenus Nero flagitiis et sceleribus velamenta quæsivit.* Il ne
pouvait souffrir Octavie, Princesse d'une bonté et d'une vertu   40
exemplaire, *fato quodam, an quia prævalent illicita. Metuebaturque
ne in stupra feminarum illustrium prorumperet.*

Je lui donne Narcisse pour confident. J'ai suivi en cela
Tacite, qui dit que Néron 'porta* impatiemment la mort de
Narcisse, parce que cet affranchi avait une conformité mer-   45
veilleuse avec les vices du Prince encore cachés', *cujus abditis adhuc
vitiis mire congruebat.* Ce passage prouve deux choses. Il prouve
et que Néron était déjà vicieux, mais qu'il dissimulait ses vices,
et que Narcisse l'entretenait dans ses mauvaises inclinations.

J'ai choisi Burrhus pour opposer un honnête homme à cette   50
peste de cour. Et je l'ai choisi plutôt que Sénèque. En voici la
raison. 'Ils étaient tous deux gouverneurs* de la jeunesse de
Néron, l'un pour les armes, l'autre pour les lettres. Et ils étaient
fameux, Burrhus pour son expérience dans les armes et pour la
sévérité* de ses mœurs', *militaribus curis et severitate morum;*   55
'Sénèque pour son éloquence et le tour agréable de son esprit',
Seneca præceptis eloquentiæ et comitate honesta. Burrhus après sa mort
'fut extrêmement regretté à cause de sa vertu', *civitati grande
desiderium ejus mansit per memoriam virtutis.*

Toute leur peine était de résister à l'orgueil et à la férocité   60
d'Agrippine, *quæ cunctis malæ dominationis cupidinibus flagrans,
habebat in partibus Pallantem.* Je ne dis que ce mot d'Agrippine,
car il y aurait trop de choses à en* dire. C'est elle que je me suis
surtout efforcé de bien exprimer, et ma tragédie n'est pas moins
la disgrâce d'Agrippine que la mort de Britannicus. Cette mort   65
fut un coup de foudre pour elle, et 'il parut* (dit Tacite) par sa
frayeur et par sa consternation qu'elle était aussi innocente de
cette mort qu'Octavie. Agrippine perdait en lui sa dernière
espérance, et ce crime lui en faisait craindre un plus grand.'
Sibi supremum auxilium ereptum, et parricidii exemplum intelligebat.   70

L'âge de Britannicus était si connu qu'il ne m'a pas été permis de le représenter autrement que comme un jeune Prince
qui avait beaucoup de cœur,* beaucoup d'amour, et beaucoup
de franchise, qualités ordinaires d'un jeune homme. Il avait

quinze ans, 'et on dit qu'il avait beaucoup d'esprit, soit qu'on   75
dise vrai, ou que ses malheurs aient fait croire cela de lui sans
qu'il ait pu en donner des marques.' *Neque segnem ei fuisse
indolem ferunt, sive verum, seu periculis commendatus retinuit famam
sine experimento.*

Il ne faut pas s'étonner s'il n'a auprès de lui qu'un aussi   80
méchant homme que Narcisse. 'Car il y avait longtemps qu'on
avait donné ordre qu'il n'y eût auprès de Britannicus que des
gens qui n'eussent ni foi ni honneur.' *Nam ut proximus quisque
Britannico neque fas neque fidem pensi haberet, olim provisum erat.*

Il me reste à parler de Junie. Il ne la faut pas confondre avec   85
une vieille coquette qui s'appelait Junia Silana. C'est ici une
autre Junie, que Tacite appelle Junia Calvina, de la famille
d'Auguste, sœur de Silanus, à qui Claudius avait promis Octavie. Cette Junie était jeune, belle, et comme dit Sénèque,
festivissima omnium puellarum. Son frère et elle s'aimaient tendre-   90
ment, et 'leurs ennemis (dit Tacite) les accusèrent tous deux
d'inceste, quoiqu'ils ne fussent coupables que d'un peu
d'indiscrétion.'* Elle vécut jusqu'au règne de Vespasien.

Je la fais entrer dans* les Vestales, quoique selon Aulu-Gelle
on n'y reçût jamais personne au-dessous de six ans, ni au-dessus   95
de dix. Mais le peuple prend ici Junie sous sa protection. Et j'ai
cru qu'en considération de sa naissance, de sa vertu, et de son
malheur, il pouvait la dispenser de l'âge prescrit par les lois,
comme il a dispensé de l'âge pour le consulat tant de grands
hommes qui avaient mérité ce privilège.   100

ACTEURS

NÉRON, Empereur, fils d'Agrippine.

BRITANNICUS, fils de l'Empereur Claudius.

AGRIPPINE, veuve de Domitius Enobarbus, père de Néron, et en secondes noces veuve de l'Empereur Claudius.

JUNIE, amante* de Britannicus.

BURRHUS, gouverneur* de Néron.

NARCISSE, gouverneur de Britannicus.

ALBINE, confidente d'Agrippine.

GARDES.

La scène est à Rome, dans une chambre du palais de Néron.

BRITANNICUS
TRAGÉDIE

ACTE I

SCÈNE I

Agrippine   Albine

ALBINE

Quoi! tandis que Néron s'abandonne au sommeil,
Faut-il que vous veniez attendre son réveil?
Qu'errant dans le palais sans suite et sans escorte
La mère de César veille seule à sa porte?
Madame, retournez dans votre appartement.   5

AGRIPPINE

Albine, il ne faut pas s'éloigner un moment.
Je veux l'attendre ici. Les chagrins* qu'il me cause
M'occuperont assez tout le temps qu'il repose.
Tout ce que j'ai prédit n'est que trop assuré.
Contre Britannicus Néron s'est déclaré.   10
L'impatient* Néron cesse de se contraindre:
Las de se faire aimer, il veut se faire craindre.
Britannicus le gêne,* Albine, et chaque jour
Je sens que je deviens importune à mon tour.

ALBINE

Quoi? vous à qui Néron doit le jour qu'il respire?   15
Qui l'avez appelé de si loin à l'Empire?
Vous qui déshéritant le fils de Claudius,
Avez nommé César l'heureux Domitius?
Tout lui parle, Madame, en faveur d'Agrippine.
Il vous doit son amour.   20

BRITANNICUS

AGRIPPINE

Il me le doit, Albine.
Tout, s'il est généreux,* lui prescrit cette loi.
Mais tout, s'il est ingrat, lui parle contre moi.

ALBINE

S'il est ingrat, Madame! Ah! toute sa conduite
Marque* dans son devoir une âme trop instruite.
Depuis trois ans entiers qu'a-t-il dit, qu'a-t-il fait,   25
Qui ne promette à Rome un Empereur parfait?
Rome, depuis deux ans par ses soins gouvernée,
Au temps de ses consuls croit être retournée:
Il la gouverne en père. Enfin Néron naissant*
A toutes les vertus d'Auguste vieillissant.   30

AGRIPPINE

Non, non, mon intérêt* ne me rend point injuste:
Il commence, il est vrai, par où finit Auguste.
Mais crains que l'avenir détruisant le passé,
Il ne finisse ainsi qu'Auguste a commencé.
Il se déguise en vain. Je lis sur son visage   35
Des fiers* Domitius l'humeur* triste,* et sauvage.
Il mêle avec l'orgueil qu'il a pris dans leur sang
La fierté des Nérons qu'il puisa dans mon flanc.
Toujours la tyrannie a d'heureuses prémices.
De Rome pour un temps Caïus fut les délices,   40
Mais sa feinte bonté se tournant en fureur,*
Les délices de Rome en devinrent l'horreur.
Que m'importe, après tout, que Néron plus fidèle*
D'une longue vertu laisse un jour le modèle?
Ai-je mis dans sa main le timon de l'Etat   45
Pour le conduire au gré du Peuple et du Sénat?
Ah! que de la Patrie il soit s'il veut le Père.
Mais qu'il songe un peu plus qu'Agrippine est sa mère.
De quel nom cependant pouvons-nous appeler
L'attentat que le jour vient de nous révéler?   50
Il sait, car leur amour* ne peut être ignorée,
Que de Britannicus Junie est adorée:
Et ce même Néron, que la vertu conduit,
Fait enlever Junie au milieu de la nuit.

Que veut-il? Est-ce haine, est-ce amour qui l'inspire?   55
Cherche-t-il seulement le plaisir de leur nuire?
Ou plutôt n'est-ce point que sa malignité
Punit sur eux l'appui que je leur ai prêté?

ALBINE

Vous leur appui, Madame?

AGRIPPINE
                    Arrête, chère Albine.
Je sais que j'ai moi seule avancé leur ruine,   60
Que du trône, où le sang l'a dû* faire monter,
Britannicus par moi s'est vu précipiter.
Par moi seule éloigné de l'hymen d'Octavie,
Le frère de Junie abandonna la vie,
Silanus, sur qui Claude avait jeté les yeux,   65
Et qui comptait Auguste au rang de ses aïeux.
Néron jouit de tout, et moi pour récompense*
Il faut qu'entre eux et lui je tienne la balance,
Afin que quelque jour par une même loi
Britannicus la tienne entre mon fils et moi.   70

ALBINE

Quel dessein!

AGRIPPINE
                    Je m'assure un port dans la tempête.
Néron m'échappera, si ce frein ne l'arrête.

ALBINE

Mais prendre contre un fils tant de soins superflus?

AGRIPPINE

Je le craindrais bientôt, s'il ne me craignait plus.

ALBINE

Une injuste frayeur vous alarme peut-être.   75
Mais si Néron pour vous n'est plus ce qu'il doit être,
Du moins son changement ne vient pas jusqu'à nous,

79

Et ce sont des secrets entre César et vous.
Quelques titres nouveaux que Rome lui défère,
Néron n'en reçoit point qu'il ne donne à sa mère.   80
Sa prodigue amitié* ne se réserve rien.
Votre nom est dans Rome aussi saint que le sien.
A peine parle-t-on de la triste* Octavie.
Auguste votre aïeul honora moins Livie.
Néron devant sa mère a permis le premier   85
Qu'on portât les faisceaux couronnés de laurier.
Quels effets voulez-vous de sa reconnaissance?

AGRIPPINE

Un peu moins de respect, et plus de confiance.
Tous ces présents, Albine, irritent* mon dépit.*
Je vois mes honneurs croître, et tomber mon crédit.   90
Non, non, le temps n'est plus que* Néron jeune encore
Me renvoyait les vœux d'une cour qui l'adore,
Lorsqu'il se reposait sur moi de tout l'Etat,
Que mon ordre au palais assemblait le Sénat,
Et que derrière un voile, invisible, et présente,   95
J'étais de ce grand corps l'âme toute-puissante.
Des volontés de Rome alors mal assuré,
Néron de sa grandeur n'était point enivré.
Ce jour, ce triste* jour frappe encor* ma mémoire,
Où Néron fut lui-même ébloui de sa gloire,   100
Quand les ambassadeurs de tant de rois divers
Vinrent le reconnaître au nom de l'univers.
Sur son trône avec lui j'allais prendre ma place.
J'ignore quel conseil prépara ma disgrâce:*
Quoi qu'il en soit, Néron, d'aussi loin qu'il me vit,   105
Laissa sur son visage éclater son dépit.*
Mon cœur même en conçut un malheureux augure.
L'ingrat, d'un faux respect colorant* son injure,
Se leva par avance, et courant m'embrasser,
Il m'écarta du trône, où je m'allais placer.   110
Depuis ce coup fatal, le pouvoir d'Agrippine
Vers sa chute, à grands pas, chaque jour s'achemine.
L'ombre seule m'en reste, et l'on n'implore plus
Que le nom de Sénèque, et l'appui de Burrhus.

ALBINE

Ah! si de ce soupçon votre âme est prévenue,   115
Pourquoi nourrissez-vous le venin* qui vous tue?
Daignez avec César vous éclaircir* du moins.

AGRIPPINE

César ne me voit plus, Albine, sans témoins.
En public, à mon heure, on me donne audience.
Sa réponse est dictée, et même son silence.   120
Je vois deux surveillants, ses maîtres, et les miens,
Présider l'un ou l'autre à tous nos entretiens.
Mais je le poursuivrai d'autant plus qu'il m'évite.
De son désordre,* Albine, il faut que je profite.
J'entends du bruit: on ouvre. Allons subitement   125
Lui demander raison de cet enlèvement.
Surprenons, s'il se peut, les secrets de son âme.
Mais quoi? déjà Burrhus sort de chez lui?

SCÈNE II

Agrippine   Burrhus   Albine

BURRHUS

                              Madame,
Au nom de l'Empereur j'allais vous informer
D'un ordre, qui d'abord a pu vous alarmer,   130
Mais qui n'est que l'effet d'une sage conduite,
Dont César a voulu que vous soyez instruite.

AGRIPPINE

Puisqu'il le veut, entrons: il m'en instruira mieux.

BURRHUS

César pour quelque temps s'est soustrait à nos yeux.
Déjà par une porte au public moins connue,   135
L'un et l'autre consul vous avaient prévenue,
Madame. Mais souffrez que je retourne exprès . . .

81

AGRIPPINE

Non, je ne trouble point ses augustes secrets.*
Cependant* voulez-vous qu'avec moins de contrainte
L'un et l'autre une fois nous nous parlions sans feinte?   140

BURRHUS

Burrhus pour le mensonge eut toujours trop d'horreur.

AGRIPPINE

Prétendez*-vous longtemps me cacher l'Empereur?
Ne le verrai-je plus qu'à titre d'importune?
Ai-je donc élevé si haut votre fortune*
Pour mettre une barrière entre mon fils et moi?   145
Ne l'osez-vous laisser un moment sur sa foi?*
Entre Sénèque et vous disputez*-vous la gloire
A qui m'effacera plutôt* de sa mémoire?
Vous l'ai-je confié pour en faire un ingrat?
Pour être sous son nom les maîtres de l'Etat?   150
Certes plus je médite, et moins je me figure
Que vous m'osiez compter pour votre créature;*
Vous, dont j'ai pu* laisser vieillir l'ambition
Dans les honneurs obscurs de quelque légion,
Et moi, qui sur le trône ai suivi mes ancêtres,   155
Moi, fille, femme, sœur, et mère de vos maîtres.
Que prétendez*-vous donc? Pensez-vous que ma voix*
Ait fait un Empereur pour m'en imposer trois?
Néron n'est plus enfant. N'est-il pas temps qu'il règne?
Jusqu'à quand voulez-vous que l'Empereur vous craigne?   160
Ne saurait-il rien voir, qu'*il n'emprunte vos yeux?
Pour se conduire enfin n'a-t-il pas ses aïeux?
Qu'il choisisse, s'il veut, d'Auguste ou de Tibère.
Qu'il imite, s'il peut, Germanicus mon père.
Parmi tant de héros je n'ose me placer.   165
Mais il est des vertus que je lui puis tracer.
Je puis l'instruire au moins combien sa confidence*
Entre un sujet et lui doit laisser de distance.

BURRHUS

Je ne m'étais chargé dans cette occasion
Que d'excuser César d'une seule action.   170

Mais puisque sans vouloir que je le justifie,
Vous me rendez garant du reste de sa vie,
Je répondrai, Madame, avec la liberté
D'un soldat, qui sait mal farder la vérité.

Vous m'avez de César confié la jeunesse,   175
Je l'avoue, et je dois m'en souvenir sans cesse.
Mais vous avais-je fait serment de le trahir,
D'en faire un Empereur qui ne sût qu'obéir?
Non. Ce n'est plus à vous qu'il faut que j'en* réponde.
Ce n'est plus votre fils. C'est le maître du monde.   180
J'en* dois compte,* Madame, à l'Empire romain,
Qui croit voir son salut ou sa perte en ma main.
Ah! si dans l'ignorance il le fallait instruire,
N'avait-on que Sénèque et moi pour le séduire?*
Pourquoi de sa conduite* éloigner les flatteurs?   185
Fallait-il dans l'exil chercher des corrupteurs?
La cour de Claudius, en esclaves fertile,
Pour deux que l'on cherchait en eût présenté mille,
Qui tous auraient brigué l'honneur de l'avilir:
Dans une longue enfance ils l'auraient fait vieillir.   190
De quoi vous plaignez-vous, Madame? On vous révère.
Ainsi que par César, on jure par sa mère.
L'Empereur, il est vrai, ne vient plus chaque jour
Mettre à vos pieds l'Empire, et grossir votre cour.
Mais le doit-il, Madame? Et sa reconnaissance   195
Ne peut-elle éclater* que dans sa dépendance?
Toujours humble, toujours le timide Néron
N'ose-t-il être Auguste et César que de nom?
Vous le dirai-je enfin? Rome le justifie.
Rome, à trois affranchis si longtemps asservie,   200
A peine respirant* du joug qu'elle a porté,
Du* règne de Néron compte sa liberté.
Que dis-je? La vertu semble même renaître.
Tout l'Empire n'est plus la dépouille* d'un maître.
Le peuple au Champ de Mars nomme ses magistrats;   205
César nomme les chefs sur la foi* des soldats.
Thraséas au Sénat, Corbulon dans* l'armée,
Sont encore innocents, malgré leur renommée.
Les déserts* autrefois peuplés de sénateurs
Ne sont plus habités que par leurs délateurs.   210

Qu'importe que César continue à nous croire,
Pourvu que nos conseils ne tendent qu'à sa gloire?
Pourvu que dans le cours d'un règne florissant
Rome soit toujours libre, et César tout-puissant?
    Mais, Madame, Néron suffit pour se conduire.   215
J'obéis, sans prétendre à l'honneur de l'instruire.
Sur ses aïeux sans doute il n'a qu'à se régler.
Pour bien faire, Néron n'a qu'à se ressembler:
Heureux, si ses vertus l'une à l'autre enchaînées
Ramènent tous les ans ses premières années!   220

AGRIPPINE

Ainsi sur l'avenir n'osant vous assurer,*
Vous croyez que sans vous Néron va s'égarer.
Mais vous, qui jusqu'ici content* de votre ouvrage,
Venez de ses vertus nous rendre témoignage,
Expliquez-nous pourquoi, devenu ravisseur,   225
Néron de Silanus fait enlever la sœur.
Ne tient-il qu'à marquer* de cette ignominie
Le sang de mes aïeux, qui brille dans Junie?
De quoi l'accuse-t-il? Et par quel attentat
Devient-elle en un jour criminelle d'Etat?   230
Elle, qui sans orgueil jusqu'alors élevée
N'aurait point vu Néron, s'il ne l'eût enlevée,
Et qui même aurait mis au rang de ses bienfaits
L'heureuse liberté de ne le voir jamais.

BURRHUS

Je sais que d'aucun crime elle n'est soupçonnée.   235
Mais jusqu'ici César ne l'a point condamnée,
Madame. Aucun objet* ne blesse ici ses yeux.
Elle est dans un palais tout plein de ses aïeux.
Vous savez que les droits qu'elle porte avec elle
Peuvent de son époux faire un prince rebelle,   240
Que le sang de César ne se doit allier
Qu'à ceux à qui César le veut bien confier;
Et vous-même avoûrez qu'il ne serait pas juste
Qu'on disposât sans lui de la nièce* d'Auguste.

AGRIPPINE

Je vous entends.* Néron m'apprend par votre voix   245
Qu'en vain Britannicus s'assure* sur mon choix.
En vain pour détourner ses yeux de sa misère,*
J'ai flatté* son amour d'un hymen qu'il espère.
A ma confusion Néron veut faire voir
Qu'Agrippine promet par delà son pouvoir.   250
Rome de ma faveur est trop préoccupée :*
Il veut par cet affront qu'elle soit détrompée,
Et que tout l'univers apprenne avec terreur
A ne confondre plus mon fils et l'Empereur.
Il le peut. Toutefois j'ose encore lui dire   255
Qu'il doit avant ce coup* affermir son empire,
Et qu'en me réduisant à la nécessité
D'éprouver contre lui ma faible autorité,
Il expose la sienne, et que dans la balance
Mon nom peut-être aura plus de poids qu'il ne pense.   260

BURRHUS

Quoi, Madame ? Toujours soupçonner son respect ?
Ne peut-il faire un pas qui ne vous soit suspect ?
L'Empereur vous croit-il du parti de Junie ?
Avec Britannicus vous croit-il réunie ?*
Quoi ! de vos ennemis devenez-vous l'appui   265
Pour trouver un prétexte à vous plaindre de lui ?
Sur le moindre discours* qu'on pourra vous redire,
Serez-vous toujours prête à partager* l'Empire ?
Vous craindrez-vous sans cesse, et vos embrassements
Ne se passeront-ils qu'en éclaircissements ?*   270
Ah ! quittez d'un censeur la triste* diligence.*
D'une mère facile* affectez l'indulgence.
Souffrez quelques froideurs sans les faire éclater,*
Et n'avertissez point la cour de vous quitter.

AGRIPPINE

Et qui s'honorerait de l'appui d'Agrippine,   275
Lorsque Néron lui-même annonce ma ruine ?
Lorsque de sa présence il semble me bannir ?
Quand Burrhus à sa porte ose me retenir ?

BURRHUS

Madame, je vois bien qu'il est temps de me taire,
Et que ma liberté commence à vous déplaire.　　　　　280
La douleur est injuste, et toutes les raisons
Qui ne la flattent* point aigrissent* ses soupçons.
Voici Britannicus. Je lui cède ma place.
Je vous laisse écouter et plaindre* sa disgrâce,*
Et peut-être, Madame, en accuser les soins*　　　　　285
De ceux que l'Empereur a consultés le moins.

SCÈNE III

Agrippine　Britannicus　Narcisse　Albine

AGRIPPINE

Ah, Prince! où courez-vous? Quelle ardeur inquiète
Parmi vos ennemis en aveugle vous jette?
Que venez-vous chercher?

BRITANNICUS

　　　　　　　Ce que je cherche? Ah, Dieux!
Tout ce que j'ai perdu, Madame, est en ces lieux.　　　290
De mille affreux* soldats Junie environnée
S'est vue en ce palais indignement traînée.
Hélas! de quelle horreur ses timides esprits*
A ce nouveau* spectacle auront été surpris!
Enfin on me l'enlève. Une loi* trop sévère　　　　　295
Va séparer deux cœurs qu'assemblait leur misère.*
Sans doute on ne veut pas que mêlant nos douleurs
Nous nous aidions l'un l'autre à porter* nos malheurs.

AGRIPPINE

Il suffit. Comme vous je ressens vos injures.*
Mes plaintes ont déjà précédé vos murmures.　　　　300
Mais je ne prétends* pas qu'un impuissant courroux
Dégage ma parole, et m'acquitte envers vous.
Je ne m'explique point. Si vous voulez m'entendre,*
Suivez-moi chez Pallas, où je vais vous attendre.

SCÈNE IV

Britannicus   Narcisse

BRITANNICUS

La croirai-je, Narcisse? Et dois-je sur sa foi*   305
La prendre pour arbitre entre son fils et moi?
Qu'en dis-tu? N'est-ce pas cette même Agrippine
Que mon père épousa jadis pour sa ruine,
Et qui, si je t'en crois, a de ses derniers jours,
Trop lents pour ses desseins, précipité le cours?   310

NARCISSE

N'importe. Elle se sent comme vous outragée.
A vous donner Junie elle s'est engagée.
Unissez vos chagrins, liez vos intérêts.
Ce palais retentit en vain de vos regrets.
Tandis* qu'on vous verra d'une voix suppliante   315
Semer ici la plainte, et non pas l'épouvante,
Que vos ressentiments se perdront en discours,
Il n'en faut point douter, vous vous plaindrez toujours.

BRITANNICUS

Ah, Narcisse! tu sais si de la servitude
Je prétends faire encore une longue habitude.   320
Tu sais si pour jamais, de* ma chute étonné,*
Je renonce à l'Empire, où* j'étais destiné.
Mais je suis seul encor.* Les amis de mon père
Sont autant d'inconnus que glace ma misère.*
Et ma jeunesse même écarte loin de moi   325
Tous ceux qui dans le cœur me réservent leur foi.*
Pour moi depuis un an qu'un peu d'expérience
M'a donné de mon sort la triste connaissance,
Que vois-je autour de moi, que* des amis vendus
Qui sont de tous mes pas les témoins assidus,   330
Qui choisis par Néron pour ce commerce infâme,
Trafiquent avec lui des secrets de mon âme?
Quoi qu'il en soit, Narcisse, on me vend tous les jours.
Il prévoit mes desseins, il entend mes discours.
Comme toi dans mon cœur il sait ce qui se passe.   335
Que t'en semble, Narcisse?

D   87

NARCISSE

Ah! quelle âme assez basse . . .
C'est â vous de choisir des confidents discrets,
Seigneur, et de ne pas prodiguer vos secrets.

BRITANNICUS

Narcisse, tu dis vrai. Mais cette défiance
Est toujours d'un grand cœur la dernière science. 340
On le trompe longtemps. Mais enfin, je te croi.*
Ou plutôt je fais vœu de ne croire que toi.
Mon père, il m'en souvient, m'assura de ton zèle.
Seul de ses affranchis tu m'es toujours fidèle.
Tes yeux, sur ma conduite incessamment ouverts, 345
M'ont sauvé jusqu'ici de mille écueils couverts.*
Va donc voir si le bruit de ce nouvel orage
Aura de nos amis excité le courage.
Examine leurs yeux. Observe leurs discours.
Vois si j'en* puis attendre un fidèle secours. 350
Surtout dans ce palais remarque avec adresse
Avec quel soin Néron fait garder la Princesse.
Sache si du péril ses beaux yeux* sont remis,
Et si son entretien m'est encore permis.
Cependant* de Néron je vais trouver la mère 355
Chez Pallas, comme toi l'affranchi de mon père.
Je vais la voir, l'aigrir,* la suivre, et s'il se peut,
M'engager sous son nom plus loin qu'elle ne veut.

ACTE II

SCÈNE I

Néron Burrhus Narcisse Gardes

NÉRON

N'en doutez point, Burrhus; malgré ses injustices,
C'est ma mère, et je veux ignorer ses caprices. 360
Mais je ne prétends* plus ignorer ni souffrir
Le ministre insolent qui les ose nourrir.

Pallas de ses conseils empoisonne ma mère;
Il séduit* chaque jour Britannicus mon frère;
Ils l'écoutent tout seul, et qui* suivrait leurs pas   365
Les trouverait peut-être assemblés chez Pallas.
C'en est trop. De tous deux il faut que je l'écarte.
Pour la dernière fois, qu'il s'éloigne, qu'il parte:
Je le veux, je l'ordonne; et que la fin du jour
Ne le retrouve pas dans Rome, ou dans ma cour.   370
Allez: cet ordre importe au salut de l'Empire.
Vous, Narcisse, approchez. Et vous, qu'on* se retire.

SCÈNE II

Néron   Narcisse

NARCISSE

Grâces aux Dieux, Seigneur, Junie entre vos mains
Vous assure* aujourd'hui du reste des Romains.
Vos ennemis, déchus de leur vaine espérance,   375
Sont allés chez Pallas pleurer leur impuissance.
Mais que vois-je? Vous-même inquiet,* étonné,*
Plus que Britannicus paraissez consterné.
Que présage à mes yeux cette tristesse* obscure,
Et ces sombres regards errants à l'aventure?   380
Tout vous rit.* La fortune obéit à vos vœux.

NÉRON

Narcisse, c'en est fait. Néron est amoureux.*

NARCISSE

Vous?

NÉRON

Depuis un moment, mais pour toute ma vie.
J'aime (que dis-je aimer?) j'idolâtre Junie.

NARCISSE

Vous l'aimez?

NÉRON

Excité d'*un désir curieux,   385
Cette nuit je l'ai vue arriver en ces lieux,
Triste, levant au ciel ses yeux mouillés de larmes,
Qui brillaient au travers des flambeaux et des armes,
Belle, sans ornements, dans le simple appareil*
D'une beauté qu'on vient d'arracher au sommeil.   390
Que veux-tu? Je ne sais si cette négligence,*
Les ombres, les flambeaux, les cris, et le silence,
Et le farouche aspect de ses fiers* ravisseurs
Relevaient de ses yeux les timides douceurs.
Quoi qu'il en soit, ravi d'une si belle vue,   395
J'ai voulu lui parler et ma voix s'est perdue:
Immobile, saisi d'un long étonnement,*
Je l'ai laissé passer dans son appartement.
J'ai passé dans le mien. C'est là que solitaire
De son image en vain j'ai voulu me distraire:*   400
Trop présente à mes yeux je croyais lui parler.
J'aimais jusqu'à ses pleurs que je faisais couler.
Quelquefois, mais trop tard, je lui demandais grâce.
J'employais les soupirs, et même la menace.
Voilà comme* occupé* de mon nouvel amour,   405
Mes yeux sans se fermer ont attendu le jour.
Mais je m'en fais peut-être une trop belle image.
Elle m'est apparue avec trop d'avantage,
Narcisse, qu'en dis-tu?

NARCISSE

Quoi, Seigneur! croira-t-on
Qu'elle ait pu si longtemps se cacher à Néron?   410

NÉRON

Tu le sais bien, Narcisse. Et soit que sa colère
M'imputât le malheur qui lui ravit son frère,
Soit que son cœur, jaloux d'une austère fierté,*
Enviât* à nos yeux sa naissante beauté,
Fidèle à sa douleur, et dans l'ombre enfermée,   415
Elle se dérobait même à sa renommée.
Et c'est cette vertu, si nouvelle à la cour,
Dont la persévérance irrite* mon amour.

Quoi, Narcisse? Tandis qu'il n'est point de Romaine
Que mon amour n'honore et ne rende plus vaine,   420
Qui dès qu'à ses regards elle ose se fier,
Sur le cœur de César ne les vienne essayer;
Seule dans son palais la modeste Junie
Regarde leurs honneurs comme une ignominie,
Fuit, et ne daigne pas peut-être s'informer   425
Si César est aimable,* ou bien s'il sait aimer?
Dis-moi: Britannicus l'aime-t-il?

NARCISSE

Quoi! s'il l'aime,
Seigneur?

NÉRON

Si jeune encor,* se connaît-il lui-même?
D'un regard enchanteur* connaît-il le poison?

NARCISSE

Seigneur, l'amour toujours n'attend pas la raison.   480
N'en doutez point, il l'aime. Instruits par tant de charmes,*
Ses yeux sont déjà faits à l'usage des larmes.
A ses moindres désirs il sait s'accommoder;*
Et peut-être déjà sait-il persuader.

NÉRON

Que dis-tu? sur son cœur il aurait quelque empire?   435

NARCISSE

Je ne sais. Mais, Seigneur, ce que je puis vous dire,
Je l'ai vu quelquefois s'arracher de ces lieux,
Le cœur plein d'un courroux qu'il cachait à vos yeux,
D'une cour qui le fuit pleurant l'ingratitude,
Las de votre grandeur, et de sa servitude,   440
Entre l'impatience* et la crainte flottant;
Il allait voir Junie, et revenait content*.

NÉRON

D'autant plus malheureux qu'il aura su lui plaire,
Narcisse, il doit plutôt souhaiter sa colère.
Néron impunément* ne sera pas jaloux.   445

91

NARCISSE

Vous? Et de quoi, Seigneur, vous inquiétez-vous?
Junie a pu le plaindre et partager ses peines:
Elle n'a vu couler de* larmes que les siennes.
Mais aujourd'hui, Seigneur, que ses yeux dessillés,
Regardant de plus près l'éclat dont vous brillez,   450
Verront autour de vous les rois sans diadème,
Inconnus dans la foule, et son amant lui-même,
Attachés sur vos yeux s'honorer d'un regard
Que vous aurez sur eux fait tomber au hasard;
Quand elle vous verra de ce degré de gloire   455
Venir en soupirant* avouer sa victoire,
Maître, n'en doutez point, d'un cœur déjà charmé,*
Commandez qu'on vous aime, et vous serez aimé.

NÉRON

A combien de chagrins* il faut que je m'apprête!
Que d'importunités!

NARCISSE

                    Quoi donc? Qui* vous arrête,   460
Seigneur?

NÉRON

                    Tout. Octavie, Agrippine, Burrhus,
Sénèque, Rome entière, et trois ans de vertus.
Non que pour Octavie un reste de tendresse
M'attache à son hymen, et plaigne* sa jeunesse.
Mes yeux, depuis longtemps fatigués de ses soins,*   465
Rarement de ses pleurs daignent être témoins.
Trop heureux si bientôt la faveur d'un divorce
Me soulageait d'un joug qu'on m'imposa par force!
Le Ciel même en secret semble la condamner.
Ses vœux depuis quatre ans ont beau l'importuner.   470
Les Dieux ne montrent point que sa vertu les touche:
D'aucun gage, Narcisse, ils n'honorent sa couche,
L'Empire vainement demande un héritier.

NARCISSE

Que* tardez-vous, Seigneur, à la répudier?

L'Empire, votre cœur, tout condamne Octavie.   475
Auguste votre aïeul soupirait* pour Livie;
Par un double divorce ils s'unirent tous deux,
Et vous devez l'Empire à ce divorce heureux.
Tibère, que l'hymen plaça dans sa famille,
Osa bien à ses yeux répudier sa fille.   480
Vous seul, jusques* ici contraire à vos désirs,
N'osez par un divorce assurer vos plaisirs.

NÉRON

Et ne connais-tu pas l'implacable Agrippine?
Mon amour inquiet déjà se l'imagine
Qui m'amène Octavie, et d'un œil enflammé   485
Atteste les saints droits d'un nœud qu'elle a formé,
Et portant à mon cœur des atteintes* plus rudes,
Me fait un long récit de mes ingratitudes.
De quel front* soutenir ce fâcheux* entretien?

NARCISSE

N'êtes-vous pas, Seigneur, votre maître et le sien?   490
Vous verrons-nous toujours trembler sous sa tutelle?
Vivez, régnez pour vous. C'est trop régner pour elle.
Craignez-vous? Mais, Seigneur, vous ne la craignez pas.
Vous venez de bannir le superbe* Pallas,
Pallas dont vous savez qu'elle soutient l'audace.   495

NÉRON

Eloigné de ses yeux, j'ordonne, je menace,
J'écoute vos conseils, j'ose les approuver,
Je m'excite contre elle et tâche* à la braver.
Mais (je t'expose ici mon âme toute nue)
Sitôt que mon malheur me ramène à sa vue,   500
Soit que je n'ose encor* démentir* le pouvoir
De ces yeux, où j'ai lu si longtemps mon devoir,
Soit qu'à tant de bienfaits ma mémoire fidèle
Lui soumette en secret tout ce que je tiens d'elle:
Mais enfin mes efforts ne me servent de rien,   505
Mon génie* étonné* tremble devant le sien.
Et c'est pour m'affranchir de cette dépendance
Que je la fuis partout, que même je l'offense,

93

Et que de temps en temps j'irrite* ses ennuis,*
Afin qu'elle m'évite autant que je la fuis.   510
Mais je t'arrête trop. Retire-toi, Narcisse:
Britannicus pourrait t'accuser d'artifice.

NARCISSE

Non, non, Britannicus s'abandonne à ma foi.*
Par son ordre, Seigneur, il croit que je vous voi,*
Que je m'informe ici de tout ce qui le touche,   515
Et veut de vos secrets être instruit par ma bouche.
Impatient surtout de revoir ses amours,*
Il attend de mes soins* ce fidèle secours.

NÉRON

J'y consens: porte-lui cette douce nouvelle.
Il la verra.   520

NARCISSE

Seigneur, bannissez-le loin d'elle.

NÉRON

J'ai mes raisons, Narcisse, et tu peux concevoir
Que je lui vendrai cher le plaisir de la voir.
Cependant* vante-lui ton heureux stratagème.
Dis-lui qu'en sa faveur on me trompe moi-même,
Qu'il la voit sans mon ordre. On ouvre, la voici.   525
Va retrouver ton maître et l'amener ici.

SCÈNE III

Néron   Junie

NÉRON

Vous vous troublez, Madame, et changez de visage.
Lisez-vous dans mes yeux quelque triste* présage?

JUNIE

Seigneur, je ne vous puis déguiser mon erreur:
J'allais voir Octavie, et non pas l'Empereur.   530

94

NÉRON

Je le sais bien, Madame, et n'ai pu sans envie
Apprendre vos bontés* pour l'heureuse Octavie.

JUNIE

Vous, Seigneur?

NÉRON

Pensez-vous, Madame, qu'en ces lieux
Seule pour vous connaître Octavie ait des yeux?

JUNIE

Et quel autre, Seigneur, voulez-vous que j'implore?   535
A qui demanderai-je un crime que j'ignore?
Vous qui le punissez, vous ne l'ignorez pas.
De grâce, apprenez-moi, Seigneur, mes attentats.

NÉRON

Quoi, Madame! Est-ce donc une légère offense
De m'avoir si longtemps caché votre présence?*   540
Ces trésors dont le ciel voulut vous embellir,
Les avez-vous reçus pour les ensevelir?
L'heureux Britannicus verra-t-il sans alarmes
Croître loin de nos yeux son amour et vos charmes?*
Pourquoi, de cette gloire exclus* jusqu'à ce jour,   545
M'avez-vous sans pitié relégué dans ma cour?
On dit plus: vous souffrez sans en être offensée
Qu'il vous ose, Madame, expliquer* sa pensée.
Car je ne croirai point que sans me consulter
La sévère Junie ait voulu le flatter,*   550
Ni qu'elle ait consenti* d'aimer et d'être aimée,
Sans que j'en sois instruit que* par la renommée.

JUNIE

Je ne vous nîrai point, Seigneur, que ses soupirs*
M'ont daigné quelquefois expliquer* ses désirs.
Il n'a point détourné ses regards d'une fille,   555
Seul reste du débris* d'une illustre famille.
Peut-être il se souvient qu'en un temps plus heureux
Son père me nomma pour l'objet de ses vœux.*

Il m'aime. Il obéit à l'Empereur son père,
Et j'ose dire encore, à vous, à votre mère: 560
Vos désirs sont toujours si conformes aux siens . . .

NÉRON

Ma mère a ses desseins, Madame, et j'ai les miens.
Ne parlons plus ici de Claude et d'Agrippine.
Ce n'est point par leur choix que je me détermine.
C'est à moi seul, Madame, à* répondre de vous;   565
Et je veux de ma main vous choisir un époux.

JUNIE

Ah, Seigneur! songez-vous que toute autre alliance
Fera honte aux Césars auteurs de ma naissance?

NÉRON

Non, Madame, l'époux dont je vous entretiens
Peut sans honte assembler vos aïeux et les siens.   570
Vous pouvez, sans rougir, consentir à sa flamme.*

JUNIE

Et quel est donc, Seigneur, cet époux?

NÉRON

Moi, Madame.

JUNIE

Vous?

NÉRON

Je vous nommerais, Madame, un autre nom,
Si j'en savais quelque autre au-dessus de Néron.
Oui, pour vous faire un choix où* vous puissiez souscrire, 575
J'ai parcouru des yeux la cour, Rome, et l'Empire.
Plus j'ai cherché, Madame, et plus je cherche encor*
En quelles mains je dois confier* ce trésor,
Plus je vois que César, digne seul de vous plaire,
En doit être lui seul l'heureux dépositaire,   580
Et ne peut dignement vous confier qu'aux mains

A qui* Rome a commis* l'empire des humains.
Vous-même, consultez* vos premières années.
Claudius à son fils les avait destinées,
Mais c'était en un temps où de l'Empire entier   585
Il croyait quelque jour le nommer l'héritier.
Les Dieux ont prononcé. Loin de leur contredire,*
C'est à vous de passer du côté de l'Empire.
En vain de ce présent ils m'auraient honoré,
Si votre cœur devait en être séparé;   590
Si tant de soins* ne sont adoucis par vos charmes;*
Si tandis que je donne aux veilles, aux alarmes,
Des jours toujours à plaindre, et toujours enviés,
Je ne vais quelquefois respirer à vos pieds.
Qu'Octavie à vos yeux ne fasse point d'ombrage.   595
Rome aussi bien que moi vous donne son suffrage,
Répudie Octavie, et me fait dénouer
Un hymen que le Ciel ne veut point avouer.*
Songez-y donc, Madame, et pesez en vous-même
Ce choix digne des soins* d'un Prince qui vous aime,   600
Digne de vos beaux yeux* trop longtemps captivés,*
Digne de l'univers à qui vous vous devez.

JUNIE

Seigneur, avec raison je demeure étonnée.*
Je me vois dans le cours d'une même journée
Comme une criminelle amenée en ces lieux;   605
Et lorsque avec frayeur je parais à vos yeux,
Que sur mon innocence à peine je me fie,*
Vous m'offrez tout d'un coup la place d'Octavie.
J'ose dire pourtant que je n'ai mérité
Ni cet excès d'honneur, ni cette indignité.   610
Et pouvez-vous, Seigneur, souhaiter qu'une fille
Qui vit presque en naissant éteindre* sa famille,
Qui dans l'obscurité nourrissant sa douleur
S'est fait une vertu conforme à son malheur,
Passe subitement de cette nuit profonde   615
Dans* un rang qui l'expose aux yeux de tout le monde,
Dont je n'ai pu de loin soutenir la clarté,
Et dont une autre enfin remplit* la majesté?

NÉRON

Je vous ai déjà dit que je la répudie.
Ayez moins de frayeur, ou moins de modestie.   620
N'accusez point ici mon choix d'aveuglement.
Je vous réponds de vous, consentez seulement.
Du sang dont vous sortez rappelez* la mémoire,
Et ne préférez point à la solide* gloire
Des honneurs dont César prétend* vous revêtir   625
La gloire d'un refus, sujet au repentir.

JUNIE

Le Ciel connaît, Seigneur, le fond de ma pensée.
Je ne me flatte point d'une gloire insensée.
Je sais de vos présents mesurer la grandeur.
Mais plus ce rang sur moi répandrait de splendeur,   630
Plus il me ferait honte et mettrait en lumière
Le crime d'en avoir dépouillé l'héritière.

NÉRON

C'est de ses intérêts prendre beaucoup de soin,
Madame, et l'amitié ne peut aller plus loin.
Mais ne nous flattons* point, et laissons le mystère.*   635
La sœur vous touche ici beaucoup moins que le frère,
Et pour Britannicus . . .

JUNIE

Il a su me toucher,
Seigneur, et je n'ai point prétendu* m'en cacher.
Cette sincérité sans doute est peu discrète;
Mais toujours de mon cœur ma bouche est l'interprète.   640
Absente de la cour, je n'ai pas dû* penser,
Seigneur, qu'en l'art de feindre il fallût m'exercer.
J'aime Britannicus. Je lui fus destinée
Quand l'Empire devait suivre son hyménée.
Mais ces mêmes malheurs qui l'en ont écarté,   645
Ses honneurs abolis, son palais déserté,
La fuite d'une cour que sa chute a bannie,
Sont autant de liens qui retiennent Junie.
Tout ce que vous voyez conspire* à vos désirs;
Vos jours toujours sereins coulent dans les plaisirs.   650

L'Empire en est pour vous l'inépuisable source,
Ou si quelque chagrin* en interrompt la course,*
Tout l'univers, soigneux* de les entretenir,
S'empresse* à l'effacer de votre souvenir.
Britannicus est seul. Quelque ennui* qui le presse,*　　655
Il ne voit dans son sort que moi qui s'intéresse,*
Et n'a pour tous plaisirs, Seigneur, que quelques pleurs
Qui lui font quelquefois oublier ses malheurs.

NÉRON

Et ce sont ces plaisirs et ces pleurs que j'envie,
Que tout autre que lui me paîrait de sa vie.　　660
Mais je garde à ce Prince un traitement plus doux.
Madame, il va bientôt paraître devant vous.

JUNIE

Ah, Seigneur! vos vertus m'ont toujours rassurée.

NÉRON

Je pouvais* de ces lieux lui défendre l'entrée.
Mais, Madame, je veux prévenir le danger　　665
Où* son ressentiment le pourrait engager.
Je ne veux point le perdre. Il vaut mieux que lui-même
Entende son arrêt de la bouche qu'il aime.
Si ses jours vous sont chers, éloignez-le de vous
Sans qu'il ait aucun lieu de me croire jaloux.　　670
De son bannissement prenez sur vous l'offense,
Et soit par vos discours,* soit par votre silence,
Du moins par vos froideurs, faites-lui concevoir
Qu'il doit porter ailleurs ses vœux* et son espoir.

JUNIE

Moi! Que je lui prononce un arrêt si sévère!*　　675
Ma bouche mille fois lui jura le contraire.
Quand même jusque-là je pourrais me trahir,
Mes yeux lui défendront, Seigneur, de m'obéir.

NÉRON

Caché près de ces lieux, je vous verrai, Madame:
Renfermez votre amour dans le fond de votre âme.　　680

99

Vous n'aurez point pour moi de langages secrets.
J'entendrai des regards que vous croirez muets.
Et sa perte sera l'infaillible salaire
D'un geste, ou d'un soupir échappé pour lui plaire.

JUNIE

Hélas! si j'ose encor* former quelques souhaits,   685
Seigneur, permettez-moi de ne le voir jamais.

SCÈNE IV

Néron   Junie   Narcisse

NARCISSE

Britannicus, Seigneur, demande la Princesse.
Il approche.

NÉRON

Qu'il vienne.

JUNIE

Ah, Seigneur!

NÉRON

Je vous laisse.

Sa fortune* dépend de vous plus que de moi.
Madame, en le voyant, songez que je vous voi.*   690

SCÈNE V

Junie   Narcisse

JUNIE

Ah! cher Narcisse, cours au-devant de ton maître.
Dis-lui . . . Je suis perdue, et je le vois paraître.

100

SCÈNE VI

Junie   Britannicus   Narcisse

BRITANNICUS

Madame, quel bonheur me rapproche de vous?
Quoi! je puis donc jouir d'un entretien si doux?
Mais parmi* ce plaisir quel chagrin* me dévore!   695
Hélas! puis-je espérer* de vous revoir encore?
Faut-il que je dérobe avec mille détours*
Un bonheur que vos yeux* m'accordaient tous les jours?
Quelle nuit! Quel réveil! Vos pleurs, votre présence*
N'ont point de ces cruels désarmé l'insolence?   700
Que faisait votre amant? Quel démon* envieux*
M'a refusé l'honneur de mourir à vos yeux?
Hélas! dans la frayeur dont vous étiez atteinte,
M'avez-vous en secret adressé quelque plainte?
Ma Princesse, avez-vous daigné me souhaiter?*   705
Songiez-vous aux douleurs que vous m'alliez coûter?
Vous ne me dites rien? Quel accueil! Quelle glace!
Est-ce ainsi que vos yeux* consolent ma disgrâce?*
Parlez. Nous sommes seuls. Notre ennemi trompé,
Tandis que je vous parle, est ailleurs occupé.   710
Ménageons* les moments de cette heureuse absence.

JUNIE

Vous êtes en des lieux tout pleins de sa puissance.
Ces murs mêmes, Seigneur, peuvent avoir des yeux,
Et jamais l'Empereur n'est absent de ces lieux.

BRITANNICUS

Et depuis quand, Madame, êtes-vous si craintive?   715
Quoi! déjà votre amour souffre qu'on le captive?*
Qu'est devenu ce cœur qui me jurait toujours
De faire à Néron même envier nos amours?
Mais bannissez, Madame, une inutile crainte.
La foi* dans tous les cœurs n'est pas encore éteinte.   720
Chacun semble des yeux approuver mon courroux;
La mère de Néron se déclare pour nous;
Rome, de sa conduite elle-même offensée . . .

JUNIE

Ah, Seigneur! vous parlez contre votre pensée.
Vous-même, vous m'avez avoué mille fois   725
Que Rome le louait d'une commune voix.
Toujours à sa vertu vous rendiez quelque hommage;
Sans doute la douleur vous dicte ce langage.

BRITANNICUS

Ce discours* me suprend, il le faut avouer.
Je ne vous cherchais pas pour l'entendre louer.   730
Quoi! pour vous confier la douleur qui m'accable,
A peine* je dérobe un moment favorable,
Et ce moment si cher,* Madame, est consumé
A louer l'ennemi dont je suis opprimé?*
Qui* vous rend à vous-même en un jour si contraire?   735
Quoi! même vos regards ont appris à se taire?
Que vois-je? Vous craignez de rencontrer mes yeux?
Néron vous plairait-il? Vous serais-je odieux?
Ah! si je le croyais . . . Au nom des Dieux, Madame,
Eclaircissez le trouble où vous jetez mon âme,   740
Parlez. Ne suis-je plus dans votre souvenir?

JUNIE

Retirez-vous, Seigneur, l'Empereur va venir.

BRITANNICUS

Après ce coup, Narcisse, à qui* dois-je m'attendre?*

SCÈNE VII

Néron   Junie   Narcisse

NÉRON

Madame . . .

JUNIE

                Non, Seigneur, je ne puis rien entendre.
Vous êtes obéi. Laissez couler du moins   745
Des larmes dont ses yeux ne seront pas témoins.

SCÈNE VIII

Néron   Narcisse

NÉRON

Hé bien! de leur amour tu vois la violence,
Narcisse: elle a paru jusque dans son silence.
Elle aime mon rival, je ne puis l'ignorer.
Mais je mettrai ma joie à le désespérer.   750
Je me fais de sa peine une image charmante,*
Et je l'ai vu douter du cœur de son amante.*
Je la suis. Mon rival t'attend pour éclater.*
Par de nouveaux soupçons, va, cours le tourmenter,
Et tandis qu'à mes yeux on le pleure, on l'adore,   755
Fais-lui payer bien cher un bonheur qu'il ignore.

NARCISSE, *seul*

La fortune t'appelle une seconde fois,
Narcisse: voudrais-tu résister à sa voix?
Suivons jusques* au bout ses ordres favorables,
Et pour nous rendre heureux, perdons les misérables.*   760

ACTE III

SCÈNE I

Néron   Burrhus

BURRHUS

Pallas obéira, Seigneur.

NÉRON

                    Et de quel œil
Ma mère a-t-elle vu confondre son orgueil?

BURRHUS

Ne doutez point, Seigneur, que ce coup* ne la frappe,
Qu'en reproches bientôt sa douleur ne s'échappe.
Ses transports* dès* longtemps commencent d'éclater   765
A d'inutiles cris puissent-ils s'arrêter!

103

NÉRON

Quoi? de quelque dessein la croyez-vous capable?

BURRHUS

Agrippine, Seigneur, est toujours redoutable.
Rome et tous vos soldats révèrent ses aïeux;
Germanicus son père est présent à leurs yeux.   770
Elle sait son pouvoir; vous savez son courage,
Et ce qui me la fait redouter davantage,
C'est que vous appuyez vous-même son courroux,
Et que vous lui donnez des armes contre vous.

NÉRON

Moi, Burrhus?   775

BURRHUS

Cet amour, Seigneur, qui vous possède . . .

NÉRON

Je vous entends,* Burrhus; le mal est sans remède.
Mon cœur s'en* est plus dit que vous ne m'en direz.
Il faut que j'aime enfin.

BURRHUS

Vous vous le figurez,
Seigneur, et satisfait de quelque résistance,
Vous redoutez un mal faible dans sa naissance.   780
Mais si dans son devoir votre cœur affermi
Voulait ne point s'entendre avec son ennemi,
Si de vos premiers ans vous consultiez* la gloire,
Si vous daigniez, Seigneur, rappeler* la mémoire
Des vertus d'Octavie, indignes* de ce prix,   785
Et de son chaste amour vainqueur de vos mépris;
Surtout si de Junie évitant la présence,
Vous condamniez vos yeux à quelque jours d'absence,
Croyez-moi, quelque amour qui semble vous charmer,*
On n'aime point, Seigneur, si l'on ne veut aimer.   790

NÉRON

Je vous croirai, Burrhus, lorsque dans les alarmes
Il faudra soutenir la gloire de nos armes,
Ou lorsque plus tranquille, assis dans le Sénat,
Il faudra décider du destin de l'Etat:
Je m'en reposerai sur votre expérience,   795
Mais, croyez-moi, l'amour est une autre science,
Burrhus, et je ferais quelque difficulté
D'abaisser jusque-là votre sévérité.*
Adieu: je souffre trop, éloigné de Junie.

SCÈNE II

BURRHUS, *seul*

Enfin, Burrhus, Néron découvre son génie.*   800
Cette férocité que tu croyais fléchir
De tes faibles liens est prête à s'affranchir.
En quels excès peut-être elle va se répandre!
O Dieux! en ce malheur quel conseil* dois-je prendre?
Sénèque, dont les soins* me devraient soulager,   805
Occupé loin de Rome, ignore ce danger.
Mais quoi? Si d'Agrippine excitant la tendresse,
Je pouvais ... La voici, mon bonheur me l'adresse.*

SCÈNE III

Agrippine   Burrhus   Albine

AGRIPPINE

Hé bien! je me trompais, Burrhus, dans mes soupçons?
Et vous vous signalez par d'illustres leçons!   810
On exile Pallas, dont le crime peut-être
Est d'avoir à l'Empire élevé votre maître.
Vous le savez trop bien. Jamais sans ses avis
Claude qu'il gouvernait* n'eût adopté mon fils.
Que dis-je? A son épouse on* donne une rivale.   815
On affranchit Néron de la foi conjugale.
Digne emploi d'un ministre, ennemi des flatteurs,
Choisi pour mettre un frein à ses jeunes ardeurs,
De les flatter* lui-même, et nourrir dans son âme
Le mépris de sa mère, et l'oubli de sa femme!   820

BURRHUS

Madame, jusqu'ici c'est trop tôt m'accuser.
L'Empereur n'a rien fait qu'on ne puisse excuser.
N'imputez qu'à Pallas un exil nécessaire:
Son orgueil dès* longtemps exigeait ce salaire,
Et l'Empereur ne fait qu'accomplir à regret   825
Ce que toute la cour demandait en secret.
Le reste est un malheur qui n'est point sans ressource.*
Des larmes d'Octavie on peut tarir la source.
Mais calmez vos transports.* Par un chemin plus doux
Vous lui pourrez plutôt* ramener son époux.   830
Les menaces, les cris le rendront plus farouche.

AGRIPPINE

Ah! l'on s'efforce en vain de me fermer la bouche.
Je vois que mon silence irrite* vos dédains,
Et c'est trop respecter l'ouvrage de mes mains.
Pallas n'emporte pas tout l'appui* d'Agrippine: 835
Le Ciel m'en laisse assez pour venger ma ruine.
Le fils de Claudius commence à ressentir*
Des crimes dont je n'ai que le seul repentir.
J'irai, n'en doutez point, le montrer à l'armée,
Plaindre* aux yeux des soldats son enfance opprimée,   840
Leur faire à mon exemple expier leur erreur.
On verra d'un côté le fils d'un Empereur
Redemandant la foi* jurée à sa famille,
Et de Germanicus on entendra la fille;
De l'autre l'on verra le fils d'Enobarbus,   845
Appuyé de* Sénèque, et du tribun Burrhus,
Qui tous deux de l'exil rappelés par moi-même,
Partagent à mes yeux l'autorité suprême.
De nos crimes communs je veux qu'on soit instruit.
On saura les chemins par où je l'ai conduit.   850
Pour rendre sa puissance et la vôtre odieuses,
J'avoûrai les rumeurs les plus injurieuses.
Je confesserai tout, exil, assassinats,
Poison même...

BURRHUS

          Madame, ils ne vous croiront pas.
Ils sauront récuser l'injuste stratagème   855

D'un témoin irrité qui s'accuse lui-même.
Pour moi, qui le premier secondai vos desseins,
Qui fis même jurer l'armée entre ses mains,
Je ne me repens point de ce zèle sincère.
Madame, c'est un fils qui succède à son père.   860
En adoptant Néron, Claudius par son choix
De son fils et du vôtre a confondu* les droits.
Rome l'a pu choisir. Ainsi sans être injuste,
Elle choisit Tibère adopté par Auguste,
Et le jeune Agrippa, de son sang descendu,   865
Se vit exclus* du rang vainement prétendu.*
Sur tant de fondements sa puissance établie
Par vous-même aujourd'hui ne peut être affaiblie.
Et s'il m'écoute encor,* Madame, sa bonté
Vous en fera bientôt perdre la volonté.   870
J'ai commencé, je vais poursuivre mon ouvrage.

SCÈNE IV

Agrippine   Albine

ALBINE

Dans quel emportement la douleur vous engage,
Madame! L'Empereur puisse-t-il l'ignorer!

AGRIPPINE

Ah! lui-même à mes yeux puisse-t-il se montrer!

ALBINE

Madame, au nom des Dieux, cachez votre colère.   875
Quoi! pour les intérêts de la sœur ou du frère
Faut-il sacrifier le repos de vos jours?
Contraindrez-vous César jusque dans ses amours?

AGRIPPINE

Quoi? tu ne vois donc pas jusqu'où l'on me ravale,*
Albine? C'est à moi qu'on donne une rivale.   880
Bientôt, si je ne romps ce funeste lien,
Ma place est occupée, et je ne suis plus rien.
Jusqu'ici d'un vain titre Octavie honorée,

Inutile à la cour, en était ignorée.
Les grâces, les honneurs par moi seule versés   885
M'attiraient des mortels les vœux intéressés.
Une autre de César a surpris* la tendresse,
Elle aura le pouvoir d'épouse et de maîtresse,
Le fruit de tant de soins,* la pompe* des Césars,
Tout deviendra le prix d'un seul de ses regards.   890
Que dis-je? L'on m'évite, et déjà délaissée . . .
Ah! je ne puis, Albine, en souffrir la pensée.
Quand je devrais du Ciel hâter l'arrêt fatal,
Néron, l'ingrat Néron . . . Mais voici son rival.

SCÈNE V

Britannicus   Agrippine   Narcisse   Albine

BRITANNICUS

Nos ennemis communs ne sont pas invincibles,   895
Madame. Nos malheurs trouvent des cœurs sensibles.
Vos amis et les miens, jusqu'alors si secrets,*
Tandis que nous perdions le temps en vains regrets,
Animés du courroux qu'allume l'injustice,
Viennent de confier leur douleur à Narcisse.   900
Néron n'est pas encor* tranquille possesseur
De l'ingrate* qu'il aime au mépris de ma sœur.
Si vous êtes toujours sensible à son injure,*
On peut dans son devoir ramener* le parjure.
La moitié du Sénat s'intéresse* pour nous.   905
Sylla, Pison, Plautus . . .

AGRIPPINE

Prince, que dites-vous?
Sylla, Pison, Plautus! Les chefs de la noblesse!

BRITANNICUS

Madame, je vois bien que ce discours* vous blesse,
Et que votre courroux tremblant, irrésolu,
Craint déjà d'obtenir tout ce qu'il a voulu.   910
Non, vous avez trop bien établi* ma disgrâce.*
D'aucun ami pour moi ne redoutez l'audace:

Il ne m'en reste plus, et vos soins* trop prudents
Les ont tous écartés ou séduits* dès* longtemps.

AGRIPPINE

Seigneur, à vos soupçons donnez moins de créance:*   915
Notre salut dépend de notre intelligence.*
J'ai promis, il suffit. Malgré vos ennemis
Je ne révoque* rien de ce que j'ai promis.
Le coupable Néron fuit en vain ma colère.
Tôt ou tard il faudra qu'il entende sa mère.   920
J'essaîrai tour à tour la force et la douceur.
Ou moi-même avec moi conduisant votre sœur,
J'irai semer partout ma crainte et ses alarmes,
Et ranger tous les cœurs du parti de ses larmes.
Adieu. J'assiégerai Néron de toutes parts.   925
Vous, si vous m'en* croyez, évitez ses regards.

SCÈNE VI

Britannicus   Narcisse

BRITANNICUS

Ne m'as-tu point flatté d'une fausse espérance?
Puis-je sur ton récit fonder quelque assurance,
Narcisse?

NARCISSE

                    Oui. Mais, Seigneur, ce n'est pas en ces lieux
Qu'il faut développer* ce mystère* à vos yeux.   930
Sortons. Qu'attendez-vous?

BRITANNICUS

                              Ce que j'attends, Narcisse?
Hélas!

NARCISSE

            Expliquez-vous.

BRITANNICUS

                              Si par ton artifice*
Je pouvais revoir . . .

BRITANNICUS

NARCISSE
Qui?

BRITANNICUS
J'en rougis. Mais enfin
D'un cœur moins agité j'attendrais mon destin.

NARCISSE
Après tous mes discours* vous la croyez fidèle?   935

BRITANNICUS
Non, je la crois, Narcisse, ingrate,* criminelle,
Digne de mon courroux. Mais je sens malgré moi
Que je ne le crois pas autant que je le doi.*
Dans ses égarements mon cœur opiniâtre
Lui prête des raisons, l'excuse, l'idolâtre.   940
Je voudrais vaincre enfin mon incrédulité,
Je la voudrais haïr avec tranquillité.
Et qui croira qu'un cœur si grand en apparence,
D'une infidèle* cour ennemi dès l'enfance,
Renonce à tant de gloire, et dès le premier jour   945
Trame une perfidie inouïe à la cour?

NARCISSE
Et qui sait si l'ingrate en sa longue retraite
N'a point de l'Empereur médité la défaite?
Trop sûre que ses yeux* ne pouvaient se cacher,
Peut-être elle fuyait pour se faire chercher,   950
Pour exciter Néron par la gloire pénible
De vaincre une fierté* jusqu'alors invincible.

BRITANNICUS
Je ne la puis donc voir?

NARCISSE
Seigneur, en ce moment
Elle reçoit les vœux* de son nouvel amant.*

BRITANNICUS
Hé bien! Narcisse, allons. Mais que vois-je? C'est elle.   955

NARCISSE

Ah, Dieux! A l'Empereur portons cette nouvelle.

SCÈNE VII

Britannicus   Junie

JUNIE

Retirez-vous, Seigneur, et fuyez un courroux
Que ma persévérance allume contre vous.
Néron est irrité. Je me suis échappée,
Tandis qu'à l'arrêter sa mère est occupée.   960
Adieu: réservez-vous, sans blesser mon amour,
Au plaisir de me voir justifier* un jour.
Votre image sans cesse est présente à mon âme.
Rien ne l'en peut bannir.

BRITANNICUS
                    Je vous entends,* Madame.
Vous voulez que ma fuite assure* vos désirs,   965
Que je laisse un champ libre à vos nouveaux soupirs.*
Sans doute, en me voyant, une pudeur secrète
Ne vous laisse goûter qu'une joie inquiète.
Hé bien! il faut partir.

JUNIE
                    Seigneur, sans m'imputer . . .

BRITANNICUS

Ah! vous deviez* du moins plus longtemps disputer.   970
Je ne murmure* point qu'une amitié* commune
Se range du parti que flatte* la fortune,
Que l'éclat d'un Empire ait pu vous éblouir,
Qu'aux dépens de ma sœur vous en vouliez jouir.
Mais que de ces grandeurs comme une autre occupée,*   975
Vous m'en ayez paru si longtemps détrompée,
Non, je l'avoue encor,* mon cœur désespéré
Contre ce seul malheur n'était point préparé.
J'ai vu sur ma ruine élever* l'injustice.
De mes persécuteurs j'ai vu le Ciel complice.   980

III

Tant d'horreurs n'avaient point épuisé son courroux,
Madame. Il me restait d'être oublié de vous.

JUNIE

Dans un temps* plus heureux ma juste impatience
Vous ferait repentir de votre défiance.
Mais Néron vous menace. En ce pressant danger,   985
Seigneur, j'ai d'autres soins* que de vous affliger.
Allez, rassurez-vous, et cessez de vous plaindre:
Néron nous écoutait, et m'ordonnait de feindre.

BRITANNICUS

Quoi! le cruel . . .

JUNIE

                    Témoin de tout notre entretien,
D'un visage sévère* examinait le mien,   990
Prêt à faire sur vous éclater la vengeance
D'un* geste confident* de notre intelligence.*

BRITANNICUS

Néron nous écoutait, Madame! Mais, hélas!
Vos yeux auraient pu feindre et ne m'abuser pas.
Ils pouvaient* me nommer l'auteur de cet outrage.   995
L'amour est-il muet, ou n'a-t-il qu'un langage?
De quel trouble un regard pouvait* me préserver!
Il fallait . . .

JUNIE

                Il fallait me taire, et vous sauver.
Combien de fois, hélas! puisqu'il faut vous le dire,
Mon cœur de son désordre* allait-il vous instruire!   1000
De combien de soupirs interrompant le cours,
Ai-je évité vos yeux que je cherchais toujours!
Quel tourment de se taire en voyant ce qu'on aime!
De l'entendre gémir, de l'affliger soi-même,
Lorsque par un regard on peut le consoler!   1005
Mais quels pleurs ce regard aurait-il fait couler!
Ah! dans ce souvenir, inquiète, troublée,
Je ne me sentais pas assez dissimulée.

De mon front* effrayé je craignais la pâleur.
Je trouvais mes regards trop pleins de ma douleur.   1010
Sans cesse il me semblait que Néron en colère
Me venait reprocher trop de soin de vous plaire.
Je craignais mon amour vainement renfermé,
Enfin j'aurais voulu n'avoir jamais aimé.
Hélas! pour son bonheur, Seigneur, et pour le nôtre,   1015
Il n'est que trop instruit de mon cœur et du vôtre.
Allez, encore un coup,* cachez-vous à ses yeux.
Mon cœur plus à loisir vous éclaircira* mieux.
De mille autres secrets j'aurais compte* à vous rendre.

BRITANNICUS

Ah! n'en voilà que trop. C'est trop me faire entendre,*   1020
Madame, mon bonheur, mon crime, vos bontés.*
Et savez-vous pour moi tout ce que vous quittez?
Quand pourrai-je à vos pieds expier ce reproche?*

JUNIE

Que faites-vous? Hélas! votre rival s'approche.

SCÈNE VIII

Néron   Britannicus   Junie

NÉRON

Prince, continuez des transports* si charmants.*   1025
Je conçois vos bontés* par ses remercîments,
Madame: à vos genoux je viens de le surprendre.
Mais il aurait aussi quelque grâce à me rendre:
Ce lieu le favorise, et je vous y retiens
Pour lui faciliter de si doux entretiens.   1030

BRITANNICUS

Je puis mettre à ses pieds ma douleur, ou ma joie,
Partout où sa bonté consent* que je la voie.
Et l'aspect de ces lieux, où vous la retenez,
N'a rien dont mes regards doivent être étonnés.*

NÉRON

Et que vous montrent-ils qui ne vous avertisse   1035
Qu'il faut qu'on me respecte, et que l'on m'obéisse?

BRITANNICUS

Ils ne nous ont pas vu l'un et l'autre élever,
Moi pour vous obéir, et vous pour me braver,
Et ne s'attendaient pas, lorsqu'ils nous virent naître,
Qu'un jour Domitius me dût parler en maître.   1040

NÉRON

Ainsi par le destin nos vœux sont traversés:*
J'obéissais alors, et vous obéissez.
Si vous n'avez appris à vous laisser conduire,
Vous êtes jeune encore, et l'on peut vous instruire.

BRITANNICUS

Et qui m'en instruira?   1045

NÉRON

Tout l'Empire à la fois,
Rome.

BRITANNICUS

Rome met-elle au nombre de vos droits
Tout ce qu'a de cruel l'injustice et la force:
Les emprisonnements, le rapt, et le divorce?

NÉRON

Rome ne porte point ses regards curieux
Jusque dans des secrets que je cache à ses yeux.   1050
Imitez son respect.

BRITANNICUS

On sait ce qu'elle en pense.

NÉRON

Elle se tait du moins: imitez son silence.

BRITANNICUS

Ainsi Néron commence à ne se plus forcer.

NÉRON

Néron de vos discours commence à se lasser.

BRITANNICUS

Chacun devait bénir le bonheur de son règne.   1055

NÉRON

Heureux ou malheureux, il suffit qu'on me craigne.

BRITANNICUS

Je connais mal Junie, ou de tels sentiments
Ne mériteront pas ses applaudissements.

NÉRON

Du moins, si je ne sais le secret de lui plaire,
Je sais l'art de punir un rival téméraire.   1060

BRITANNICUS

Pour moi, quelque péril qui me puisse accabler,
Sa seule* inimitié peut me faire trembler.

NÉRON

Souhaitez-la. C'est tout ce que je vous puis dire.

BRITANNICUS

Le bonheur de lui plaire est le seul où* j'aspire.

NÉRON

Elle vous l'a promis, vous lui plairez toujours.   1065

BRITANNICUS

Je ne sais pas du moins épier ses discours.*
Je la laisse expliquer* sur tout ce qui me touche,
Et ne me cache point pour lui fermer la bouche.

NÉRON

Je vous entends.* Hé bien, gardes!

JUNIE
Que faites-vous?

C'est votre frère. Hélas! C'est un amant jaloux,   1070
Seigneur, mille malheurs persécutent sa vie.
Ah! son bonheur peut-il exciter votre envie?
Souffrez que de vos cœurs rapprochant les liens,
Je me cache à vos yeux, et me dérobe aux siens.
Ma fuite arrêtera vos discordes fatales,   1075
Seigneur, j'irai remplir* le nombre des Vestales.
Ne lui disputez plus mes vœux* infortunés,
Souffrez que les Dieux seuls en soient importunés.

NÉRON
L'entreprise,* Madame, est étrange et soudaine.
Dans son appartement, gardes, qu'on la remène.*   1080
Gardez Britannicus dans celui de sa sœur,

BRITANNICUS
C'est ainsi que Néron sait disputer un cœur.

JUNIE
Prince, sans l'irriter, cédons à cet orage.

NÉRON
Gardes, obéissez, sans tarder davantage.

SCÈNE IX

Néron   Burrhus

BURRHUS
Que vois-je? O Ciel!   1085

NÉRON, *sans voir Burrhus*
Ainsi leurs feux* sont redoublés.
Je reconnais la main qui les a rassemblés.*
Agrippine ne s'est présentée à ma vue,
Ne s'est dans ses discours si longtemps étendue,
Que pour faire jouer ce ressort* odieux.
Qu'on* sache si ma mère est encore en ces lieux.   1090

Burrhus, dans ce palais je veux qu'on la retienne,
Et qu'au lieu de sa garde, on lui donne la mienne.

BURRHUS

Quoi, Seigneur? sans l'ouïr?* Une mère?

NÉRON

Arrêtez.

J'ignore quel projet, Burrhus, vous méditez.
Mais depuis quelques jours tout ce que je désire   1095
Trouve en vous un censeur prêt à me contredire.
Répondez-m'en,* vous dis-je, ou sur votre refus
D'autres me répondront et d'elle, et de Burrhus.

ACTE IV

SCÈNE I

Agrippine   Burrhus

BURRHUS

Oui, Madame, à loisir vous pourrez vous défendre.
César lui-même ici consent* de vous entendre.   1100
Si son ordre au palais vous a fait retenir,
C'est peut-être à dessein de vous entretenir.
Quoi qu'il en soit, si j'ose expliquer* ma pensée,
Ne vous souvenez plus qu'il vous ait offensée.
Préparez-vous plutôt à lui tendre les bras.   1105
Défendez-vous, Madame, et ne l'accusez pas.
Vous voyez, c'est lui seul que la cour envisage.*
Quoiqu'il soit votre fils, et même votre ouvrage,
Il est votre Empereur. Vous êtes comme nous
Sujette à ce pouvoir qu'il a reçu de vous.   1110
Selon qu'il vous menace, ou bien qu'il vous caresse,*
La cour autour de vous ou s'écarte, ou s'empresse.
C'est son appui qu'on cherche, en cherchant votre appui.
Mais voici l'Empereur.

117

AGRIPPINE

Qu'on* me laisse avec lui.

SCÈNE II

Agrippine   Néron

AGRIPPINE, *s'asseyant*

Approchez-vous, Néron, et prenez votre place.   1115
On veut sur vos soupçons que je vous satisfasse.
J'ignore de quel crime on a pu me noircir.
De tous ceux que j'ai faits je vais vous éclaircir.*
    Vous régnez. Vous savez combien votre naissance
Entre l'Empire et vous avait mis de distance.   1120
Les droits de mes aïeux, que Rome a consacrés,
Etaient même sans moi d'inutiles degrés.
Quand de Britannicus la mère condamnée
Laissa de Claudius disputer l'hyménée,
Parmi tant de beautés qui briguèrent son choix,   1125
Qui de ses affranchis mendièrent les voix,
Je souhaitai son lit, dans la seule pensée
De vous laisser au trône où* je serais placée.
Je fléchis mon orgueil, j'allai prier Pallas.
Son maître, chaque jour caressé dans mes bras,   1130
Prit insensiblement dans les yeux de sa nièce
L'amour où je voulais amener sa tendresse.
Mais ce lien du sang qui nous joignait tous deux
Ecartait Claudius d'un lit incestueux.
Il n'osait épouser la fille de son frère.   1135
Le Sénat fut séduit.* Une loi moins sévère
Mit Claude dans mon lit, et Rome à mes genoux.
C'était beaucoup pour moi, ce n'était rien pour vous.
Je vous fis sur mes pas entrer dans sa famille.
Je vous nommai son gendre, et vous donnai sa fille.   1140
Silanus, qui l'aimait, s'en* vit abandonné,
Et marqua* de son sang ce jour infortuné.
Ce n'était rien encore. Eussiez-vous pu prétendre*
Qu'un jour Claude à son fils dût préférer son gendre?
De ce même Pallas j'implorai le secours: 1145
Claude vous adopta, vaincu par ses discours,*

118

Vous appela Néron, et du pouvoir suprême
Voulut avant le temps vous faire part lui-même.
C'est alors que chacun, rappelant* le passé,
Découvrit mon dessein, déjà trop avancé;   1150
Que de Britannicus la disgrâce* future
Des amis de son père excita le murmure.
Mes promesses aux uns éblouirent les yeux;
L'exil me délivra des plus séditieux.
Claude même, lassé de ma plainte éternelle,   1155
Eloigna de son fils tous ceux de qui le zèle,
Engagé dès* longtemps à suivre son destin,
Pouvait du trône encor* lui rouvrir le chemin.
Je fis plus: je choisis moi-même dans ma suite
Ceux à qui je voulais qu'on livrât sa conduite.*   1160
J'eus soin de vous nommer, par un contraire choix,
Des gouverneurs* que Rome honorait de sa voix.*
Je fus sourde à la brigue, et crus la renommée.
J'appelai de l'exil, je tirai de l'armée,
Et ce même Sénèque, et ce même Burrhus,   1165
Qui depuis... Rome alors estimait leurs vertus.
De Claude en même temps épuisant les richesses,
Ma main, sous votre nom, répandait ses largesses.
Les spectacles, les dons, invincibles appâts,
Vous attiraient les cœurs du peuple, et des soldats,   1170
Qui d'ailleurs réveillant leur tendresse première,
Favorisaient en vous Germanicus mon père.
Cependant Claudius penchait vers son déclin.
Ses yeux longtemps fermés s'ouvrirent à la fin.
Il connut* son erreur. Occupé* de sa crainte,   1175
Il laissa pour son fils échapper quelque plainte,
Et voulut, mais trop tard, assembler ses amis.
Ses gardes, son palais, son lit m'étaient soumis.
Je lui laissai sans fruit consumer sa tendresse;
De ses derniers soupirs je me rendis maîtresse;   1180
Mes soins,* en apparence épargnant ses douleurs,
De son fils, en mourant, lui cachèrent les pleurs.
Il mourut. Mille bruits en courent à ma honte.
J'arrêtai de sa mort la nouvelle trop prompte:
Et tandis que Burrhus allait secrètement   1185
De l'armée en vos mains exiger le serment,

E   119

Que vous marchiez au* camp, conduit sous mes auspices,
Dans Rome les autels fumaient de sacrifices,
Par mes ordres trompeurs tout le peuple excité
Du Prince déjà mort demandait la santé.   1190
Enfin des légions l'entière obéissance
Ayant de votre empire affermi la puissance,
On vit Claude, et le peuple, étonné* de son sort,
Apprit en même temps votre règne, et sa mort.
   C'est le sincère aveu que je voulais vous faire.   1195
Voilà tous mes forfaits. En voici le salaire.
   Du fruit de tant de soins à peine jouissant
En avez-vous six mois paru reconnaissant,
Que lassé d'un respect qui vous gênait* peut-être,
Vous avez affecté de ne me plus connaître.   1200
J'ai vu Burrhus, Sénèque, aigrissant* vos soupçons,
De l'infidélité* vous tracer des leçons,
Ravis d'être vaincus dans leur propre science.
J'ai vu favoriser de votre confiance
Othon, Sénécion, jeunes voluptueux,   1205
Et de tous vos plaisirs flatteurs respectueux.
Et lorsque, vos mépris excitant mes murmures,
Je vous ai demandé raison de tant d'injures,*
(Seul recours d'un ingrat qui se voit confondu)
Par de nouveaux affronts vous m'avez répondu.   1210
Aujourd'hui je promets Junie à votre frère,
Ils se flattent tous deux du choix de votre mère :
Que faites-vous ? Junie, enlevée à la cour,
Devient en une nuit l'objet de votre amour.
Je vois de votre cœur Octavie effacée,   1215
Prête* à sortir du lit où je l'avais placée.
Je vois Pallas banni, votre frère arrêté,
Vous attentez enfin jusqu'à ma liberté :
Burrhus ose sur moi porter ses mains hardies.
Et lorsque convaincu de tant de perfidies,   1220
Vous deviez* ne me voir que pour les expier,
C'est vous qui m'ordonnez de me justifier.

NÉRON

Je me souviens toujours que je vous dois l'Empire.
Et sans vous fatiguer du soin* de le redire,

120

Votre bonté, Madame, avec tranquillité   1225
Pouvait se reposer sur ma fidélité.

Aussi bien ces soupçons, ces plaintes assidues*
Ont fait croire à tous ceux qui les ont entendues
Que jadis (j'ose ici vous le dire entre nous)
Vous n'aviez sous mon nom travaillé que pour vous.   1230
Tant d'honneurs (disaient-ils) et tant de déférences,
Sont-ce de ses bienfaits de faibles récompenses?
Quel crime a donc commis ce fils tant condamné?
Est-ce pour obéir qu'elle l'a couronné?
N'est-il de son pouvoir que le dépositaire?   1235
Non que si jusque-là j'avais pu vous complaire,
Je n'eusse pris plaisir, Madame, à vous céder
Ce pouvoir que vos cris semblaient redemander:
Mais Rome veut un maître, et non une maîtresse.

Vous entendiez les bruits qu'excitait ma faiblesse.   1240
Le Sénat chaque jour, et le peuple, irrités
De s'ouïr* par ma voix dicter vos volontés,
Publiaient qu'en mourant Claude avec sa puissance
M'avait encor* laissé sa simple* obéissance.

Vous avez vu cent fois nos soldats en courroux   1245
Porter en murmurant leurs aigles devant vous,
Honteux de rabaisser par cet indigne usage
Les héros dont encore elles portent l'image.

Toute autre se serait rendue à leurs discours,*
Mais si vous ne régnez, vous vous plaignez toujours.   1250

Avec Britannicus contre moi réunie*,
Vous le fortifiez du parti de Junie,
Et la main de Pallas trame tous ces complots.
Et lorsque, malgré moi, j'assure mon repos,
On vous voit de colère et de haine animée.   1255
Vous voulez présenter mon rival à l'armée.
Déjà jusques* au camp le bruit en a couru.

 AGRIPPINE

Moi, le faire Empereur, ingrat? L'avez-vous cru?
Quel serait mon dessein? Qu'aurais-je pu prétendre?*
Quel honneur dans sa cour, quel rang pourrais-je attendre?   1260
Ah! si sous votre empire on ne m'épargne pas,
Si mes accusateurs observent tous mes pas,

BRITANNICUS

Si de leur Empereur ils poursuivent la mère,
Que ferais-je au milieu d'une cour étrangère?
Ils me reprocheraient, non des cris impuissants,   1265
Des desseins étouffés aussitôt que naissants,
Mais des crimes pour vous commis à votre vue,
Et dont je ne serais que trop tôt convaincue.
Vous ne me trompez point, je vois tous vos détours:
Vous êtes un ingrat, vous le fûtes toujours.   1270
Dès vos plus jeunes ans mes soins et mes tendresses
N'ont arraché de vous que de feintes caresses.
Rien ne vous a pu vaincre, et votre dureté
Aurait dû dans son cours arrêter ma bonté.
Que je suis malheureuse! Et par quelle infortune   1275
Faut-il que tous mes soins me rendent importune?
Je n'ai qu'un fils. O Ciel, qui m'entends aujourd'hui,
T'ai-je fait quelques vœux qui ne fussent pour lui?
Remords, crainte, périls, rien ne m'a retenue.
J'ai vaincu ses mépris, j'ai détourné ma vue   1280
Des malheurs qui dès lors me furent annoncés.
J'ai fait ce que j'ai pu: vous régnez, c'est assez.
Avec ma liberté, que vous m'avez ravie,
Si vous le souhaitez, prenez encor* ma vie;
Pourvu que par ma mort tout le peuple irrité   1285
Ne vous ravisse pas ce qui m'a tant coûté.

NÉRON

Hé bien donc! prononcez: que voulez-vous qu'on* fasse?

AGRIPPINE

De mes accusateurs qu'on* punisse l'audace,
Que de Britannicus on calme le courroux,
Que Junie à son choix puisse prendre un époux,   1290
Qu'ils soient libres tous deux, et que Pallas demeure,
Que vous me permettiez de vous voir à toute heure,

Burrhus rentre

Que ce même Burrhus, qui nous vient écouter,
A votre porte enfin n'ose plus m'arrêter.

122

NÉRON

Oui, Madame, je veux que ma reconnaissance   1295
Désormais dans les cœurs grave votre puissance,
Et je bénis déjà cette heureuse froideur
Qui de notre amitié* va rallumer l'ardeur.
Quoi que Pallas ait fait, il suffit, je l'oublie.
Avec Britannicus je me réconcilie,   1300
Et quant à cet amour qui nous a séparés,
Je vous fais notre arbitre, et vous nous jugerez.
Allez donc, et portez cette joie à mon frère.
Gardes, qu'on obéisse aux ordres de ma mère.

SCÈNE III

Néron   Burrhus

BURRHUS

Que cette paix, Seigneur, et ces embrassements   1305
Vont offrir à mes yeux des spectacles charmants!*
Vous savez si jamais ma voix lui fut contraire,
Si de son amitié* j'ai voulu vous distraire,*
Et si j'ai mérité cet injuste courroux.

NÉRON

Je ne vous flatte* point, je me plaignais de vous,   1310
Burrhus: je vous ai crus tous deux d'intelligence.
Mais son inimitié vous rend ma confiance.
Elle se hâte trop, Burrhus, de triompher.
J'embrasse* mon rival, mais c'est pour l'étouffer.

BURRHUS

Quoi, Seigneur!   1315

NÉRON

               C'en est trop. Il faut que sa ruine
Me délivre à jamais des fureurs d'Agrippine.
Tant qu'il respirera, je ne vis qu'à demi.
Elle m'a fatigué de ce nom ennemi,
Et je ne prétends* pas que sa coupable audace
Une seconde fois lui promette ma place.   1320

BURRHUS

Elle va donc bientôt pleurer Britannicus.

NÉRON

Avant la fin du jour je ne le craindrai plus.

BURRHUS

Et qui* de ce dessein vous inspire l'envie?

NÉRON

Ma gloire, mon amour, ma sûreté, ma vie.

BURRHUS

Non! quoi que vous disiez, cet horrible dessein   1325
Ne fut jamais, Seigneur, conçu dans votre sein.

NÉRON

Burrhus!

BURRHUS

De votre bouche, ô Ciel! puis-je l'apprendre?
Vous-même sans frémir avez-vous pu l'entendre?
Songez-vous dans quel sang vous allez vous baigner?
Néron dans tous les cœurs est-il las de régner?   1330
Que dira-t-on de vous? Quelle est votre pensée?

NÉRON

Quoi! toujours enchaîné de* ma gloire passée,
J'aurai devant les yeux je ne sais quel amour
Que le hasard nous donne et nous ôte en un jour?
Soumis à tous leurs vœux, à mes désirs contraire,   1335
Suis-je leur Empereur seulement pour leur plaire?

BURRHUS

Et ne suffit-il pas, Seigneur, à vos souhaits
Que le bonheur public soit un de vos bienfaits?
C'est à vous à* choisir, vous êtes encor* maître.
Vertueux jusqu'ici, vous pouvez toujours l'être.   1340
Le chemin est tracé, rien ne vous retient plus.
Vous n'avez qu'à marcher de vertus en vertus.

Mais si de vos flatteurs vous suivez la maxime,
Il vous faudra, Seigneur, courir de crime en crime,
Soutenir vos rigueurs par d'autres cruautés,   1345
Et laver dans le sang vos bras ensanglantés.
Britannicus mourant excitera le zèle
De ses amis, tout prêts à prendre sa querelle.*
Ces vengeurs trouveront de nouveaux défenseurs,
Qui même après leur mort auront des successeurs.   1350
Vous allumez un feu qui ne pourra s'éteindre.
Craint de tout l'univers, il vous faudra tout craindre,
Toujours punir, toujours trembler dans vos projets,
Et pour vos ennemis compter tous vos sujets.
Ah! de vos premiers ans l'heureuse expérience   1355
Vous fait-elle, Seigneur, haïr votre innocence?
Songez-vous au bonheur qui les a signalés?
Dans quel repos, ô Ciel! les avez-vous coulés!
Quel plaisir de penser et de dire en vous-même:
Partout, en ce moment, on me bénit, on m'aime.   1360
On ne voit point le peuple à mon nom s'alarmer,
Le Ciel dans tous leurs pleurs ne m'entend point nommer.
Leur sombre inimitié ne fuit point mon visage,
Je vois voler partout les cœurs à mon passage!
Tels étaient vos plaisirs. Quel changement, ô Dieux!   1365
Le sang le plus abject vous était précieux.
Un jour, il m'en souvient, le Sénat équitable
Vous pressait de souscrire* à la mort d'un coupable;
Vous résistiez, Seigneur, à leur sévérité,
Votre cœur s'accusait de trop de cruauté,   1370
Et plaignant* les malheurs attachés à l'empire,
Je voudrais, disiez-vous, *ne savoir pas écrire.*
Non, ou vous me croirez, ou bien de ce malheur
Ma mort m'épargnera la vue et la douleur.
On ne me verra point survivre à votre gloire.   1375
Si vous allez commettre une action si noire,
                                    (Il se jette à genoux)
Me voilà prêt, Seigneur: avant* que de partir,
Faites percer ce cœur qui n'y peut consentir.
Appelez les cruels qui vous l'ont inspirée;
Qu'ils viennent essayer leur main mal assurée.   1380
Mais je vois que mes pleurs touchent mon Empereur,

Je vois que sa vertu frémit de leur fureur.
Ne perdez point de temps, nommez-moi les perfides
Qui vous osent donner ces conseils parricides.*
Appelez votre frère, oubliez dans ses bras . . .   1385

NÉRON
Ah! que demandez-vous?

BURRHUS

                              Non, il ne vous hait pas,
Seigneur, on le trahit, je sais son innocence,
Je vous réponds pour lui de son obéissance.
J'y cours. Je vais presser un entretien si doux.

NÉRON
Dans mon appartement qu'il m'attende avec vous.   1390

SCÈNE IV

Néron Narcisse

NARCISSE
Seigneur, j'ai tout prévu pour une mort si juste.
Le poison est tout prêt. La fameuse Locuste
A redoublé pour moi ses soins* officieux.
Elle a fait expirer un esclave à mes yeux;
Et le fer est moins prompt pour trancher une vie   1395
Que le nouveau poison que sa main me confie.

NÉRON
Narcisse, c'est assez; je reconnais* ce soin,*
Et ne souhaite pas que vous alliez plus loin.

NARCISSE
Quoi! pour Britannicus votre haine affaiblie
Me défend . . .   1400

NÉRON
Oui, Narcisse, on nous réconcilie.

126

NARCISSE

Je me garderai bien de vous en détourner,
Seigneur. Mais il s'est vu tantôt emprisonner.
Cette offense en son cœur sera longtemps nouvelle.*
Il n'est point de secrets que le temps ne révèle:
Il saura que ma main lui devait présenter   1405
Un poison que votre ordre avait fait apprêter.
Les Dieux de ce dessein puissent-ils le distraire!*
Mais peut-être il fera ce que vous n'osez faire.

NÉRON

On répond de son cœur, et je vaincrai le mien.

NARCISSE

Et l'hymen de Junie en est-il le lien?   1410
Seigneur, lui faites-vous encor* ce sacrifice?

NÉRON

C'est prendre trop de soin.* Quoi qu'il en soit, Narcisse,
Je ne le compte plus parmi mes ennemis.

NARCISSE

Agrippine, Seigneur, se l'était bien promis.
Elle a repris sur vous son souverain empire.   1415

NÉRON

Quoi donc? Qu'a-t-elle dit? Et que voulez-vous dire?

NARCISSE

Elle s'en est vantée assez publiquement.

NÉRON

De quoi?

NARCISSE

      Qu'elle n'avait qu'à vous voir un moment:
Qu'à tout ce grand éclat, à ce courroux funeste
On verrait succéder un silence modeste,   1420
Que vous-même à la paix souscririez le premier,
Heureux que sa bonté daignât tout oublier.

NÉRON

Mais, Narcisse, dis-moi, que veux-tu que je fasse?
Je n'ai que trop de pente à punir son audace.
Et si je m'en* croyais, ce triomphe indiscret*   1425
Serait bientôt suivi d'un éternel regret.
Mais de tout l'univers quel sera le langage?
Sur les pas des tyrans veux-tu que je m'engage,
Et que Rome, effaçant tant de titres d'honneur,
Me laisse pour tous noms celui d'empoisonneur?   1430
Ils mettront ma vengeance au rang des parricides.*

NARCISSE

Et prenez-vous, Seigneur, leurs caprices pour guides?
Avez-vous prétendu* qu'ils se tairaient toujours?
Est-ce à vous de prêter l'oreille à leurs discours?*
De vos propres désirs perdrez-vous la mémoire?   1435
Et serez-vous le seul que vous n'oserez croire?
Mais, Seigneur, les Romains ne vous sont pas connus.
Non, non, dans leurs discours* ils sont plus retenus.
Tant de précaution affaiblit votre règne.
Ils croiront en effet mériter qu'on les craigne.   1440
Au joug depuis longtemps ils se sont façonnés.
Ils adorent la main qui les tient enchaînés.
Vous les verrez toujours ardents à vous complaire.
Leur prompte* servitude* a fatigué Tibère.
Moi-même, revêtu d'un pouvoir emprunté,   1445
Que je reçus de Claude avec la liberté,
J'ai cent fois dans le cours de ma gloire passée
Tenté leur patience, et ne l'ai point lassée.
D'un empoisonnement vous craignez la noirceur?
Faites périr le frère, abandonnez la sœur: 1450
Rome, sur ses autels prodiguant les victimes,
Fussent-ils innocents, leur trouvera des crimes.
Vous verrez mettre au rang des jours infortunés
Ceux où jadis la sœur et le frère sont nés.

NÉRON

Narcisse, encore un coup,* je ne puis l'entreprendre.   1455
J'ai promis à Burrhus, il a fallu me rendre.
Je ne veux point encore, en lui manquant de foi,*

Donner à sa vertu des armes contre moi.
J'oppose à ses raisons un courage* inutile,
Je ne l'écoute point avec un cœur tranquille.   1460

NARCISSE

Burrhus ne pense pas, Seigneur, tout ce qu'il dit.
Son adroite vertu ménage son crédit.
Ou plutôt ils n'ont tous qu'une même pensée,
Ils verraient par ce coup* leur puissance abaissée,
Vous seriez libre alors, Seigneur, et devant vous   1465
Ces maîtres orgueilleux fléchiraient comme nous.
Quoi donc! ignorez-vous tout ce qu'ils osent dire?
Néron, s'ils en sont crus, n'est point né pour l'Empire.
Il ne dit, il ne fait que ce qu'on lui prescrit.
Burrhus conduit son cœur, Sénèque son esprit.   1470
Pour toute ambition, pour vertu singulière,**
Il excelle à conduire un char dans la carrière,
A disputer des prix indignes de ses mains,
A se donner lui-même en spectacle aux Romains,
A venir prodiguer sa voix sur un théâtre,   1475
A réciter des chants qu'il veut qu'on idolâtre,*
Tandis que des soldats de moments en moments
Vont arracher pour lui les applaudissements.
Ah! ne voulez-vous pas les forcer à se taire?

NÉRON

Viens, Narcisse. Allons voir ce que nous devons faire.   1480

ACTE V

SCÈNE I

Britannicus   Junie

BRITANNICUS

Oui, Madame, Néron (qui l'aurait pu penser?)
Dans son appartement m'attend pour m'embrasser.
Il y fait de sa cour inviter la jeunesse.

129

Il veut que d'un festin la pompe* et l'allégresse
Confirment à leurs yeux la foi* de nos serments,   1485
Et réchauffent l'ardeur de nos embrassements.
Il éteint cet amour, source de tant de haine,
Il vous fait de mon sort arbitre souveraine.
Pour moi, quoique banni du rang de mes aïeux,
Quoique de leur dépouille* il se pare à mes yeux,   1490
Depuis qu'à mon amour cessant d'être contraire,
Il semble me céder la gloire de vous plaire,
Mon cœur, je l'avoûrai, lui pardonne en secret,
Et lui laisse le reste avec moins de regret.
Quoi! je ne serai plus séparé de vos charmes?*   1495
Quoi! même en ce moment je puis voir sans alarmes
Ces yeux, que n'ont émus ni soupirs ni terreur,
Qui m'ont sacrifié l'Empire et l'Empereur?
Ah, Madame! Mais quoi? Quelle nouvelle crainte
Tient parmi mes transports* votre joie en contrainte?   1500
D'où vient qu'en m'écoutant, vos yeux, vos tristes yeux
Avec de longs regards se tournent vers les cieux?
Qu'est-ce que vous craignez?

JUNIE
Je l'ignore moi-même.

Mais je crains.

BRITANNICUS
Vous m'aimez?

JUNIE
Hélas! si je vous aime?

BRITANNICUS
Néron ne trouble plus notre félicité.   1505

JUNIE
Mais me répondez-vous de sa sincérité?

BRITANNICUS
Quoi! vous le soupçonnez d'une haine couverte?*

ACTE V SCÈNE I

JUNIE

Néron m'aimait tantôt, il jurait votre perte.
Il me fuit, il vous cherche. Un si grand changement
Peut-il être, Seigneur, l'ouvrage d'un moment ?   1510

BRITANNICUS

Cet ouvrage, Madame, est un coup* d'Agrippine.
Elle a cru que ma perte entraînait sa ruine.
Grâce aux préventions de son esprit jaloux,
Nos plus grands ennemis ont combattu pour nous.
Je m'en* fie aux transports* qu'elle m'a fait paraître.*   1515
Je m'en fie à Burrhus. J'en* crois même son maître.
Je crois qu'à mon exemple impuissant à trahir,
Il hait à cœur ouvert, ou cesse de haïr.

JUNIE

Seigneur, ne jugez pas de son cœur par le vôtre.
Sur des pas différents vous marchez l'un et l'autre.   1520
Je ne connais Néron et la cour que d'*un jour.
Mais (si je l'ose dire) hélas! dans cette cour
Combien tout ce qu'on dit est loin de ce qu'on pense!
Que la bouche et le cœur sont peu d'intelligence!
Avec combien de joie on y trahit sa foi!*   1525
Quel séjour étranger et pour vous et pour moi!

BRITANNICUS

Mais que son amitié soit véritable ou feinte,
Si vous craignez Néron, lui-même est-il sans crainte?
Non, non, il n'ira point par un lâche attentat
Soulever contre lui le Peuple et le Sénat.   1530
Que dis-je? il reconnaît sa dernière injustice.
Ses remords ont paru* même aux yeux de Narcisse.
Ah! s'il vous avait dit, ma Princesse, à quel point ...

JUNIE

Mais Narcisse, Seigneur, ne vous trahit-il point?

BRITANNICUS

Et pourquoi voulez-vous que mon cœur s'en* défie?   1535

131

JUNIE

Et que sais-je? Il y va, Seigneur, de votre vie.
Tout m'est suspect. Je crains que tout ne soit séduit.*
Je crains Néron. Je crains le malheur qui me suit.
D'un noir pressentiment malgré moi prévenue,
Je vous laisse à regret éloigner* de ma vue.   1540
Hélas! si cette paix dont vous vous repaissez
Couvrait* contre vos jours quelques pièges dressés!
Si Néron, irrité de notre intelligence,*
Avait choisi la nuit pour cacher sa vengeance!
S'il préparait ses coups tandis que je vous vois!   1545
Et si je vous parlais pour la dernière fois!
Ah, Prince!

BRITANNICUS

      Vous pleurez! Ah, ma chère Princesse!
Et pour moi jusque-là votre cœur s'intéresse?*
Quoi, Madame! en un jour où plein de sa grandeur
Néron croit éblouir vos yeux de sa splendeur,   1550
Dans des lieux où chacun me fuit et le révère,
Aux pompes* de sa cour préférer ma misère!*
Quoi! dans ce même jour, et dans ces mêmes lieux,
Refuser un Empire et pleurer à mes yeux!
Mais, Madame, arrêtez ces précieuses larmes;   1555
Mon retour va bientôt dissiper vos alarmes.
Je me rendrais suspect par un plus long séjour.*
Adieu: je vais, le cœur tout plein de mon amour,
Au milieu des transports* d'une aveugle jeunesse,
Ne voir, n'entretenir que ma belle Princesse.   1560
Adieu.

JUNIE

   Prince . . .

BRITANNICUS

   On m'attend, Madame, il faut partir.

JUNIE

Mais du moins attendez qu'on vous vienne avertir.

SCÈNE II

Agrippine   Britannicus   Junie

AGRIPPINE

Prince, que* tardez-vous? Partez en diligence.*
Néron impatient se plaint de votre absence.
La joie et le plaisir de tous les conviés   1565
Attend pour éclater que vous vous embrassiez.*
Ne faites point languir une si juste envie:
Allez. Et nous, Madame, allons chez Octavie.

BRITANNICUS

Allez, belle Junie, et d'un esprit* content*
Hâtez-vous d'embrasser ma sœur qui vous attend.   1570
Dès que je le pourrai, je reviens sur vos traces,
Madame, et de vos soins* j'irai vous rendre grâces.

SCÈNE III

Agrippine   Junie

AGRIPPINE

Madame, ou je me trompe, ou durant vos adieux
Quelques pleurs répandus ont obscurci vos yeux.
Puis-je savoir quel trouble a formé ce nuage?   1575
Doutez-vous d'une paix dont je fais mon ouvrage?

JUNIE

Après tous les ennuis* que ce jour m'a coûtés,
Ai-je pu rassurer mes esprits* agités?
Hélas! à peine encor* je conçois ce miracle.
Quand même à vos bontés je craindrais quelque obstacle,   1580
Le changement, Madame, est commun à la cour,
Et toujours quelque crainte accompagne l'amour.

AGRIPPINE

Il suffit, j'ai parlé, tout a changé de face.
Mes soins* à vos soupçons ne laissent point de place.
Je réponds d'une paix jurée entre mes mains: 1585

133

Néron m'en a donné des gages trop certains.
Ah! si vous aviez vu par combien de caresses*
Il m'a renouvelé la foi* de ses promesses!
Par quels embrassements il vient de m'arrêter!
Ses bras dans nos adieux ne pouvaient me quitter.   1590
Sa facile* bonté, sur son front* répandue,
Jusqu'aux moindres secrets est d'abord descendue.
Il s'épanchait en fils, qui vient en liberté
Dans le sein de sa mère oublier sa fierté.
Mais bientôt reprenant un visage sévère,   1595
Tel que d'un Empereur qui consulte sa mère,
Sa confidence* auguste a mis entre mes mains
Des secrets d'où* dépend le destin des humains.
Non, il le faut ici confesser à sa gloire,
Son cœur n'enferme point une malice* noire,   1600
Et nos seuls* ennemis, altérant sa bonté,
Abusaient contre nous de sa facilité.*
Mais enfin à son tour leur puissance décline.
Rome encore une fois va connaître Agrippine.
Déjà, de ma faveur on adore le bruit.   1605
Cependant en ces lieux n'attendons pas la nuit,
Passons chez Octavie, et donnons-lui le reste
D'un jour autant* heureux que je l'ai cru funeste.
Mais qu'est-ce que j'entends? Quel tumulte confus?
Que peut-on faire?   1610

JUNIE
O Ciel! sauvez Britannicus!

SCÈNE IV

Agrippine   Junie   Burrhus

AGRIPPINE
Burrhus, où courez-vous? Arrêtez. Que veut dire...

BURRHUS
Madame, c'en est fait, Britannicus expire.

JUNIE
Ah, mon Prince!

134

AGRIPPINE

Il expire?

BURRHUS

Ou plutôt il est mort,

Madame.

JUNIE

Pardonnez, Madame, à ce transport.*

Je vais le secourir, si je puis, ou le suivre.   1615

SCÈNE V

Agrippine   Burrhus

AGRIPPINE

Quel attentat, Burrhus!

BURRHUS

Je n'y pourrai survivre,

Madame, il faut quitter la cour et l'Empereur.

AGRIPPINE

Quoi! du sang de son frère il n'a point eu d'horreur?

BURRHUS

Ce dessein s'est conduit avec plus de mystère.*

A peine l'Empereur a vu venir son frère,   1620

Il se lève, il l'embrasse,* on se tait, et soudain

César prend le premier une coupe à la main.

Pour achever ce jour sous de meilleurs auspices,

Ma main de cette coupe épanche les prémices,*

Dit-il; *Dieux, que j'appelle à cette effusion,**   1625

*Venez favoriser notre réunion.**

Par les mêmes serments Britannicus se lie.

La coupe dans ses mains par Narcisse est remplie.

Mais ses lèvres à peine en ont touché les bords,

Le fer ne produit point de si puissants efforts,*   1630

Madame, la lumière à ses yeux est ravie,

Il tombe sur son lit sans chaleur et sans vie.

135

Jugez combien ce coup* frappe tous les esprits.
La moitié s'épouvante et sort avec des cris.
Mais ceux qui de la cour ont un plus long usage   1635
Sur les yeux de César composent* leur visage.
Cependant* sur son lit il demeure penché,*
D'aucun étonnement* il ne paraît touché.
Ce mal dont vous craignez, dit-il, la violence
A souvent sans péril attaqué son enfance.   1640
Narcisse veut en vain affecter quelque ennui,*
Et sa perfide joie éclate malgré lui.
Pour moi, dût l'Empereur punir ma hardiesse,
D'une odieuse cour j'ai traversé la presse,*
Et j'allais, accablé de cet assassinat,   1645
Pleurer Britannicus, César et tout l'Etat.

AGRIPPINE

Le voici. Vous verrez si c'est moi qui l'inspire.

SCÈNE VI

Agrippine   Néron   Burrhus   Narcisse

NÉRON, *voyant Agrippine*

Dieux!

AGRIPPINE

Arrêtez, Néron. J'ai deux mots à vous dire.
Britannicus est mort, je reconnais les coups.
Je connais l'assassin.   1650

NÉRON

Et qui, Madame?

AGRIPPINE

Vous.

NÉRON

Moi! Voilà les soupçons dont vous êtes capable.
Il n'est point de malheurs dont je ne sois coupable.
Et si l'on veut, Madame, écouter vos discours,*

Ma main de Claude même aura tranché les jours.
Son fils vous était cher, sa mort peut vous confondre.   1655
Mais des coups du destin je ne puis pas répondre.

AGRIPPINE

Non, non, Britannicus est mort empoisonné.
Narcisse a fait le coup,* vous l'avez ordonné.

NÉRON

Madame, mais qui peut vous tenir ce langage?

NARCISSE

Hé, Seigneur! ce soupçon vous fait-il tant d'outrage?   1660
Britannicus, Madame, eut des desseins secrets
Qui vous auraient coûté de plus justes regrets.
Il aspirait plus loin qu'à l'hymen de Junie.
De vos propres bontés il vous aurait punie.
Il vous trompait vous-même, et son cœur offensé   1665
Prétendait* tôt ou tard rappeler* le passé.
Soit donc que malgré vous le sort vous ait servie,
Soit qu'instruit des complots qui menaçaient sa vie,
Sur ma fidélité César s'en soit remis,*
Laissez les pleurs, Madame, à vos seuls* ennemis.   1670
Qu'ils mettent ce malheur au rang des plus sinistres.
Mais vous . . .

AGRIPPINE

       Poursuis, Néron, avec de tels ministres.
Par des faits* glorieux tu te vas signaler.
Poursuis. Tu n'as pas fait ce pas pour reculer.
Ta main a commencé par le sang de ton frère.   1675
Je prévois que tes coups viendront jusqu'à ta mère.
Dans le fond de ton cœur, je sais que tu me hais.
Tu voudras t'affranchir du joug de mes bienfaits.
Mais je veux que ma mort te soit même inutile:
Ne crois pas qu'en mourant je te laisse tranquille.   1680
Rome, ce ciel, ce jour que tu reçus de moi,
Partout, à tout moment, m'offriront devant toi.
Tes remords te suivront comme autant de furies.
Tu croiras les calmer par d'autres barbaries.

137

Ta fureur, s'irritant soi-même* dans son cours,   1685
D'un sang toujours nouveau marquera* tous tes jours.
Mais j'espère qu'enfin le Ciel, las de tes crimes,
Ajoutera ta perte à tant d'autres victimes,
Qu'après t'être couvert de leur sang et du mien,
Tu te verras forcé de répandre le tien ;   1690
Et ton nom paraîtra dans* la race* future
Aux plus cruels tyrans une cruelle injure.
   Voilà ce que mon cœur se présage de toi.
Adieu, tu peux sortir.

NÉRON
Narcisse, suivez-moi.

SCÈNE VII

Agrippine   Burrhus

AGRIPPINE
Ah, Ciel! de mes soupçons quelle était l'injustice!   1695
Je condamnais Burrhus, pour écouter Narcisse!
Burrhus, avez-vous vu quels regards furieux
Néron en me quittant m'a laissés pour adieux?
C'en est fait. Le cruel n'a plus rien qui l'arrête :
Le coup qu'on m'a prédit va tomber sur ma tête.   1700
Il vous accablera vous-même à votre tour.

BURRHUS
Ah, Madame! pour moi j'ai vécu trop d'un jour.
Plût au Ciel que sa main heureusement cruelle
Eût fait sur moi l'essai de sa fureur nouvelle!
Qu'il ne m'eût pas donné par ce triste* attentat   1705
Un gage trop certain des malheurs de l'Etat!
Son crime seul n'est pas ce qui me désespère ;
Sa jalousie a pu l'armer contre son frère.
Mais, s'il vous faut, Madame, expliquer* ma douleur,
Néron l'a vu mourir sans changer de couleur.   1710
Ses yeux indifférents ont déjà la constance*
D'un tyran dans le crime endurci dès l'enfance.
Qu'il achève, Madame, et qu'il fasse périr

Un ministre importun qui ne le peut souffrir.
Hélas! Loin de vouloir éviter sa colère,   1715
La plus soudaine mort me sera la plus chère.*

SCÈNE VIII

Agrippine Burrhus Albine

ALBINE

Ah, Madame! ah, Seigneur! Courez vers l'Empereur.
Venez sauver César de sa propre fureur.*
Il se voit pour jamais séparé de Junie.

AGRIPPINE

Quoi? Junie elle-même a terminé sa vie?   1720

ALBINE

Pour accabler César d'un éternel ennui,*
Madame, sans mourir elle est morte pour lui.
Vous savez de ces lieux comme* elle s'est ravie.*
Elle a feint de passer chez la triste* Octavie.
Mais bientôt elle a pris des chemins écartés,   1725
Où mes yeux ont suivi ses pas précipités.
Des portes du palais elle sort éperdue.
D'abord* elle a d'Auguste aperçu la statue;
Et mouillant de ses pleurs le marbre de ses pieds,
Que de ses bras pressants elle tenait liés: 1730
*Prince, par ces genoux, dit-elle, que j'embrasse,**
Protège en ce moment le reste de ta race.
Rome dans ton palais vient de voir immoler
Le seul de tes neveux qui te pût ressembler.*
On veut après sa mort que je lui sois parjure.   1735
Mais pour lui conserver une foi toujours pure,*
Prince, je me dévoue à ces Dieux immortels,
Dont ta vertu t'a fait partager les autels.*
Le peuple cependant* que ce spectacle étonne,*
Vole de toutes parts, se presse, l'environne,   1740
S'attendrit à ses pleurs, et plaignant* son ennui,*
D'une commune voix la prend sous son appui.
Ils la mènent au temple où depuis tant d'années

Au culte des autels nos vierges destinées
Gardent fidèlement le dépôt précieux 1745
Du feu toujours ardent* qui brûle pour nos Dieux.
César les voit partir sans oser les distraire.*
Narcisse, plus hardi, s'empresse pour lui plaire.
Il vole vers Junie, et sans s'épouvanter,
D'une profane main commence à l'arrêter. 1750
De mille coups mortels son audace est punie.
Son infidèle sang rejaillit sur Junie.
César, de tant d'objets* en même temps frappé,
Le laisse entre les mains qui l'ont enveloppé.
Il rentre. Chacun fuit son silence farouche. 1755
Le seul* nom de Junie échappe de sa bouche.
Il marche sans dessein, ses yeux mal assurés
N'osent lever au ciel leurs regards égarés.
Et l'on craint, si la nuit jointe à la solitude
Vient de son désespoir aigrir* l'inquiétude,* 1760
Si vous l'abandonnez plus longtemps sans secours,
Que sa douleur bientôt n'attente* sur ses jours.
Le temps presse. Courez. Il ne faut qu'un caprice.
Il se perdrait,* Madame.

AGRIPPINE
Il se ferait justice.
Mais, Burrhus, allons voir jusqu'où vont ses transports.* 1765
Voyons quel changement produiront ses remords,
S'il voudra désormais suivre d'autres maximes.

BURRHUS
Plût aux Dieux que ce fût le dernier de ses crimes!

VARIANTS

Le voici. Vous verrez si je suis sa complice: 1647
Demeurez.

SCÈNE VI

Néron Agrippine Junie Burrhus Narcisse

NÉRON, *a Junie*
De vos pleurs j'approuve la justice.
Mais, Madame, évitez ce spectacle odieux.
Moi-même en frémissant j'en détourne les yeux.
Il est mort. Tôt ou tard il faut qu'on vous l'avoue.
Ainsi de nos desseins la fortune* se joue.
Quand nous nous rapprochons, le Ciel nous désunit.

JUNIE
J'aimais Britannicus, Seigneur, je vous l'ai dit.
Si de quelque pitié ma misère* est suivie,
Qu'on me laisse chercher dans le sein d'Octavie
Un entretien conforme à l'état où je suis.

NÉRON
Belle Junie, allez: moi-même je vous suis.
Je vais par tous les soins* que la tendresse inspire
Vous...

SCÈNE VII

Agrippine Néron Burrhus Narcisse

AGRIPPINE
Arrêtez,   (1670)

Madame, il vous trompait, et son cœur offensé (1670–76)   1665
Tu te fatigueras d'entendre tes forfaits. (1670–76)   1677

ACTE III, SCÈNE I[1]

Burrhus Narcisse

BURRHUS
Quoi! Narcisse au palais obsédant* l'Empereur,
Laisse Britannicus en proie à sa fureur,

[1] Scene first published by L. Racine in 1747. See note, p. 161.

Narcisse, qui devrait d'une amitié sincère
Sacrifier au fils tout ce qu'il tient du père?
Qui devrait en plaignant* avec lui son malheur,   5
Loin des yeux de César détourner sa douleur?
Voulez-vous qu'accablé d'horreur, d'inquiétude,
Pressé du désespoir qui suit la solitude,
Il avance sa perte en voulant l'éloigner,
Et force l'Empereur à ne plus l'épargner?   10
Lorsque de Claudius l'impuissante vieillesse
Laissa de tout l'Empire Agrippine maîtresse,
Qu'instruit du successeur que lui gardaient les Dieux,
Il vit déjà son nom écrit dans tous les yeux;
Ce Prince, à ses bienfaits mesurant votre zèle,   15
Crut laisser à son fils un gouverneur* fidèle,
Et qui sans s'ébranler verrait passer un jour
Du côté de Néron la fortune et la cour.
Cependant aujourd'hui sur la moindre menace
Qui de Britannicus présage la disgrâce,*   20
Narcisse, qui devait le quitter le dernier,
Semble dans le malheur le plonger le premier:
César vous voit partout attendre son passage.

NARCISSE
Avec tout l'univers je viens lui rendre hommage,
Seigneur: c'est le dessein qui m'amène en ces lieux.   25

BURRHUS
Près de Britannicus vous le servirez mieux.
Craignez-vous que César n'accuse votre absence?
Sa grandeur lui répond de votre obéissance.
C'est à Britannicus qu'il faut justifier
Un soin* dont ses malheurs se doivent défier.   30
Vous pouvez sans péril respecter sa misère:*
Néron n'a point juré la perte de son frère.
Quelque froideur qui semble altérer leurs esprits,
Votre maître n'est point au nombre des proscrits.
Néron même en son cœur touché de votre zèle,   35
Vous en tiendrait peut-être un compte plus fidèle
Que de tous ces respects vainement assidus,*
Oubliés dans la foule aussitôt que rendus.

143

NARCISSE

Ce langage, Seigneur, est facile à comprendre;
Avec quelque bonté César daigne m'entendre;   40
Mes soins* trop bien reçus pourraient vous irriter . . .
A l'avenir, Seigneur, je saurai l'éviter.

BURRHUS

Narcisse, vous réglez mes desseins sur les vôtres:
Ce que vous avez fait, vous l'imputez aux autres.
Ainsi lorsqu'inutile au reste des humains,   45
Claude laissait gémir l'Empire entre vos mains,
Le reproche éternel de votre conscience
Condamnait devant lui Rome entière au silence.
Vous lui laissiez à peine écouter vos flatteurs,
Le reste vous semblait autant d'accusateurs,   50
Qui prêts à s'élever contre votre conduite,
Allaient de nos malheurs développer* la suite,
Et lui portant les cris du Peuple et du Sénat
Lui demander justice au nom de tout l'Etat.
Toutefois pour César je crains votre présence: 55
Je crains, puisqu'il vous faut parler sans complaisance,
Tous ceux qui comme vous, flattant tous ses désirs,
Sont toujours dans son cœur du parti des plaisirs.
Jadis à nos conseils l'Empereur plus docile,
Affectait pour son frère une bonté facile,*   60
Et de son rang pour lui modérant la splendeur,
De sa chute à ses yeux cachait la profondeur.
Quel soupçon aujourd'hui, quel désir de vengeance
Rompt du sang des Césars l'heureuse intelligence?*
Junie est enlevée, Agrippine frémit;   65
Jaloux et sans espoir, Britannicus gémit:
Du cœur de l'Empereur son épouse bannie
D'un divorce à toute heure attend l'ignominie,
Elle pleure; et voilà ce que leur a coûté
L'entretien d'un flatteur qui veut être écouté.   70

NARCISSE

Seigneur, c'est un peu loin pousser la violence;
Vous pouvez tout, j'écoute, et garde le silence.
Mes actions un jour pourront vous repartir:
Jusque-là . . .

BURRHUS
Puissiez-vous bientôt me démentir!
Plût aux Dieux qu'en effet ce reproche vous touche!   75
Je vous aiderai même à me fermer la bouche.
Sénèque, dont les soins* devraient me soulager,
Occupé loin de Rome, ignore ce danger.
Réparons, vous et moi, cette absence funeste:
Du sang de nos Césars réunissons* le reste.   80
Rapprochons-les, Narcisse, au plutôt*, dès ce jour,
Tandis qu'ils ne sont point séparés sans retour.

NOTES

EPÎTRE AU DUC DE CHEVREUSE

Duc de Chevreuse. See Introduction, p. 13–14. The family of the Luynes-Chevreuse was influential at Court mainly through the Duke's grandmother, the Duchess of Chevreuse, widow of the first Duke of Luynes, minister and favourite of Louis XIII. The Duchess had been a life-long friend of the Queen Mother, Anne of Austria, and what was more important, one of the small circle of friends who helped the young Louis XIV to get rid of Foucquet. She protected Colbert, and arranged her grandson's marriage with Colbert's daughter.

4 *que de cacher.* de cacher.
6 *se puisse taire.* puisse se taire: the construction is extremely frequent in the seventeenth century. It is still found nowadays in the literary language (*Une voiture te peut broyer,* Alain. *Ce qui nous doit occuper,* Duhamel). Cf. Grevisse, 483. It is becoming old-fashioned and should not be imitated.
9 *mes amis mêmes* . . . An obscure, but obviously challenging allusion.
11 *un homme* . . . Colbert.
17 *il serait dangereux* . . . By inclination and policy Colbert discouraged flattery: all praise had to be addressed to the King.
23 *avec toutes les qualités* . . . Cf. Saint-Simon, *Mémoires,* IV, 86 (Pléiade).
25 *l'expérience de plusieurs années.* The Duke of Chevreuse was twenty-three.
26 *vos amis particuliers* . There is no reason to doubt the friendship Racine recalls with a touch of familiarity. But he was not displeased to let it be known that he was an 'ami particulier' of Colbert's son-in-law.

PREMIÈRE PRÉFACE

1670. This Preface is found only in the first edition published at the beginning of 1670.

8 *trop cruel.* Perhaps an allusion to Saint-Evremond (see Introduction, p. 7), who thought the atrocious crimes of Néron and the other characters ruined the play, or to similar views.
14 *Il ne s'agit point* . . . *des affaires du dehors.* Racine will not deal with the administration of the Empire or the wars on its borders.
19 *trop bon.* Boursault found Néron 'cruel sans malice' (*Artémise et Poliante,* see Mesnard edition). In the *Gazette* Robinet wished Néron had 'plus de véhémence et de passion'.
22 *mis le feu à Rome.* It is not certain that the great fire that destroyed Rome in A.D. 64 was ordered by Nero.
23 *sa mère.* Agrippina was murdered in A.D. 59 (*Annals,* XIV, 8).
sa femme. Octavia was first accused of adultery and exiled, then executed in particularly horrible circumstances in A.D. 62.

ses gouverneurs . . . Burrhus died in A.D. 62. He was seriously ill, and it was only a rumour that Nero had ordered him to be poisoned (*Ann.* XIV, 51).

Seneca's part in Piso's conspiracy was not proved, but Nero ordered him to commit suicide. He died with stoic serenity, and his wife chose to die with him (A.D. 65).

37 *de dix-sept ans.* Britannicus was not fifteen when he was murdered in A.D. 55. Cf. Seconde Préface.

45 *un homme.* Corneille.

46 *un Empereur.* In *Héraclius*, the Emperor Phocas.

51 *Junia Silana.* See Tacitus, *Ann.*, XIII, 19.

56 *Junia Calvina. Ann.*, XII, 4.

58 *festivissima* . . . 'the liveliest girl', Seneca, *Apokolokyntosis*, 8.2.

65 *la délicatesse est grande* . . . The scene referred to followed, in the first edition, the present scene 5, in Act v. In spite of Racine's heated self-justification he finally cancelled it. It can be found in the Variants; there is no doubt it is a weak scene: Junie's grief seems inadequate; Néron's *galanterie* ('Belle Junie') is out of place.

74 *la pièce est finie* . . . See Introduction, p. 7.

82 *Antigone.* Represented in Athens in 442 B.C. The end of the tragedy is essentially lyrical.

90 *Au lieu d'une action simple* . . . See Introduction, p. 10.

99 *quelque héros ivre* . . . Attila may have been a drunken barbarian, but he does not appear so in Corneille's *Attila* (1667).

qui se voudrait faire haïr . . .
　　'L'amour chez Attila n'est pas un bon suffrage;
　　Ce qu'on m'en donnerait me tiendrait lieu d'outrage,
　　Et tout exprès ailleurs je porterais ma foi,
　　De peur qu'on eût par là trop de pouvoir sur moi.' 　(*Attila*, I, 2)
As in fact he is in love with Ildione, he tries to keep her away from him:
　　'Pour l'obliger à fuir, peins-lui bien tout l'affront
　　Que va mon hyménée imprimer sur son front.
　　Ose plus: fais-lui peur d'une prison sévère . . .
　　Fais-m'en haïr . . .
　　Fais qu'elle me dédaigne et me préfère un autre.' 　(Id., III, 1)

100 *un Lacédémonien grand parleur.* The Spartans were supposed to express themselves in a brief, *laconic* way. Racine accuses Corneille's hero, in *Agésilas* (1666), of speaking too much.

101 *un conquérant qui ne débiterait* . . . This has sometimes been read as a reference to Corneille's César in *La Mort de Pompée* (1644). It is more probable that it is aimed at Quinault's *Pausanias* (1668): 'The hero of it, after leading the Greek armies to victory over the Persians, is represented as so desperately in love with a captive that he meditates deserting his country and his allies for her sake' (C. Lancaster).

102 *une femme qui donnerait des leçons* . . . This again has been referred to *La Mort de Pompée.* According to C. Lancaster it would fit better Hannibal's daughter addressing the Roman Flaminius in a more recent play, Thomas Corneille's *Mort d'Annibal* (1669).

106 *ces grands hommes de l'antiquité* . . . See Introduction, p. 9.

114 *Quid de te alii* ... 'What other people will say about you is their own business; in any case they will talk' (Cicero, *De Re publica*, VI, 23).

121 *malevoli* ... The 'vieux poète malintentionné' (Luscius Lanuvinus) is of course an indirect allusion to Corneille. 'The poet, when he first applies himself to writing, believes his main task is to produce plays that will please his audience. But soon he understands things are not that way at all, for he must waste his time writing prologues, not to expound his plot, but to answer the slanders of a malevolent old poet.' Terence, *Andr.*, Prol.

124 *Occœpta est* ... 'The play begins: he exclaims (that this is the work of a thief, not of a poet ...', etc.). Terence, *Eunuch.*, Prol., 22.

128 *les Vestales.* See Note 1076.

129 *Aulu-Gelle.* A. Gellius (*Noct. Attic.*, I, 12).

151 *Homine imperito* ... Racine quotes from memory: *Homine inperito numquam quicquam iniustiust:* 'In no circumstances is there any man more unfair than an ignorant man' (the quotation goes on: 'Nothing is right to him except what he does himself ...', etc.). Terence, *Adelphœ*, 98.

SECONDE PRÉFACE

1676. The new Preface replaced the first one in all editions from 1676.

29 *qui ont été heureuses.* See Note 28.

33 *sa mère, sa femme* ... See First Preface.

36 *factus natura* ... 'Inclined by nature to conceal his hatred behind false embraces' (*Ann.*, XIV, 56).

39 *hactenus Nero* ... 'So far Nero had tried to disguise his vices and his crimes' (*Ann.*, XIII, 47).

41 *fato quodam* ... 'Because it was so fated, or because things forbidden have a stronger appeal (...). It was feared that he could not be prevented from seducing women of rank' (*Ann.*, XIII, 12).

46 *cujus abditis* ... Racine has just translated this passage.

51 *cette peste* ... Narcisse.
En voici la raison. Burrhus offered a more marked contrast with Narcisse than Seneca would have done.

55 *militaribus curis* ... *Seneca praeceptis* ... *civitati grande desiderium* ... Racine himself translates all these passages. (*Ann.*, XIII, 2; XIV, 51).

61 *quae cunctis malae* ... 'Agrippina was burning with the desires of a tyrannic domination, and she had on her side Pallas' (*Ann.*, XIII, 2).

70 *Sibi supremum auxilium* ... *Neque segnem ei* ... *Nam ut proximus* ... Racine has translated these passages (*Ann.*, XIII, 16; XII, 26; XIII, 15).

86 *Junia Silana*, etc. Cf. First Preface.

93 *jusqu'au règne de Vespasien.* Cf. Suetonius, *Vesp.* 23.

ACT I

SCENE I

Racine did not have at his disposal modern stage-lighting and scenic means. But for a modern producer the beginning of *Britannicus* has impressive possibilities. The theatre is still in almost total darkness, but dawn is coming, and the gold and marble of the Imperial palace glimmer faintly. The stage seems deserted, except perhaps for a praetorian guard on sentry duty in the background; yet a woman is there, waiting, motionless. In a few moments, with a shock of surprise—for at the French Court as in Imperial Rome pageantry filled every moment in the life of the great—the spectators will learn that this lonely woman is the Empress Mother, the all-powerful Agrippine, who always appears surrounded by a 'suite' of ladies-in-waiting, and followed by an 'escorte' of guards. Agrippine, whom the Romans have seen sitting on a throne by the side of the Emperor, preceded by legionaries carrying the eagles, or lictors bearing the fasces, is in Rome a *sacred* character, the object of public veneration and awe: 'Votre nom est dans Rome aussi *saint* que le sien' (82) . . . 'Ainsi que par César on jure par sa mère' (192).

Day is breaking slowly in the course of the first scene, while the secrets of the Imperial Court gradually emerge into light. It is the dawn of that single, decisive day which encompasses the whole action of a classical tragedy: within that single day each character will risk and lose all; within that single place, *à huis clos*, they will fight their battle to a finish. When darkness comes again the power of the great Empress will be crumbling, and utter ruin will be her only prospect, Britannicus will be dead, and Néron a murderer half crazy with rage and despair.

The first scene—and practically the whole of the first Act—is one of *exposition*, one, that is, in which the author's main preoccupation is to acquaint the spectator with his characters and with the initial situation in which they find themselves. This will be taken up again and developed later, but the main facts are given to us clearly in less than fifteen lines: Néron's mother is waiting behind the closed doors of his private rooms; a dangerous conflict has broken out between Néron and Britannicus; the power of Agrippine is on the wane.

Albine. The use of 'confidents' and 'confidentes' in Corneille, Racine, and their later imitators has often been criticized, not without reason. It is said that they have no character of their own, are present on the stage only to listen to the main actors of the drama, and add nothing to it. This is not always true: some of Racine's confidants do reach the full status of a real character: such is Oenone in *Phèdre*, and Burrhus and Narcisse are confidants who have a marked personality and influence the action. But Albine is not in the same category. Her usefulness is obvious; in the first Act her part— not very convincing in one who is supposed to be so close to Agrippine—is to voice the current opinions of the Roman in the street, who sees the political situation as most satisfactory, and grows sentimental at Néron's filial love and Agrippine's maternal devotion. Later (III, 4) her fears and warnings will set off Agrippine's rage and fury, and loss of all self-control. In the last scene of the play she will fulfil the functions of that traditional character of ancient and modern tragedy: the messenger. But she remains colourless and impersonal.

4 *César.* 'Caesar' and the 'Prince' (*princeps*) are the expressions used most frequently by Roman historians when referring to the Emperor.

12 *Las de se faire aimer, il veut se faire craindre.* Paraphrase of a line in an old Latin tragedy; Racine probably found it in Seneca's *De clementia*, XII, 4: *Oderint, dum metuant!* 'Let them hate me, as long as they fear me!' It was Caligula's favourite maxim (Suet., *Calig.*, 30). Cf., too, Seneca, *Octavia*, 457, 1056.

18 ... *l'heureux Domitius.* Lucius Domitius Ahenobarbus was the name of the son Agrippine had by her first marriage; when he was legally adopted into the Claudian family, he changed his name, according to Roman usage, to Tiberius Claudius Nero.
heureux. fortunate, lucky.

25, 27 ... *depuis trois ans* ... *depuis deux ans.* Britannicus was murdered one year after Nero's accession. Racine, probably trying to conform to history more closely, corrected line 27 (see Variants), but forgot to correct line 25.

28 *Au temps de ses consuls croit être retournée.* Suetonius and Tacitus (XIII, 4, 5) agree that in the first year of Nero's reign Imperial despotism was moderated and the old Republican institutions (Senate, consuls, ...) allowed to regain some prestige.

32–4 *Il commence, il est vrai* ... Partly for the sake of clarity, mainly to express Agrippine's sombre energy, Racine makes use in this scene of every kind of parallel constructions, antitheses, repetitions, strong caesurae dividing the line into equally balanced half-lines:
'Il *commence* ... par où *finit* Auguste ...
Il ne *finisse* ainsi qu'Auguste a *commencé*.
... l'*avenir* détruisant le *passé* ...'
Cf. line 21: '*Tout*, s'il est *généreux*, ...
            Mais *tout*, s'il est *ingrat*, ...'
       line 12: 'Las de se faire *aimer*, / il veut se faire *craindre*.'
And already in line 10 the names of the two rivals defy each other from each side of the caesura:
        'Contre *Britannicus Néron* s'est déclaré.'
A number of similar examples can be found in the rest of the scene; they give the style its tense, heavy, brooding quality.

34 ... *ainsi qu'Auguste a commencé.* The domination of the *triumviri*, Octavius, who was to become Augustus, Antony, and Lepidus, had started with the *proscriptions* in appalling bloodshed, and Augustus established his final supremacy by armed force. With the cessation of all organized resistance he was able to relax his despotism and to rule peacefully.

35–8 *Je lis sur son visage* ... Racine, in presenting his character, does not fail to mention Néron's heredity, but it would be an unbalanced view to explain the whole play in terms of these four lines.

36 *Des fiers Domitius* ... Suetonius tells revolting stories about the brutality of Nero's father (*Nero*, 5,1): once on the Appian Way he deliberately crushed a child under the hoofs of his horses, for the fun of it.

38 ... *des Nérons.* The family of the Emperor Tiberius and his nephew Germanicus, Agrippine's father.

39 *prémices.* First fruits, firstlings. Here: beginnings.

40 *Caïus.* The Emperor Caligula, Agrippine's own brother.

41 ... *fureur.* Caligula actually became insane.

43 *Que m'importe ... que Néron ... | D'une longue vertu laisse un jour le modèle?*
Let us remember this contemptuous declaration of Agrippine's indifference about the moral or immoral character of Néron's actions.

46 *... au gré du Peuple et du Sénat.* Agrippine uses scornfully the ancient
formula which defined the power of the State in the old Roman Republic:
Senatus Populusque Romanus.

47 *... de la Patrie ... le Père.* The traditional title of *Pater Patriae*, which the
Senate conferred upon a citizen who had saved Rome from mortal peril:
it was conferred upon Cicero after the crushing of Catiline's conspiracy,
and later upon Augustus. It was offered to Nero, who had in fact refused
it (Suet., *Nero*, 8).

50 *L'attentat que le jour vient de nous révéler.* This is the initial fact of the drama,
the one that sets it in motion.

60 *...j'ai moi seule avancé leur ruine.* Agrippine will tell the whole story later
(IV, 2). Cf. Tacitus, *Ann.*, Book XII.

63 *hymen, hyménée*, belong to the literary style exclusively, but are always
used by Racine instead of the common word 'mariage'.

65 *Silanus, sur qui Claude avait jeté les yeux.* Claudius had officially agreed to
his marrying his daughter Octavia; Agrippina wanted her to marry Nero.
An accusation of incest was brought against Silanus and his sister (cf.
Racine's Prefaces) and he committed suicide ('abandonna la vie'). In the
play therefore Junie has already suffered at the hands of Agrippina and
lost her brother thanks to her intrigues.

66 *... Auguste au rang de ses aïeux.* He and Junie were the great-great-grand-
children of Augustus. See Appendix II.

68 *... entre eux et lui je tienne la balance.* The true relationship between mother
and son is indeed very different from the touching picture earlier presented
by Albine.

83 *... la triste Octavie.* Britannicus' sister. The marriage had been arranged
for purely dynastic reasons. Nero was not sixteen yet, Octavia thirteen.
Nero disliked Octavia, and naturally enough resented the enforced
marriage (cf. 468).

84 *Auguste votre aïeul.* Your ancestor (see Appendix II).

86 *... les faisceaux couronnés de laurier.* The *fasces laureati* had been the privilege
of the general who had won a great victory (*imperator*), and was granted
a triumph. They then became associated with the Prince. It was unheard
of that they should be carried in front of a woman.

93 *Lorsqu'il se reposait sur moi de tout l'Etat.* In contrast with the dreams of a
return to Republican forms of government Agrippine stands for personal
rule and the pure, unadulterated despotism towards which Rome is
gradually moving.

95 *... un voile.* Tradition was still strong enough to prevent a woman
from openly attending the deliberations of the Senate: a curtain hid the
known presence of Agrippine.

114 *Sénèque ... Burrhus.* See First Preface.

125 *J'entends du bruit: on ouvre.* Stage indications are rare in Racine, but
according to Aristotle's principle they are usually embodied in the text.
Allons subitement ... Agrippine springs up, ready to do battle.

128 *Mais quoi?* . . . Keen disappointment.

129 *Au nom de l'Empereur . . . vous informer | D'un ordre . . . Dont César a voulu* . . . Even before the discussion has started every word uttered by Burrhus suggests that he speaks on behalf of the highest authority in Rome, one to which even Agrippine is 'sujette' (1110): she is not consulted but *informed* of the Emperor's *order*.
   . . . *un ordre*. The arrest of Junie.

133 *Puisqu'il le veut* . . . (i.e.: that I should be informed about it).
   . . . *il m'en instruira mieux* (better than if I stay outside with you). Agrippine at once snubs Burrhus, and prepares to walk in.

136 *L'un et l'autre consul* . . . Latinism: *uterque consul*.
   . . . *vous avaient prévenue*. Had arrived before you.

138 . . . *ses augustes secrets*. There is a harsh sneer in several of Agrippine's remarks. Examples were to be found in Scene 1 already ('Las de se faire aimer, il veut se faire craindre'. 'Les délices de Rome en devinrent l'horreur'. 'Néron, que la vertu conduit'), and there will be many more later in the play.

142 *Prétendez-vous* . . . Furious at being foiled in her attempt to see Néron, Agrippine now sets upon Burrhus, and her onslaught has the terrifying violence that shook her enemies and awed even Néron (cf. 506: 'Mon génie étonné tremble devant le sien'). Almost every line is a question, and each question is like a blow, and does not wait for an answer.

143 *à titre de*. Literally: by right of, in one's capacity as; here simply: as.

145 *Pour mettre* . . . 'Pour que vous mettiez.' Similarly, 150: *Pour être* . . . 'Pour que vous soyez.' The construction is more rapid and direct, but it is no longer correct.

153, 155 *Vous, . . . Et moi,* . . . Main stops after the first and second syllables.

156 *Moi, fille, femme, sœur, et mère de vos maîtres*. Racine's line can lash like a whip. Agrippine's towering pride reaches here its climax. Behind it is all the patrician arrogance of ancient Rome and of seventeenth-century France.

159 *N'est-il pas temps qu'il règne?* Bad faith of Agrippine.

164 . . . *Germanicus mon père*. After winning brilliant victories against the Germans and in the East, Germanicus had become a hero in the eyes of the people and the army (cf. 770, 1170), and aroused his uncle Tiberius' ill-will. When he died there was strong suspicion of poison.

170 . . . *une seule action*. Junie's arrest, which we had almost forgotten in the turmoil of Agrippine's accusations.

171 . . . *sans vouloir que je le justifie, | Vous me rendez garant* . . . without allowing me to defend him (on that particular point), you make me responsible ('garant') for all his actions ('du reste de sa vie').

174 . . . *un soldat,* . . . a man who has spent his life in the army. Burrhus was *praefectus praetorii*, commander of the praetorians, the Emperor's life-guards.

180 *Ce n'est plus votre fils* . Cf. 48: 'Qu'il songe un peu plus qu'Agrippine est sa mère.'

181 *J'en dois compte* . . . 'en' i.e. 'de Néron' (cf. Glossary).

182 . . . *son salut* . . . 'Le salut de Néron.'

183 'Instruire dans l'ignorance' is a daring combination of terms.

186 . . . *dans l'exil* . . . Seneca had been brought back from exile by Agrippine.

200 . . . *trois affranchis* . . . Pallas, Narcissus, Callistus had been all-powerful during the reign of Claudius.

202 . . . *compte sa liberté.* Only after Néron's accession did Rome begin to feel free.

205 *Le peuple au Champ de Mars* . . . The Roman elections were held at the *Campus Martius*. Those concessions were only apparent: the Prince remained the real master.

207 *Thraséas au Sénat* . . . Thrasea Paetus, one of the few Senators who, later, showed dignity and independence under Nero's tyranny.

. . . *Corbulon dans l'armée.* A harsh but very capable general, whom Nero had just put in command of his eastern armies. Later Nero became jealous of his fame, and ordered him to kill himself.

228 *Le sang de mes aïeux* . . . Both Agrippine and Junie were descended from Julia, daughter of Augustus (see Appendix II).

239 . . . *les droits qu'elle porte avec elle.* Racine has been taken to task for presenting things as if Junie was a Hapsburg or a Bourbon princess. Of course the order of succession for the Emperors was not fixed as in modern monarchies, and Junie, or for that matter Britannicus, did not have *rights* to the throne. But the first four successors of Augustus were all descended from Livia, and in the case of Nero, from Augustus and Livia. All took the name of Caesar, the adoptive father of Octavius Augustus, and the real founder of the new system. A dynastic feeling was in the making.

241 . . . *le sang de César.* His blood relations.

247 . . . *pour détourner ses yeux de sa misère.* Agrippine's true motives are very different.

256 *son empire.* His power.

258 *éprouver.* To test.

271 *censeur.* Roman magistrate who periodically reviewed the roll of senators, closely scrutinizing their life and all their actions.

274 *Et n'avertissez point la cour de vous quitter.* After deploring Agrippine's suspicions of her son and denying all possibilities of a conflict between them, Burrhus slips in a veiled threat: in the trial of force Agrippine is contemplating she will have the worst.

280 *ma liberté.* Free, uninhibited way of speaking.

286 . . . *a consultés le moins.* Burrhus drops a hint that *he* is not the one who advised Néron to have Junie arrested.

SCENE III

Sudden change in the tempo and the tone of the play. Britannicus comes *running* in (cf. Note 125); he has not given a thought to the danger of putting himself at the mercy of his rival, but Agrippine at once remarks upon his rashness ('en aveugle vous jette...'), and expresses her displeasure: Britannicus is now a valuable weapon in her hands, nothing must happen to him. But Britannicus is beside himself with worry and grief; his speech is halting, and almost incoherent.

299 *Il suffit.* Agrippine is not really interested in Britannicus' feelings.

301–2 ... *qu'un impuissant courroux | Dégage ma parole*... To make good her promise Agrippine does not mean to confine herself to giving vent to an ineffective anger.

304 *Pallas.* Claudius' chief minister, and Agrippine's long-standing and powerful ally in her struggle for power. That the Empress should ask the young Pretender, Néron's rival, to a conference with Pallas creates a new situation. Junie's arrest was Néron's answer to Agrippine's first move: the betrothal of Britannicus and Junie. This is Agrippine's countermove.

SCENE IV

305 *La croirai-je* ... Britannicus is well aware of the implications of Agrippine's offer, but he remains hesitant and suspicious: he has suffered too much from her.

313 ... *liez vos intérêts.* Narcisse encourages Britannicus and seems to be on his side. It will soon be clear, however, that he is only trying to involve him further in a dangerous situation.

319–26 An important passage for the understanding of Britannicus and the play. Britannicus will not accept for a moment more than necessary what he calls 'servitude', submission to Néron. He has not renounced what he considers to be his right to the throne ('l'Empire, où j'étais destiné'). Only his youth and isolation make him harmless, but he represents a grave, if only a potential, threat to Néron's power.
tu sais si ...je prétends ... | Tu sais si ...je renonce ... You know I shall never renounce ...

335 *Comme toi dans mon cœur il sait ...* The spectator does not suspect yet the irony of these words and of the whole passage: Narcisse is of course Néron's chief spy. Cf. 437, etc.

339–40 ... *cette défiance | Est toujours d'un grand cœur la dernière science.* (The last knowledge he acquires.) Racine does not wish us to despise Britannicus for his trustfulness. Even his *naïveté* is lessened by the fact that his dead father recommended Narcisse to him (343). On the help Claudius expected Narcisse to give his son, see the scene which Racine suppressed, but which was preserved by his son (Variants, p. 142).

349 *Examine leurs yeux.* A simple, yet highly suggestive expression, which evokes the guarded, suspicious atmosphere of the Court, where much can be conveyed, or betrayed, by a single look.

358 *M'engager sous son nom plus loin qu'elle ne veut.* Racine has tried to give Britannicus an active role: he is not merely Agrippine's tool.

ACT II

SCENE I

At the beginning of the Act Néron appears giving his orders to a silent circle of respectful subordinates. Unresentful of his mother's 'injustices', implicitly excusing his 'brother', he will only punish a subversive schemer; nor is the sentence inhuman: Pallas will leave Rome and go into exile. In spite of his youth (he is eighteen or nineteen) Néron speaks and behaves with all the dignity and authority of his high office, and his decision is motivated by the good of the State, 'le salut de l'Empire'.

362 . . . *nourrir* (ses caprices). To foster them.

366 *Les trouverait . . . assemblés chez Pallas.* A shrewd guess—which the presence of Narcisse will soon explain....

369 *Je le veux, je l'ordonne.* 'Sic volo, sic jubeo' (Juvenal, *Sat.*, VI, 223: *Hoc volo, sic jubeo*). But the expression goes back to the ancient Roman formula by which a law was proposed to the Assembly of the people: *Velitis, jubeatis, uti . . . vos, quirites, rogo.* 'Whether it is your will, whether it is your command that . . . I put it to you, citizens.' Néron is assuming the ultimate power that used to reside in the people.

372 *Et vous,* . . . To the Guards.

SCENE II

A long scene, in which, behind the majestic figure of the Emperor, will gradually appear—no monster yet, but a moody, yearning, insecure, rebellious adolescent.

373 *Junie entre vos mains / Vous assure . . . du reste des Romains.* It is important to remember that Junie has been arrested for political reasons, in order to check Agrippine and prevent the rise of Britannicus: Néron had never seen her before.

377–80 *Mais que vois-je? Vous-même inquiet, étonné,* . . . Néron's love, significantly in the Racinian world, first appears as a darkening expression on his face ('une tristesse obscure'): Néron is not elated but dismayed, 'consterné'.

379 *Que présage* . . . In Racine's time the verb often agrees with the nearest subject (with 'tristesse', and not with 'regards').

380 . . . *errants à l'aventure.* The present participle does not nowadays agree in gender or number.

385 There is nothing monstrous in the passage that follows, although some critics have tried hard to see it as such. It is a picture, rare, indeed unique in Racine, of a youth falling in love, and we must forget for the time being that his name is Néron. The unsuspecting Néron (he was there out of curiosity), the baroque splendour of the background, with its violent *chiaroscuri*—flaming torches and glittering arms against the darkness of night—its violent contrasts—the sharp words of command in the quiet of night—and, in this dramatic setting, the *strangeness* of Junie, a very young girl, frightened and in tears, in the middle of a rough soldiery,

all this does nothing to explain Néron's love, but it magnificently conveys its magic and its 'charme'.

At this moment Néron is no longer 'le maitre du monde' or le 'fier Domitius'; his throat contracts, no sound comes out of it, and he cannot think of anything but Junie for the rest of the night.

387, 389 *Triste, . . . | Belle, . . .* Position of the words, and value of the stops —and the almost Baudelairian climate they create.

397 *Immobile, saisi d'un long étonnement.* The climax of the passage, and, with its internal echoes (of 'i' 's and muffled nasal sounds), one of Racine's mysteriously suggestive lines.

401, 405 Racine's syntax is particularly free in this almost lyrical passage. *Trop présente à mes yeux je croyais lui parler . . .* 'présente' should normally refer to the subject ('je'). *Voilà comme occupé de mon nouvel amour | Mes yeux . . .* 'occupé' refers to the idea of 'je' contained in 'mes yeux'.

407 *je m'en fais peut-être une trop belle image.* Néron seems almost to wish Narcisse to say so, just as he tried hard to tear himself from Junie's memory. He feels trapped, rather than pleased with himself.

412 *. . . qui lui ravit son frère.* Cf. 64.

413 *jaloux de.* Anxious to preserve.

419–422 *Tandis qu'il n'est point de Romaine | . . .* This has not the intensity of what precedes: the novelty of the adventure attracts the already *blasé*, and not a little self-satisfied, Néron, used to the eager advances of the ladies of the Court. For this there is no equivalent in Tacitus: it is the French Court and its young King Racine has in mind.

424 *leurs honneurs.* What other women consider to be an honour.

427 *. . . l'aime-t-il?* The abruptness of the question corresponds to Néron's sudden concern.

428 *Si jeune encor . . .* According to the Second Preface Britannicus is fifteen: Néron may well think the projected marriage is only one of Agrippine's schemes, like his own marriage.

432 *. . . sont faits à l'usage . . .* Have learnt to know.

437–42 Cf. 335.

445 *Néron impunément ne sera pas jaloux.* The first distant thunder of the storm and the first brief awakening of the murderous violence that will take hold of Néron.

451 *. . . les rois sans diadème.* The subject kings of the Empire will not wear their crown in the presence of their master.

452 *. . . et son amant lui-même.* Her lover, Britannicus, will be lost in the crowd of the onlookers.

455 *. . . sa victoire.* Her victory over you. Cf. note 948.

456 *Maître, n'en doutez point, . . .* Master, as you will be no doubt . . . 'Maître', apposition to the subject of the imperative 'commandez' (Néron).

470 *Ses vœux.* Vows, promises made to the gods, in expectation of a favour.

472 *gage.* Token, sign of their favour (the birth of a child).

473 *L'Empire . . . demande un héritier.* The anachronism here is more marked than in 239: the idea of a Crown Prince was not clearly established in Rome.

BRITANNICUS

476 *aïeul*. Ancestor. See Appendix II.

477 *Par un double divorce* . . . Livia divorced her husband Tiberius Claudius Nero, father of her son, the future Emperor Tiberius, and Augustus divorced Scribonia, mother of his daughter Julia.

479 *hymen*. See Note 63.

480 . . . *répudier sa fille*. Tiberius was for a while married to Julia.

489 *De quel front soutenir ce fâcheux entretien?* 'Le maître du monde' is afraid of his mother.

496–510 A sensitive, almost sympathetic, analysis of a very young, very real human being—no personification of Evil.

In Néron's feelings towards Agrippine, there is the memory of his not very distant childhood ('ces yeux où j'ai lu si longtemps mon devoir'); there is, unexpectedly, gratitude ('tout ce que je tiens d'elle'); there is fear ('. . . tremble . . .'), but who does not fear Agrippine? Particularly irksome to a young man, there is a feeling of dependence, and in rebelling against it he rebels against a part of himself: if he deliberately, gratuitously, avoids, defies, or annoys her, it is to prove his independence, because it is sorely in need of being proved.

513–18 . . . *Il attend de mes soins ce fidèle secours*. Narcisse expresses only irony and derision towards the boy who was entrusted to him, and who believes in him.

SCENE III

527 . . . *et changez de visage*. Junie is obviously upset at meeting unexpectedly the Emperor. Face and eyes (see *Glossary: Yeux*) are almost as important in Racine as in a film close-up.

532 . . . *l'heureuse Octavie*. Fortunate to receive Junie's visit.

539 *et seq*. The whole passage is full of expressions, often associated with *préciosité*, which belong to the conventional language of *galanterie* in the seventeenth century, and this is characterized by the constant use of elaborate compliments and studied exaggerations.

The clichés were in universal use at the time, and Racine himself is not always beyond reproach in that respect. Here, however, they have, at least up to a point, a dramatic justification. It is the first time Junie sees Néron, and an immediate expression of his passion would only bewilder and frighten her. The *précieux* compliments are less a way of expressing his love than a means of allowing her gradually to understand that he loves her. Addressed to a girl who is in fact his prisoner, however, they cannot but have some undertones of irony.

540 Junie is guilty of a crime ('une offense') in concealing herself from Néron.

545 It is glorious ('cette gloire') to be in her presence.

546 To be away from her is to be in exile ('relégué dans ma cour'); he complains of her inhumanity ('sans pitié') Cf. earlier (531) the envy he pretends to feel for the fortunate Octavie.

549–52 Néron's last lines, dismissing with apparent unconcern Junie's love, of which he is aware, are meant to warn and to embarrass her:

Néron cannot believe that a well-behaved, and a strictly educated, Princess ('la sévère Junie') could have encouraged a lover.

553-558 Junie, speaking of intimate feelings to a stranger, uses at first the same conventional language ('ses soupirs, . . . ses vœux'), except that, whereas Néron relies on exaggeration and hyperbole, she shelters behind understatement and litotes ('. . . m'ont daigné quelquefois . . .' 'Il n'a point détourné ses regards . . .').

558 This is an answer to Néron's innuendo: there is no impropriety in her behaviour; they were promised to each other by Claudius himself ('l'Empereur son père').

561 *Vos désirs sont toujours si conformes aux siens* . . . A piece of monumental naïveté.

562 *Ma mère a ses desseins, Madame, et j'ai les miens.* Sharp interruption—end of the *précieux* arabesques.

567-8 . . . *toute autre alliance* | *Fera honte aux Césars* . . . Not of course Junie's real motive, but the first one she can think of to gain time: her rank does not allow her to marry below herself.

573-4 . . . *un autre nom,* | *Si j'en savais quelque autre au-dessus de Néron.* Néron's declaration, and an impassioned attempt at convincing Junie; but his plea is framed in a way that is, to us, peculiar. Junie's extraordinary beauty as well as her high birth make it a duty for her to marry not a fallen Prince without hopes or expectations, but the greatest person in the Empire, the Emperor. The argument was familiar in literature, as well as in a society based on birth and privilege, in which marriages were arranged by parents according to rank and family interests. The girl's 'duty' was to conform:

'De quelque amant pour moi que mon père eût fait choix . . .
J'en aurais soupiré, mais j'aurais obéi.'

(Pauline, in Corneille's *Polyeucte*, II, 2.)

What was striking at the time was not that such a plea should be made, but that it should be rejected.

590-1 Insinuating subtlety of the rhythm: however outmoded Néron's courting may seem to us, there is no doubt about his longing for Junie, and his genuine need of her.

603-618 *Seigneur, avec raison je demeure étonnée.* . . . Junie is still stone-walling, and her attitude shows remarkable self-mastery.

612 . . . *éteindre sa famille.* After her brother's suicide (Octavie's fiancé, cf. 64) Agrippine had had Junie's other brother poisoned, for fear he might avenge him (Tacitus, XIII, 1).

617 *clarté.* Éclat, gloire (*claritas*).

619 *Je vous ai déjà dit* . . . Change in the style: how do Néron's impatience and imperiousness express themselves?

635 . . . *laissons le mystère.* From now on the gloves are off: we are far from the compliments of the beginning.

637-58 *Il a su me toucher,* | . . . *J'aime Britannicus.* . . . Junie rises to Néron's challenge, and meets his frontal attack fearlessly: she too leaves off pretending.

639 *Cette sincérité sans doute est peu discrète.* According to *précieux* ideas it was

unbecoming to a girl to admit her love ('cet aveu qui fait tant de peine', *Préc. Ridic.*); Racine's heroines are aware of the convention, even when they do not submit to it.

645–8 ... *ces mêmes malheurs* ... / *Sont autant de liens* ... Junie loves Britannicus *because* he is fallen, deserted, humiliated. To the fierce, pitiless struggle of *Britannicus* Junie adds a touch of tenderness, and she also strikes a new chord in seventeenth-century tragedy (cf. Note 573). 'Le tendre Racine' is as real as 'le cruel Racine'.

656 ... *que moi qui s'intéresse.* One would expect: 'qui m'intéresse'. What is in Racine's mind is: 'il ne voit personne qui s'intéresse à son sort sauf moi'.

659 *Et ce sont ces plaisirs et ces pleurs que j'envie.* At the very moment when Néron is choosing the path of violence, it is something that, in the middle of his Imperial omnipotence, he realizes the priceless value of an unselfish, loving heart; but like most Racinian lovers (Pyrrhus, Roxane, Mithridate), he cannot resign himself to the loss of what he so passionately desires: what can only be given freely he will try and wrest by force.

660 *paîrait*: paierait *or* payerait.

665 *je veux prévenir le danger.* .... Politically Néron's plan is quite ingenious: it will avoid further antagonizing his rival and possibly creating trouble in Rome. Humanly its cruelty is breath-taking: it involves the maximum suffering for the two lovers.

669 *ses jours*: sa vie.

675 *prononcer un arrêt:* to pronounce judgment.

679 *Caché près de ces lieux* ... It is a measure of the silliness of some of Racine's contemporaries' criticism (among them, alas, Boileau) that they thought the hidden presence of the Emperor 'une situation de comédie'.

682 *J'entendrai des regards* ... This is an answer to 678: 'Mes yeux lui défendront de m'obéir', and is one of those striking combinations of words of which Racine is a master.

683 *sa perte.* His death.

686 *de ne le voir jamais:* 'de ne jamais le voir' is now the usual form.

SCENE VI

693 *bonheur*: chance, fortunate circumstance.

707 *Vous ne me dites rien?* So moved and agitated is Britannicus that he has only just noticed that Junie is standing rigid and unresponsive.

709 *Notre ennemi* ... With all the rashness of his fifteen years Britannicus speaks at the very doors of his 'enemy'.

713–14 *Ces murs* ... *peuvent avoir des yeux / Et jamais l'Empereur n'est absent de ces lieux.* At all costs Britannicus must be stopped: silence has become more dangerous than words. The warning Junie gives him should be clear: he understands nothing.

718 ... *envier nos amours.* Truer than Britannicus imagines.

722 *La mère de Néron se déclare pour nous.* These are life-and-death secrets which Britannicus eagerly blurts out. Again Junie tries desperately to shut him up and save him from himself.

729–35 *Ce discours me suprend*, . . . Britannicus hardly succeeds in containing his irritation: why must she spoil everything?

735 *en un jour:* since yesterday.

737–41 *Vous craignez de rencontrer mes yeux?* The thoughtless youngster who had been deaf and blind to every warning suddenly awakes to that small, momentous fact: Junie's eyes will not meet his own. In a few seconds he passes from sulking and complacency to uneasiness, suspicion, alarm, then to a desperate appeal for reassurance. His final prayer is none the less moving for its humble understatement. 'Don't you remember me any more?'

738 *Néron vous plairait-il?* Is it possible that . . . Could you possibly be attracted by . . .

742 *Retirez-vous, Seigneur, l'Empereur va venir.* Hardly a better example could be found of those bare Racinian lines, which the context and situation make heavy with tragedy.

743 *A qui dois-je m'attendre?* 'S'attendre à', in Racine's time, often meant: 'se confier à', and the meaning is probably: 'whom shall I ever be able to trust?' But 's'attendre' also had the modern meaning of: to expect, and 'qui' in several cases meant: what. 'What but the worst shall I expect now?'

SCENE VII

744 *Non, Seigneur,* . . . After the extreme tension of the previous scene Junie's nerve suddenly snaps: she bursts into tears, and rushes out.

SCENE VIII

747–9 Néron has nothing to be triumphant about: to him too the scene has been cruel, in a different way. Hence the outburst of violence that follows.

751 *Je me fais de sa peine une image charmante.* His jealousy of Britannicus has awakened Néron's latent cruelty. If he cannot have Junie's love, he will at least enjoy Britannicus' grief (see Introduction, p. 34).

757 *La fortune t'appelle une seconde fois* . . . Racine assumes that Narcisse, after wielding, and losing, great power under Claudius—which was true— is now attempting a come-back: this 'second life' of Narcisse is of course entirely fictitious; Narcisse died (thanks to Agrippine) at the very beginning of Nero's reign (see Racine's Prefaces, and Tacitus, XIII, 1).

ACT III

Louis Racine, Racine's son, tells us that this Act began with a long scene between Burrhus and Narcisse (see *Variants*, p. 142), which Boileau had persuaded Racine to cancel. Louis Racine's information is often suspect, and according to some critics the variant took its place *between* Scene 1 and Scene 2. Either hypothesis implies several other changes, and a fair amount of re-writing. But whatever the truth, the play has gained by the suppression, which illustrates Racine's willingness to sacrifice details for the benefit of the whole.

BRITANNICUS

SCENE I

766 *S'arrêter.* To go no further than.

767 *Dessein.* Plan, plot.

770 *Germanicus.* Cf. Note 164. One of Agrippine's main sources of power is briefly recalled: her prestige with the army—main prop of the Imperial *régime*—which saw in her the daughter of its beloved, and still lamented general.

774 *vous lui donnez des armes* ... Burrhus looks at the situation from a political point of view; what he means will become clear in Scene 5.

776 *le mal est sans remède.* Love as a disease, or a source of suffering (cf. 380).

777 *mon cœur s'en est plus dit* ... Cf. 407, 459, 461.

778 *Il faut que j'aime* ... See Introduction, p. 33.
     enfin. When all is said.

786 ... *vainqueur de vos mépris.* Octavie's love has survived Néron's indifference.

790 *On n'aime point* ... *si l'on ne veut aimer.* 'Et sur mes passions ma raison souveraine ...' Corneille, *Polyeucte*, II, 2. 'Je suis maître de moi comme de l'univers', Auguste, in *Cinna*, V, 3, etc.

791 ... *les alarmes.* In its original, etymological meaning: dangers on the battle-field. (Italian: *all'arme!* To arms!)

SCENE II

800 ... *Néron découvre son génie.* Given the circumstances (Néron had been married against his will) and the frequency of divorces in Rome, Burrhus' forebodings appear at first sight excessive. What rightly frightens him, however, is that Néron is prepared to satisfy his passion whatever the consequences to his throne and to Rome. Again, the political aspect of the situation is what worries him, not the moral one, and we shall see him a little later spring to the defence of Néron (822): 'L'Empereur n'a rien fait qu'on ne puisse excuser.'

806 *Occupé loin de Rome* ... Racine's invention: one 'gouverneur' was enough.

807 *Si d'Agrippine excitant la tendresse* ... This shows Burrhus' political sense of responsibility and moral selflessness: it cannot be easy for him to make advances to Agrippine after her insults in Act I.

808 *mon bonheur me l'adresse.* Racine usually manages his characters' entrances with more subtlety.
     bonheur. Cf. 693

SCENE III

This is a new, and at first sight puzzling, Agrippine: her fury at Pallas' dismissal was to be expected, but not that it would blind her to everything else.

810 ... *d'illustres leçons.* A cutting allusion to Burrhus' functions as a tutor. A fine tutor indeed!

813 *Jamais sans ses avis* ... Cf. 1146, and Tacitus, XII, 25.

162

817 *Digne emploi d'un ministre* . . . A fine tutor *and* a fine minister! It now appears that the 'on' of 815 and 816 meant 'vous'. Burrhus is made responsible for everything: a first, but ominous, sign that Agrippine is losing her lucidity and her grip.

824 *Son orgueil* . . . According to Tacitus (XIII, 23), although Pallas had been cleared of a charge of conspiracy, 'there was resentment at his arrogance rather than relief at his innocence; for his accusers having named some of his freedmen as his accomplices, he replied that in his house he never communicated with them except by a gesture or a nod, and if he had more to convey to them, he did it in writing, not wishing to have any verbal exchange with them'.

827–8 . . . *un malheur qui n'est point sans ressource.* / . . . The gist of what Burrhus has to say to Agrippine, and a discreet but plain offer of alliance.

832 *l'on* . . . Again: 'vous'.

832 . . . *de me fermer la bouche.* Agrippine not only misinterprets Burrhus' advice: she disregards his proposal that they might work together. Extraordinary as it may seem, she has not heard it. She is too upset to understand or to hear anything.

834 . . . *l'ouvrage de mes mains.* Néron's power.

841 . . . *leur erreur.* In choosing Néron instead of Britannicus.

842–54 When Agrippine had Néron proclaimed Emperor she prepared everything in secret, and then presented Rome with a *fait accompli*. Now she gives due warning to the Emperor's minister that she will have the Emperor replaced by another, which can only mean death to Néron: there cannot be two masters of Rome, and Caesars do not go into peaceful retirement. Has Agrippine gone out of her mind?

845 *le fils d'Enobarbus.* In so far as it is in her power, Agrippine annuls the adoption and denies Néron's right to be on the throne.

848 *Partagent* . . . Have a share in.

852–4 *rumeurs* . . . Cf. IV, 2.

863–4 *Rome l'a pu choisir.* . . . / *Elle choisit Tibère* . . . Rome had very little to say in the choice of Néron (cf. Tacitus, XII, 69), or of Tiberius.

865 *Agrippa.* Agrippa Postumus, Augustus' own grandson. He was considered unfit to rule; Augustus sent him into exile, and under pressure from Livia gave precedence to her son, Tiberius. The moment he was on the throne Tiberius had him executed. He possessed a Herculean strength, and the Roman centurion who attacked him, unarmed and unsuspecting, had a hard task overcoming him (Tacitus, I, 6).

SCENE IV

A scene of capital importance for our understanding of Agrippine.

873 *L'Empereur puisse-t-il l'ignorer.* Albine is terrified by the risks Agrippine is taking.

876 . . . *les intérêts de la sœur ou du frère.* Octavie and Britannicus do not seem to be worth a fight to the death with the Emperor.

878 . . . *jusque dans ses amours.* The idea that the ruler's 'amours' should not be interfered with could not be missed as a passing reference to the private life of the very amorous Louis XIV.

880 *C'est à moi qu'on donne une rivale.* An entirely new angle on the situation, and on the face of it an extraordinary statement.

882 *Ma place est occupée, et je ne suis plus rien.* Agrippine then fears for her power: Néron no doubt will listen more to a wife he loves than to the 'triste Octavie'. But Junie is a very young, totally inexperienced girl: she hardly seems to present such a threat to the Empress Mother. And we discover that Agrippine wanted her son to have a wife he did *not* love.

886 . . . *des mortels.* Agrippine speaks like a goddess.

887 *Une autre de César a surpris la tendresse.* Agrippine gives herself away: no doubt she wants power over Rome and the Empire; but she also wants power over Néron and Néron's heart. She will not share her power, and she will not share Néron. The two feelings are so entwined together that the ambitious, domineering Empress can hardly be separated from the jealous, possessive mother, who hates, before she has even set eyes upon her, the daughter-in-law who will take her son away from her.

891–4 . . . *L'on m'évite, et déjà délaissée . . . | Ah! je ne puis . . . en souffrir la pensée . . . | Néron, l'ingrat Néron . . .* The powerful mind of the Agrippine we saw in Act I is overcome by her passions: she is hardly able to speak, even less to reason. Now we understand the blindness and rage of the previous scene.

893 . . . *l'arrêt fatal.* Fixed by Destiny: astrologers had predicted to Agrippine that her son would become Emperor, but that he would kill his mother. 'Let him kill me, provided he becomes Emperor', she answered (Tacitus, xiv, 9).

SCENE V

However aggrieved he feels about Junie's apparent desertion, Britannicus knows that the quarrel between Agrippine and Néron is his great opportunity and he has been quick to exploit it, and to devise his tactics accordingly (cf. 357: 'Je vais la voir, l'aigrir, la suivre, et s'il se peut, | M'engager sous son nom plus loin qu'elle ne veut'). The following scene shows how successful he has been, and Agrippine's reaction should be watched carefully.

895–6 *Nos ennemis communs . . . Nos malheurs . . . Vos amis et les miens . . .* Britannicus intentionally emphasizes their common interest.

903 . . . *son injure.* The wrong she (Octavie) has suffered.

906 *Sylla, Pison, Plautus . . .* Sylla, of the same family as the dictator, was a member of the *Cornelii*, one of the greatest names in Rome. C. Piso, of the illustrious *gens Calpurnia*, was later to lead against Nero the great conspiracy in which the most famous writers of the time, Seneca and Lucan, were implicated. Plautus was a great-grandson of Tiberius; Agrippine was later to try to use him against Nero as she had tried to use Britannicus. All three were to die by Nero's order.

Prince, que dites-vous? This is a turning point in the drama. Agrippine is obviously taken by surprise, and in no mood of elation. Why? Is this not what she wanted? What goes on in her mind will be made clearer in IV, 2.

907 *la noblesse.* The senatorial order.

908 *je vois bien que ce discours vous blesse.* Britannicus has sensed at once Agrippine's new mood, and he tries to reassure her. How? Why?

924 *Et ranger tous les cœurs du parti de ses larmes.* But this is not at all what the angry Agrippine was telling Burrhus and Albine in the two previous scenes! She was not thinking much of Octavie: she was threatening to have Britannicus proclaimed by the soldiers. . . .

926 *évitez ses regards.* Every moment Britannicus spends in his enemy's palace is fraught with dangers. Agrippine has already warned him (287); Junie will do the same again (1017). Thus does Racine prepare the momentous meeting of the two rivals in III, 8.

927 *. . .flatté d'une fausse espérance.* The crestfallen Britannicus realizes that Agrippine is backing out. Her *volte-face* will have tremendous consequences; for herself: it is dangerous to utter such threats and then do nothing (cf. 1320–1); for Britannicus: without her his great political ambitions will never be achieved. From a dramatic point of view, with Néron secure on his throne and Britannicus powerless, the action of the play comes to a standstill.

932–3 and 938 *Si par ton artifice | Je pouvais revoir . . . J'en rougis . . . je ne le crois pas autant que je le doi.* After his very creditable performance with Agrippine this is a rather bashful, very naïve, and pathetically trusting, Britannicus. Racine's characters often try, unsuccessfully, to feel the way they know they ought to feel.

942 *Je la voudrais haïr avec tranquillité.* A chilling notion, alien from the Britannicus we know.

948 *. . . la défaite.* In the conventional language of *galanterie* a man who falls in love with a woman has been 'vanquished' by her. Cf. Junie's 'victoire' (456).

954 *Elle reçoit les vœux de son nouvel amant.* Cf. Néron's order to Narcisse: 'Fais-lui payer bien cher un bonheur qu'il ignore' (756).

955 *Mais que vois-je? . . . Coup de théâtre.*

956 *Ah, Dieux! . . .* For once Fate seems to be kind to the lovers, and Néron's plans have gone wrong.

In spite of Narcisse hurrying to warn the Emperor, the menace of tragedy recedes in this scene, just as the dramatic tension has relaxed in the previous one. It is one of the 'régions ensoleillées' (Vinaver) in *Britannicus.*

958 *. . . ma persévérance.* Junie still refuses to give up Britannicus, and since Act II the Emperor's attitude has stiffened into anger.

960 *arrêter*. To delay, to detain. Cf. 1086–9.

961 *Adieu* . . . Almost Junie's first word; she knows the risk she is taking: in her mind the interview should last only a few seconds.
blesser. To wrong, to offend (by your distrust).

964 *Je vous entends,* . . . Britannicus, who a moment ago longed to see Junie, now chooses to stand on his dignity. He must speak out all the grievances he has been nursing against Junie; a 'querelle d'amoureux'.

966 *vos nouveaux soupirs*. Your love for Néron.

967 *en me voyant*. Free construction: 'lorsque vous me voyez.'
Pudeur: 'honte'.

969 *il faut partir*. He does not leave, of course, and goes on accusing Junie before she has had time to say a word in her defence, or even to beg him to stay.

970 *Ah! vous deviez du moins* . . . What Junie has said should have been enough to dispel Britannicus' doubts. But his highly emotional state carries its own impetus, and has little to do with reason and logic: he is not far from tears.

971 *une amitié commune*. Ordinary, vulgar, lacking in passion and generosity. Every word that follows is meant to hurt.

976 *détrompée*. Not: realizing one's mistake, but: immune from such illusions.

980 *De mes persécuteurs j'ai vu le Ciel complice*. The absence of a providential design is often more explicit in Racine's theatre: the gods do not care about justice or injustice, the order of the world shows no moral purpose.

982 *Il me restait d'être oublié de vous*. There is eloquence in the previous lines, and a firm sustained rhythm, which suddenly breaks down, and ends in a sentence as brief as a sob.

983 . . . *ma juste impatience*. Only a flicker of resentment: Junie understands and forgives; she will not indulge in counter-recriminations.

985–8 *Mais Néron vous menace* . . . / *Néron nous écoutait* . . . Short, urgent sentences: time is short.

987 *Allez, rassurez-vous* . . . Not for the first or the last time Junie appears more mature than the boy she is trying to soothe and quieten.

989 *Quoi! le cruel* . . . Realization at last dawns upon Britannicus.

994 *Vos yeux auraient pu feindre* . . . There is something almost obsessive about the eyes in *Britannicus*.

998–1019 *Il fallait me taire et vous sauver*. Junie has no more to say: she must go now. But she cannot resist the temptation of sharing with Britannicus the cruel experience she has suffered. The brief message she has come to deliver gradually turns into a lyrical monologue: time stands still. But not for Narcisse and Néron.

1003 . . . *ce qu'on aime*. 'Celui, ou celle qu'on aime.' The neutral pronoun is sometimes used in this way in the seventeenth century ('L'on veut faire tout le bonheur, ou si cela ne se peut ainsi, tout le malheur de ce qu'on aime', La Bruyère).

1003–5 *Quel tourment de se taire* . . . / *Lorsque par un regard on peut le consoler*. We are very far from Néron here: there is much more variety among Racine's lovers than was once believed.

1007 ... *dans ce souvenir.* A very elliptical phrase: every time I remembered (Néron's stratagem).

1008-14 *Je ne me sentais pas assez dissimulée.* | ... *Je trouvais mes regards trop pleins de ma douleur.* | ... *Je craignais mon amour.* In the violently distorted world of *Britannicus* lying becomes a duty and a virtue, compassion a crime, love an object of fear.

1015-6 ... *pour son bonheur et pour le nôtre* | *Il n'est que trop instruit* ... Néron knows too much of their love for him, or for them, to feel happy.

1017 *Allez, encore un coup* ... Junie first regains a notion of the passage of time.

1020 *Ah! n'en voilà que trop.* At last Britannicus' mood has been reversed: he is now ready for a long lyrical monologue of his own. He will not be given time.

1021 ... *mon bonheur.* A precarious, Racinian 'bonheur'! But for one instant, after their long, painful misunderstanding, nothing stands between them, and they are one in blissful happiness.

1024 *Que faites-vous?* Cf. 1027.

SCENE VIII

Again a striking change in rhythm and tone—first in the grating irony of the first six lines, above all in the long-expected confrontation of the two Emperors, or so each one considers himself. This is the only scene in which we see them together, and there could be only one, for when it has begun its climax cannot be long delayed. Neither of the two rivals can afford to acknowledge for one moment the other's precedence: youthful pride forbids it—the girl they both love is watching—but it is as if the whole Empire was watching this trial of strength. (Cf. Introduction, p. 55.)

1031 *Je puis mettre* ... Britannicus at once makes it clear he takes no order from the usurper.

1033-4 *L'aspect de ces lieux* ... | *N'a rien dont mes regards doivent être étonnés.* Britannicus is at home, in the palace where he was born and brought up, where his father lived and reigned.

... *où vous la retenez,* ... Sharp thrust at Néron's abuse of his power.

1035 Néron loses no time in asserting his authority—in two heavy lines, made up of four groups of six syllables, full of harsh explosives and r's. The heavy regularity of the rhythm and caesurae in the whole passage emphasizes the gravity of the moment.

1038 *Moi* ... *vous* ... *obéir* ... *braver* ... The constant play of antitheses is as significant here as in the first scene of the play.

... *vous pour me braver.* 'Braver' means: to dare a stronger opponent, or a superior authority. The challenge is none the less effective for being dropped almost unconcernedly: *Néron* is defying the Imperial authority.

1040 *Domitius.* A deadly insult, again delivered *en passant* and with icy contempt. As before in Agrippine's threats ('le fils d'Enobarbus'), it implicitly denies the validity of the adoption, and Néron's right to the throne. It seems foolish to say, as some critics said, even perhaps Boileau, that Racine has made Britannicus 'too small' in the presence of Néron.

1041–4 Néron's re-assertion of supremacy is coupled with derisive allusions to Britannicus' junior status: he is a mere child, a schoolboy.

1046 *Rome met-elle au nombre de vos droits* | ... Néron not only usurps his authority, he abuses it. The attack is switched from the dynastic to the political plane.

1047 ... *ce qu'a de cruel.* Agreement with *l'injustice et la force* considered as one.

1048 *Rome.* For the third time repeated in four lines. Rome is the ideal spectator, and the main stake in the battle.

1053 *Ainsi Néron* ... The attack now becomes personal. And Britannicus is the one who uses irony: Néron is losing ground.

1056 *Heureux ou malheureux* ... Violently elliptical construction (cf. 12).

1056–60 ... *il suffit qu'on me craigne* | ... *si je ne sais le secret de lui plaire.* As a ruler and as a lover Néron has been forced by Britannicus into a naked assertion of brute force: fear and punishment are all he can dispose of; right and love are not for him.

1062 *Sa seule inimitié peut me faire trembler.* Britannicus in one sentence expresses his love and his respect for Junie, as well as his indifference to Néron's threats.

1065 ... *vous lui plairez toujours.* This is meant to be derisive, and is in fact an admission of defeat.

1066–8 *Je ne sais pas du moins* ... The final, crushing blow to Néron's pride and to his love: the mighty Emperor 'se cache'; the lover knows so well Junie feels nothing for him that he must 'lui fermer la bouche'. Néron is reeling back; but Britannicus' victory is a Pyrrhic one. Every success of his brings nearer the moment when Néron will use the one weapon Britannicus cannot counter, force.

1069 *Je vous entends. Hé bien,* ... The rhythm disintegrates at the same time as Néron's defences.

... *gardes!* The stage fills with praetorians.

1069–73. *Que faites vous?* | *C'est votre frère. Hélas!* ... Junie's terror and despair are expressed in the short, halting sentences, and the broken rhythm.

1070–1 *C'est un amant jaloux,* | *Seigneur,* ... Junie tries to excuse what must seem to Néron unbearable provocation: Britannicus' jealousy, and the bitterness of his fall deserve indulgence.

1072 ... *son bonheur.* Cf. 649–58.

1073–8 These lines prepare the *dénouement.*

1074 *Je me cache à vos yeux, et me dérobe aux siens.* Like Bérénice, unlike Hermione or Roxane, Junie, to save her lover, is prepared for total sacrifice.

1076 *Vestales.* The priestesses of Vesta had as their main task to keep burning a flame which must never go out. They were not allowed to marry. Part of the anachronism has already been mentioned by Racine himself in his

Prefaces: a convent was, in the seventeenth century, the only place where a girl could escape her father's absolute authority. It was used too as a means of enforcing obedience upon a recalcitrant daughter.

SCENE IX

1086–9 *Je reconnais la main qui les a rassemblés.* 960 gives some substance to the accusation.

1092 . . . *au lieu de sa garde on lui donne la mienne.* Agrippine's escort will take their orders from Néron, not from her: Agrippine will be virtually under arrest.

1097–8 *Répondez-m'en, vous dis-je,* . . . After Britannicus, Junie, and Agrippine, Burrhus himself is now threatened. No longer does Néron carry out Agrippine's commands, or take Burrhus' and Seneca's advice, or even listen to Narcisse's suggestions. At the end of the Act his thundering voice exacts obedience from all: he is the master.

ACTE IV

The drama in this act becomes more intense, and at the same time more interior: the field of the battle is almost entirely Néron's mind.

SCENE I

Brief introductory scene to the great debate of Scene 2: Burrhus attempts once more to make reason prevail, to avoid a clash which will make the situation worse, and to consolidate his master's position, and his own.

1100 *César . . . consent de vous entendre.* This is the interview which Agrippine has sought from the very first scene. The word 'consent' is not used at random by Burrhus.

1101–2 Attempt at soothing Agrippine (cf. 1091–3 and 1219).

1103–6 Sensible advice (Burrhus knows Néron's exasperation), which also fits in with Burrhus' policy.

1104 . . . *qu'il vous ait offensée.* The subjunctive suggests this is Agrippine's subjective impression, not an objective fact.

1110 *Sujette à.* Soumise à.

1114 *Qu'on me laisse avec lui.* Agrippine dismisses Burrhus curtly, not troubling to answer him directly.

SCENE II

The scene begins with two carefully prepared speeches, in which the two opponents state their case. Agrippine's defence and accusation (1115–222), to which Néron listens in complete silence, is followed by Néron's briefer, but strongly argued, reply (1223–57). After this, passion takes over, and the issue of the discussion will, for a while, be in doubt, but Agrippine will

169

finally lose the battle she was so keen to fight, and had nearly won. The scene is packed with allusions to Tacitus, as a careful study of Appendix I will show, and they are not listed here.

AGRIPPINE, *s'asseyant*. One of Racine's rare stage indications, and an important one: Agrippine sits down first, then graciously gives the Emperor permission to be seated. . . . She has not even listened to Burrhus. At the Court of the Sun-King such questions of etiquette were the subject of keenly fought battles, in which the honour of the opponents was engaged.

1118 *De tous ceux que j'ai faits* . . . Agrippine's line of defence: her crimes, which she does not deny, have been committed for Néron's sake.

1119 *Vous régnez.* Racine derives peculiar effects from such bare statements, or understatements; this one summarizes all Agrippine's crimes, and the whole of Agrippine's defence. Cf. 1183: 'Il mourut', with all its sinister implications.

votre naissance . . . Some anachronism; but see Note 239.

1123 *la mère condamnée.* Latinism: 'la condamnation de sa mère' (Messaline).

1126 *ses affranchis.* Cf. Note 200.

1137, 1144 *Claude.* Nowadays the usual form in French for Claudius.

1139 . . . *entrer dans sa famille.* Explained in following line: Néron married Octavie, and became Claudius' son-in-law.

1141 *Silanus.* Cf. Note 65.

1147 . . . *vous appela Néron.* Cf. Note 18.

1147-9 . . . *pouvoir suprême* . . . *avant le temps.* Néron received the consulship before he had reached the legal age (Tacitus, XII, 41).

1159 . . . *dans ma suite.* Therefore devoted to *me*.

1163 . . . *brigue* . . . *renommée* . . . Opposes those who relied on influence and intrigue to obtain the position to those who were considered worthy of it by universal consent.

1164 *J'appelai de l'exil, je tirai de l'armée.* The first verb refers to Seneca, the second to Burrhus. Construction more frequent in Latin than in French.

1166 *Qui depuis* . . . Sarcastic innuendo (cf. 809-20).

. . . *alors.* The sarcastic intention emphasized by the caesura.

1171-2 . . . *leur tendresse* . . . *Germanicus* . . . Cf. Notes 164, 770.

1179 . . . *sans fruit.* Uselessly: Claudius' love for his son could no longer be translated into acts.

1180 . . . *je me rendis maîtresse.* This ambiguous line is made clear by 309-10.

1182 . . . *en mourant* . . . 'Quand il mourut'. Construction no longer possible nowadays.

1183 *Il mourut.* Cf. 1119. It was never doubted that Agrippine had poisoned her husband. The two short sentences, each one followed by a long pause, suddenly slows down the rapid course of the narration.

1185 *Burrhus* . . . Cf. 857.

1187 . . . *au camp.* The praetorians' camp, at the gates of Rome.

1191 . . . *légions* . . . Again the praetorians.

1193 *On vit Claude.* People were allowed to see the corpse which had been hidden from them.

1196 *Voilà ... voici ...* Strongly marks the division between the two parts of Agrippine's speech.

1197–1200 *... à peine jouissant ... Que ...* Less than six months after being put in possession of the throne I had won for you ... (you pretended ...).

1205 *Othon.* Emperor in A.D. 69. The title character in Corneille's play (cf. Introduction, '*Britannicus* and its Sources').
Sénécion. Cf. Tacitus, XIII, 12 (Appendix I). Senecio will also become involved in Piso's great conspiracy.

1209 *Seul recours ...* Refers to the following line.

1214 *... en une nuit ...* Contemptuous: infatuation, not love.

1219 *Burrhus ... ses mains hardies.* Cf. 1091.

1220 *convaincu.* Convicted.

1223–57 Néron's answer: he justifies himself, and accuses Agrippine. He stands his ground as he has never done before.

1224–5 *... vous fatiguer ... | Votre bonté ...* Derisive.

1234 *pour obéir.* 'Pour qu'il obéisse'.

1236–7 *... si ... j'avais pu vous complaire, | Je n'eusse pris plaisir ...* The formal politeness, while emphasizing Néron's coldness, is touched with sarcasm.

1237–8 *... à vous céder | Ce pouvoir ...* The *enjambement* throws emphasis upon this *pouvoir*, which seems to be Agrippine's only preoccupation.

1239 *... un maître ... une maîtresse ...* Tacitus often underlines the amazement felt at the power wielded by a woman in Rome, used to being led by men.

1243 *publiaient.* Openly, loudly stated.

1250 *Mais si vous ne régnez ...* The whole first scene in the play substantiates the accusation.

1251–6 A fair summary of Agrippine's activities.

1258 From now on the scene takes a livelier and more personal character.
Moi ...? Indignant protest ... Did Agrippine think of making Britannicus Emperor or not?

1259–68 All very good reasons why she could not possibly think of such a thing ... What should we believe?

1266 *Des desseins étouffés aussitôt que naissants ...* Some truth here: Agrippine did back out of the plot, but was it only a passing thought?

1268 *convaincue.* As in 1220.

1269–85 This is no longer reasoning and rationalizing, but a cry of anguish, the sudden explosion of a long frustrated love, even though Agrippine may be deceiving herself on her own disinterestedness (cf. I, 1).

1282 Cf. Note 893.

1284 *... prenez encor ma vie ...* Agrippine's despair and death-wish are unexpected and disconcerting, but utterly sincere: the character and the play become unintelligible if we think she is play-acting in cold blood.

1287 A dramatic moment in the scene: Néron is shaken by his mother's grief; he is ready to yield. Hypocrisy? But why should he pretend now, when a moment ago he was defying and accusing Agrippine to her face?

If he had wished to deceive her he would have pretended all the time.

1288–94 Agrippine's terms: unconditional surrender.

1295–1304 *Now* Néron is lying: it is for the actor to make us sense his sudden reversal; in dictating her terms, Agrippine has overreached herself.

SCENE III

Scenes 3 and 4 are, with the clash of Burrhus' and Narcisse's policies, the culminating scenes in the political drama. But Néron, not Burrhus or Narcisse, is at the centre of the stage.

1305 *ces embrassements.* Stage direction, found, as often in Racine, in the text: there is a long emotional pause at the end of Scene 2.

1307 *Vous savez si . . .* 'Vous savez que je n'ai pas (mérité)'.
ma voix. My opinion, my advice.

1312 *Mais son inimitié vous rend ma confiance.* Néron's disposition towards Burrhus at the end of Act III was far from trusting. Agrippine's hostility explains why Néron will now reveal his secret to Burrhus.

1315–6 *. . . sa ruine | Me délivre . . . des fureurs d'Agrippine.* What is at the moment uppermost in Néron's mind is revolt against Agrippine's arrogance. The death of Britannicus is first of all a way of depriving her of her weapon and breaking her power.

1320 *. . . lui promette ma place.* It must not be forgotten that Agrippine has threatened to do just that.

1322 *. . . je ne le craindrai plus.* Néron had then, before the interview, given the order for the murder.

1323 *Qui. . .?* Néron's answer shows that here the word means: 'Qu'est-ce qui . . .?'

1324 *Ma gloire . . .* The threats to Néron's prestige and to his life are real enough, whatever may be thought of Néron's way of defending himself.

1325 *Non!* Sudden, dramatic turn in the scene: Burrhus openly challenges the authority of the Emperor.

1329–31 Summarizes Burrhus' arguments: the moral one (murder of a brother), the political one (the just ruler versus the despot), the personal one (the honour of the Emperor).

1332 *. . . enchaîné de ma gloire passée.* Néron refuses to be tied to his past, or to the self others have built and shaped for him.

1333 *je ne sais quel amour.* A fickle, too often groundless, popularity.

1335 *leurs vœux.* The wishes of the Romans. As often in Racine, the construction becomes more elliptical when passion takes control. Cf. 1362, 1369.

1337–72 Burrhus' arguments, and the opposition between the tyrant and the good ruler are drawn from Seneca, and have been analysed in the chapter on '*Britannicus* and its Sources'. A good example of Racine's eloquence, using all devices of rhetoric, parallels, antitheses, and repetitions, rhetorical questions, metaphors, etc.

1347 *Britannicus mourant.* 'La mort de Britannicus'.

1377 *Il se jette à genoux.* The gesture may appear exaggerated, it is justified not only by Burrhus' emotion, but by the daring, almost unimaginable in an absolute monarchy, of a subject trying to dictate to the monarch.

1381 *mes pleurs* . . . New dramatic turn in the action, by now an entirely psychological action. Against all expectations Néron is moved.

1386 *Ah! que demandez-vous?* Néron's resistance here is an indication of his sincerity.

. . . *il ne vous hait pas.* Burrhus' intentions are admirable, but his case weakens when he comes to the specific instance of the two rivals: is it true that Britannicus does not hate Néron? and is he not conspiring against him?

SCENE IV

The elaborate character of the opposition between the two scenes is obvious, but the differences in composition and tone, the *volte-face* of Néron, who is now using Burrhus' arguments against Narcisse, prevent the opposition from appearing artificial and contrived.

1391 *j'ai tout prévu.* I have made all arrangements.

1392 *Locuste.* The quasi-official poisoner for the Imperial Court.

1394 *Elle a fait expirer un esclave.* This trait of particular ferocity is not in Tacitus; it is of Racine's invention.

1398 . . . *ne souhaite pas que vous alliez plus loin.* Néron is now alone with Narcisse, and has no reason to pretend when he cancels the order of execution.

1399 *votre haine affaiblie.* Cf. 1347, *Britannicus mourant.*

1400 . . . *on nous réconcilie.* Some embarrassment perhaps in this 'on'.

1401 *Je me garderai bien* . . . Narcisse now starts to work on Néron, but with great caution. He begins by stepping back: he too is all for peace and reconciliation. But . . .

1403–8 Narcisse's first offensive: the risk Britannicus has run may make him dangerous.

1409 . . . *je vaincrai le mien.* Néron will master the resentment in his heart: Burrhus *has* made a deep impression upon him.

1410–1 *Junie* . . . Narcisse's second line of attack.

. . . *en est-il le lien?* 'en', i.e. 'de vos deux cœurs'.

. . . *encor.* In addition.

1412 . . . *trop de soin.* Sharp rebuff.

1413 Néron's resolve is getting firmer and more positive.

1414 *Agrippine* . . . Third line of attack, directed at Néron's pride and impatience of his mother's interference.

1416 *Quoi donc?* . . . Touché! Néron is startled.

1418–22 Narcisse now turns the knife: every word hurts a sensitive nerve: *un moment, grand éclat,* ironical rhymes of *courroux funeste* and *silence modeste,* etc.

1423 . . . *que veux-tu que je fasse?* The 'tu' shows that Narcisse has reassumed his place as a familiar adviser, and Néron is now on the defensive.

1427–31 Néron speaks with the voice of Burrhus: 'Mais de tout l'univers quel sera le language?' Cf. 1331: 'Que dira-t-on de vous?' 'Sur le pas des tyrans . . .', the gist of Burrhus' argument; '. . . au rang des parricides', and Burrhus (1384): ' . . . ces conseils parricides'.

1431 *Ils*... Cf. 1362, etc.

1432–54 Narcisse's explicit statement of Machiavellism, and the counter-blast to Burrhus' political theory (cf. 'The political drama in *Britannicus*').

1434 *Est-ce à vous* . . . The ruler must not consult his subjects: it is his privilege to make decisions and carry them out.

1440 *Ils croiront* . . . *mériter qu'on les craigne.* Subjects must not be encouraged to believe that their opinions matter, for fear that they become fractious.

1442 *Ils adorent* . . . The servile mob respects only force, and enjoys being dominated by a strong master.

1452 *fussent-ils innocents.* . . . The mob dislikes being on the side of a loser: he must therefore be the guilty one.

1453 . . . *jours infortunés.* 'Dies nefasti', anniversaries of unfavourable events, on which it was unlucky to start anything.

1455–60 Néron's resistance is still unimpaired.

1456 *J'ai promis* . . . Néron still finds it unthinkable he might break his word.

1459–60 *J'oppose à ses raisons* . . . Burrhus' arguments are reasonable ones: Néron still feels he cannot disregard reason.

1461 *Burrhus ne pense pas* . . . Direct thrust at Burrhus himself, who seems to embody what holds Néron back, and at his sincerity: Burrhus' self-identification with 'virtue' brings him respect, influence, power; he has everything to gain by it. But Narcisse briefly dismisses Burrhus.

1463–79 The final assault; Narcisse tries to exasperate first Néron's pride, then his vanity.

1465 *Vous seriez libre* . . . With uncanny shrewdness Narcisse appeals to Néron's deepest yearning, the wish to be free; free from a moralizing Burrhus and a domineering Agrippine, free from the threat of Britannicus, free from a wife he has never loved, free to marry the girl he has chosen, free to be himself. No word could be better chosen to rally all his energies.

1471–78 . . . *conduire un char* | . . . *prodiguer sa voix* . . . The young Emperor's sportive performances were not in themselves scandalous, and Seneca, who had taught him, praised his literary and musical talents (see '*Britannicus* and its Sources'). But Néron was to become inordinately vain of such accomplishments, and Racine supposes he already was. The argument is irrelevant to the real debate, but is cunningly chosen to confuse and irritate Néron.

1480 *Allons voir* . . . For psychological, as well as dramatic, reasons Racine ends the act on a note of uncertainty; what is clear is that everything again is in the balance, whereas at the beginning of the scene everything seemed settled.

ACT V

The act of the *dénouement*, and how it affects every one of the characters in the play, Britannicus and Junie, Néron and Agrippine, Burrhus and Narcisse. The fateful day of the tragedy is nearing its end; night is falling (1606).

Strong, deliberate contrast between the furious debate at the end of Act
IV, and the beginning of Act V: Britannicus' happiness, and the melancholy, elegiac quality of the lovers' farewell.

1481 ... *qui l'aurait pu penser?* A kind of *coup de théâtre* which, however, leaves
us unconvinced.

1485 ... *leurs yeux.* Cf. 1335. The eyes of 'jeunes gens' implicit in 'jeunesse'.

1487 *Il éteint cet amour, source* ... Not very coherent metaphors.

1493 ... *lui pardonne en secret.* Britannicus feels his love is strong enough
to make him forget his ambition.

1501 ... *en m'écoutant.* 'Pendant que vous m'écoutez'.

1503 *Je l'ignore* ... Junie herself does not understand, and will only
gradually explain, the reasons for her deep, irrational premonition and
fear.

1504 *Vous m'aimez?* Not an expression of doubt, but of reassurance: if
she loves him as he loves her, what is there to fear?
Hélas! ... There is no doubt in Julie's mind about the answer to Britannicus' question, but love has been, and will be to her, mainly a source of
suffering.

1505–62 Little by little around the names of Néron, Narcisse, Junie's
anxiety crystallizes, and far from being soothed by Britannicus, builds up
to a climax of terror.

1508–10 *Néron* ... | *Il me fuit, il vous cherche* ... Gropingly, in an almost
instinctive way, Junie becomes aware of the reasons for her fear.

1511–18 ... *un coup d'Agrippine.* A perceptive analysis of what occurred in
Agrippine's mind (blind preconceptions, jealousy), and a fair assessment
of Burrhus' part: here again it is clear Racine does not want us to think
of Britannicus as a simpleton. Only about Néron is he hopelessly mistaken.

1519 *ne jugez pas de son cœur* ... But Junie is not: in one day she has seen
through the lies and intrigues of Néron and his Court, and cannot forget
the experience.

1520 *Sur des pas différents vous marchez* ... Along different ways (cf. 'marcher
sur les pas de quelqu'un', to follow in someone's tracks).

1522 ... *dans cette cour.* Obvious reminiscence of the intrigues at the French
Court, and perhaps of the young Racine's first reactions at the Louvre.

1530 *Soulever contre lui le Peuple* ... Even in the case of Néron, Britannicus'
attitude has some rational, if mistaken, foundation.

1534 *Mais Narcisse* ... Alone among all the characters, by a kind of divina-
tion, Junie has seen through Narcisse, who has deceived Agrippine
herself (cf. 1696).

1535 See Variants. Racine has cancelled a passage which would have made
Britannicus look too naïve.

1536–8 Irregular rhythm, mounting, obsessive value of the repeated 'je
crains'.

1538 *Je crains le malheur qui me suit.* Junie has seen two brothers die a violent
death. Like Oreste in *Andromaque*, if with much less emphasis, she feels
marked for misfortune, almost predestined.

1540 *Je vous laisse à regret éloigner de ma vue.* The clearest expression of Junie's *protective* love.

1543–6 *Si Néron . . . | Avait choisi la nuit . . . | S'il préparait ses coups . . .* Junie's premonitions here amount to hallucination. In the gathering shadows—in a modern production—Britannicus' life is almost engulfed.

1554 *Refuser un Empire et pleurer à mes yeux.* Britannicus too 'aime jusqu'à ces pleurs qu'il *fait* couler'; they are Junie's most precious gift.

1560 *Ne voir . . . que ma belle Princesse.* Naïve expression of his love, to which the circumstances give a particular pathos: Britannicus' last thought will be of Junie.

1561 *Prince . . .* Supreme appeal: Junie now *knows*.

. . . il faut partir. Britannicus' words, from the circumstances again, assume a strange gravity.

1562 *. . . attendez qu'on vous vienne avertir.* Junie clings to the last straw: she insists, even after Britannicus has made his last, formal bow.

SCENE II

To Agrippine is reserved the role of the Exterminating Angel. She has come, unwittingly, to hurry Britannicus to his death, and, unwittingly too, to consummate her own ruin.

1565 *La joie et le plaisir . . . | Attend . . .* Joie et plaisir considered a single notion.

1571 *. . . je reviens sur vos traces, | Madame, . . .* Addressed to Agrippine; he will retrace his steps along the way she has led him.

SCENE III

Agrippine at her proudest, such as we have not seen her before, in full possession of her old assurance, dominates the scene, during which Junie vainly tries to control her tears.

1576 *Doutez-vous d'une paix . . .* Junie's tears are to Agrippine almost a personal offence.

1580 *Quand même à vos bontés je craindrais quelque obstacle, | Le changement . . .* Elliptical construction: Supposing I had such fears (you should forgive them for) . . .

1583–6 *Il suffit, j'ai parlé, . . .* Agrippine's enormous pride . . . Narcisse was not exaggerating.

1585 *. . . une paix jurée entre mes mains.* 'Jurer entre les mains de': 'to sweare unto . . . ; for the old fashion was that he which tooke an oath held his hand within his that received it' (Cotgrave, 1650).

1587–1602 Agrippine's lyrical praise of her son; no doubt is possible here about her love.

1592 ... *moindres secrets.* Secrets of lesser importance, opposed to 'secrets d'où dépend le destin des humains' (1598): Agrippine at last feels she is again sharing in ruling the Empire.

1601 *altérant.* Not: altering.

1608 ... *autant heureux que je l'ai cru funeste.* The collapse will come just when Agrippine believes herself at the summit of power and happiness.

1610 *Que peut-on faire? ... sauvez Britannicus!* Agrippine is so sure of herself that she is slow to understand; Junie guesses at once.

SCENE IV

A short scene, in which the news is given rapidly by one who is in no mood to make a long narration. Tumult and disorder, in the vacillating light of torches.

1611 ... *où courez-vous?* Stage indication: Burrhus comes rushing in, beside himself with horror.

Que veut dire ... The great Agrippine, caught utterly unaware, is almost speechless in this scene and in the next one; she can only exclaim in bewilderment.

1614 *Pardonnez, Madame,* ... So strong is the hold of etiquette that, in the middle of her grief, Junie can still remember to apologize to the Empress for her hasty withdrawal.

1615 ... *ou le suivre.* We shall not see Junie again.

SCENE V

A quieter scene: Burrhus is now able to tell the full story.

1619 ... *avec plus de mystère.* Blood has not been shed.

1624 *prémices.* Here: first drops, as an offering to the gods.

1625 *Dieux* ... Sacrilege is added to murder.

1632 ... *sur son lit.* The Romans took their meals reclining on a couch.

1638 *D'aucun étonnement* ... Néron's impassiveness is what most horrifies Burrhus (Cf. 1710).

1639–40 *Ce mal* ... Britannicus had had epileptic fits.

1643 *dût l'Empereur* ... 'Même si l'Empereur devait' ...

1646 ... *si c'est moi qui l'inspire.* Agrippine, sworn enemy of Britannicus and his family, realizes she is suspect.

SCENE VI

The original Scene 6, defended in the First Preface, but later cancelled by Racine, will be found in the Variants. The reappearance of Junie could only be an anticlimax; Néron's compliments were at such a time out of tune. The present Scene 6 (originally Scene 7) is the final confrontation between Agrippine and Néron. Agrippine has lost the battle, but none of her pride, and once more she will subdue Néron into silence.

1648 *Dieux!* Néron is still afraid of his mother.

... *J'ai deux mots à vous dire.* Agrippine at once seizes the initiative.

1651–6 Néron's answer is a strange mixture of fear and aggressiveness. He does not dare to assume the responsibility for the deed, to allege, as he might, the Reason of State. But he slyly reminds Agrippine she has no right to judge him: it is not he who has killed Claudius.

1659 ... *mais qui peut vous tenir ce langage?* Perhaps a veiled threat to Burrhus.

1660–71 Narcisse intervenes to prop a vacillating Néron: lying to his mother is another way of admitting her superiority.

1661 ... *eut des desseins secrets.* True. Cf. 319, 358.

1663 ... *aspirait plus loin qu'à l'hymen de Junie.* True again.

1667 ... *malgré vous le sort vous ait servie.* Now that Agrippine is vanquished, Narcisse cunningly tries to reconcile her to the new situation, which has advantages for her too.

1672–3 *Poursuis, Néron, avec de tels ministres.* Punctuation of most seventeenth-century editions. Eighteenth- and nineteenth-century editions have: *Poursuis, Néron: avec de tels ministres, | Par des faits glorieux* etc. True to herself, Agrippine ignores Narcisse as contemptuously as she used to ignore Burrhus.

1672–94 Agrippine's curse upon her son is at the same time a kind of prophetic vision of Néron's career and end. See '*Britannicus* and its sources'. *Poursuis ... | ... glorieux ... signaler.* Sarcasm is seldom absent from Agrippine's words.

1676 ... *jusqu'à ta mère.* Agrippine foresees her own death. See Appendix I (Tacitus, XIV, 3–10).

1677 ... *tu me hais.* Néron's feelings were far more complex.

1681 *Rome, ce ciel, ce jour.* Agrippine's ghost, or presence will for ever accompany Néron.

1683 *Tes remords ...* It is difficult to forget that Agrippine has committed many more murders than Néron, and does not seem to be troubled by remorse.

furies. Ancient divinities of revenge.

1686 *D'un sang toujours nouveau....* Cf. Burrhus' warnings (1344).

1690 ... *forcé de répandre le tien.* Another accurate prediction: Néron will be compelled to commit suicide.

1694 ... *tu peux sortir.* Agrippine disdainfully dismisses the Emperor from her presence, and Néron meekly goes out. But he will no doubt remember this last insult: in his 'regards furieux' (1697), there is now hatred.

SCENE VII

The quiet of the battle-field, after the defeat. Increasing darkness.

1700 *Le coup qu'on m'a prédit ...* Cf. note 893.

1701 *Il vous accablera ...* Burrhus was also numbered, wrongly it seems, among Néron's victims.

1702 ... *j'ai vécu trop d'un jour.* 'Un jour de trop'. For the third time (cf. 1378, 1616) Burrhus expresses a wish to die (cf., too, 1713). See 'The political drama in *Britannicus*'.

1707 *Son crime seul n'est pas ce qui me désespère.* Burrhus makes a distinction between the murder, and the way in which Néron behaved, and reacted to it. See 'Néron.'

1714 *qui ne le peut souffrir.* Who cannot bear such behaviour.

1715 *Loin de vouloir.* 'Loin que je veuille'.

SCENE VIII

Only Junie's fate, it seems, is now in doubt. But we still have to learn something about Néron, as well as about Narcisse.

1718 *... sauver César.* Unexpected reversal at such a late stage in the play.

1719 *... pour jamais séparé de Junie.* Néron triumphant in the political battle, has lost his love.

1725-6 *... des chemins écartés, | Où mes yeux ont suivi ses pas ...* This is not very clear or convincing.

1731 *... par ces genoux.* The traditional gesture of supplication in the ancient world.

1732 *le reste de ta race.* Herself, the last descendant of Augustus.

1734 *le seul de tes neveux.* Britannicus was a descendant of Livia and Tiberius, and only by adoption of Augustus.

1737 *je me dévoue.* In its full religious meaning of: to consecrate oneself to a god.

1738 *... partager les autels.* Augustus, after his death, had been deified and was worshipped like the other gods.

1739 *Le peuple ...* Although never appearing on the stage, the people often plays a part in Racine's *dénouements*.

1741 *S'attendrit à ses pleurs.* The people does not behave in the brutal, heartless way described by Narcisse.

1743 *... au temple.* The Temple of the Vestals. Cf. Note 1076. Cf., too, the Prefaces.

1747 *... sans oser les distraire.* It seems unnecessary to accuse Néron of cowardice, as some do, for failing to rescue Junie or Narcisse in the confusion of sudden, violent rioting.

1751 *De mille coups mortels ...* There is poetic justice in Narcisse's death: the contemner of the people is massacred by the people. His death must also give some satisfaction to those spectators who expect the punishment of the wicked at the *dénouement*.

1752 *... rejaillit sur Junie.* A brief detail, which gives reality to the killing.

1756 *Le seul nom de Junie ...* So his love for Junie also mattered to Néron, not just the defeat of Agrippine, and the elimination of a dangerous rival. Néron was not lying when he told Junie that power was not enough (589).

1757-8 *Il marche sans dessein ... | ... regards égarés ...* Néron is on the verge of collapsing into madness.

1761 *... sans secours.* The all-powerful Caesar needs help.

1762 *... n'attente sur ses jours.* Second mention of the suicide which will end Néron's life.

1766–7 . . . *ses remords.* | . . . *suivre d'autres maximes.* There has been no mention of Néron's remorse, only of his despair at having lost Junie. Agrippine's moral reflexions give the tragedy a dignified ending, but it is difficult to see where Néron's 'maximes' differ from those of Agrippine. Such an attitude is of course quite consistent with Agrippine's character.

1768 . . . *le dernier de ses crimes.* As in Agrippine's prophecy, Racine is anxious to remind us that Britannicus' murder is only the prelude to Néron's reign. The tragedy opens out dark vistas in the future; the *dénouement* is only the end of the beginning.

GLOSSARY

of seventeenth-century words and expressions

à, 498, 566, 654, 1339: 'de'; 1187: 'vers'.

d'abord, 1728: straightway, at once.

s'accommoder à, 433: to comply with.

adresser, 808: 'amener'.

affreux, Not: hideous. 291: fearsome, terrifying. (Cf. 'les affres de la mort'.)

aigrir, to exacerbate (282, 1201, 1760), to exasperate (357).

aimable, 426: 'digne d'être aimé' (Not: 'affable').

amant, amante, 701, etc.: one whose love is returned, 'fiancé(e)'.

amour, 51: There was hesitation about the gender of this word, and from lengthy discussions among the grammarians the present rule finally emerged: that it should be masculine in the singular, and feminine in the plural. The tendency is to make it masculine in all cases.

amours, 517: love, person one loves.

amitié, 81, 971, 1298, 1308: affection, love.

amoureux, 382: one whose love has not yet been accepted or declared, not necessarily one whose love has been rejected.

appareil, 389: apparel, garb, appearance ('ensemble des signes extérieurs avec lesquels une personne se présente; tenue' Cayrou).

apparence, Epître au Duc de Chevreuse: 'vraisemblance, possibilité'. *Quelle apparence que...?* Is it likely that...?

appui, 835: power and influence ('crédit').

ardent, 1746: in its Latin, literal meaning of: burning.

artifice, 932: resourcefulness. (Also in the modern meaning of: deceit, 512.)

assidu, 1227: continuous, persistent, unceasing.

assurer, to make sure, or safe, to remove all obstacles to (965), or all fears from (374).

s'assurer sur, 221, 246: to trust in.

atteinte, 487: blow (fig.), wound.

s'attendre à, 743: to trust, to rely on. (Also: to expect. See Note.)

attenter sur, 1762: 'attenter à'.

autant, 1608: could be used before an adjective instead of: 'aussi'.

autant que... autant, Première Préface: 'autant... autant...'

avant que de+infinitive, 1377: archaic for: 'avant de'.

avouer, 598: to approve of, to make one's approval manifest ('ratifier'). (Cf. in modern French: 'sans l'aveu de'.)

bon homme, Première Préface: 'homme de bien'. Written in one or two words it did not necessarily suggest irony or condescension.

bonté, Seconde Préface: 'valeur, intérêt, agrément'.

bontés, Epître au Duc de Chevreuse, 532, 1021, 1026: marks of preference or kindness (often given by a woman to a man).

captiver, Lit.: to make a prisoner ('captif' = prisoner of war, hence in antiquity: slave). 601, 716: fig., to capture, to enslave. Nowadays: to captivate, to fascinate.

caresses, Seconde Préface, 1587: demonstrations of friendship or love.

caresser, 1111: See *caresses*.

cependant, 139, 355, 1637, 1739: meanwhile ('pendant ce temps').

chagrin (noun), 7, 459: cause of irritation, displeasure, discontent. Not: grief.

charme, 431, 544, 591, 1495: Retains more frequently its stronger meaning of magic spell ('sortilège'), but also means inexplicable charm, beauty that deeply moves.

charmant, 751: enchanting, exquisite. Also (1025, 1306): moving, touching.

charmer, 789: to cast a spell, to bewitch ('ensorceler, enchanter').

charmé, 457: spellbound.

cher, 733, 1716: more strongly emotional: precious, priceless.

cœur, Première Préface: 'courage'. (But in Racine usually with its modern meaning.)

colorer, 108: to disguise, to give a favourable appearance.

comme, 405, 1723: Sometimes used instead of 'comment'.

commettre, 582: to commit to someone's care ('confier').

composer, 1636: 'composer son visage', to compose one's countenance in order to deceive.

avoir compte à rendre, 1019: to clear up, to explain.

devoir compte, 181: 'devoir rendre compte'.

conduite, 185, 1160: action of directing, function of one who guides someone's actions. Also (23, 131, 341) in the modern sense of: behaviour.

confidence, 167, 1597: complete trust.

confident de (adj.) 992: disclosing, betraying.

confier en, 578: 'confier à' is the normal construction but the context ('mettre dans les mains de', cf. 581;) justifies 'en' ('se confier en' is in common use).

confondre, 862: Not: to confuse, but: to make equal, undistinguishable.

connaître, 1175: to realize, to become aware.

conseil, 804: firm decision. (*Quel conseil dois-je prendre?* = 'A quel parti dois-je m'arrêter?')

consentir de, 551, 1100: 'consentir à'.

consentir que, 1032: 'consentir à ce que'. (Today 'consentir que' = to grant, to concede, to admit.)

conspirer, 649: to concur, to tend.

constance, 1711: unshakable firmness of purpose (in good things or bad); here: callousness.

consulter quelque chose, 583, 783: to examine with care, to review.

content, 223, 442, 1569: satisfied, content, not asking for more; *d'un esprit content* = with a mind at rest, not: gladly.

contredire à quelqu'un, 587: 'contredire quelqu'un'.

couleurs, Seconde Préface: pretexts, specious reasons, false appearances.

coup, 256, 763, 1464, 1511, 1658: daring, unexpected act (as in: 'coup d'Etat'). Often too in the modern meaning of: blow (743).

encore un coup, 1017, 1455: 'encore une fois'.

courage, 1459: Not: bravery, but: will-power.

course, 652: 'cours'.

couvrir, 346, 1507, 1542: to conceal, to dissimulate.

créance, 915: Doublet of: 'croyance'. Apart from its financial meaning (debt), is now used only in a few set expressions: 'accorder créance à', etc.

créature, 152: one who is under an obligation, who owes something to someone.

croire, je croi (341); *je voi* (514, 690); *je doi* (938): Archaic spellings preserved for the rhyme.

dans, 'à' (207, 616, 904: 'ramener dans'). 'chez' (Première et Seconde Préfaces: 'dans les Vestales'). 'au temps de' (1691: 'dans la race future').

de, 'par' (321, 385, 846, 1332, etc.); 'depuis' (1521), 'à partir de' (202). Partitive (448: 'Elle n'a vu couler de larmes que les siennes'). Objective (991/2: 'la vengeance/D'un geste . . .' Néron's revenge for a gesture). Not repeated, against modern usage (819).

débris, 556: ruin, downfall.

déclarer à, Première Préface: to make something quite clear to someone.

délicatesse, Première Préface: fastidiousness, excessive refinement.

démentir, Not just: to deny or to belie, but: actively to oppose the acts of, or to defy the power of (501).

demeurer, Seconde Préface: to endure.

démon, 701: in the Greek sense of: divinity.

dépit, 89, 106: violent irritation, or resentment caused by hurt pride. Nowadays much weaker.

dépouille (singular), 204, 1490: inheritance, what is the indisputed property of someone.

dès longtemps, 765, 1157: 'depuis long-temps' is now the usual expression.

désert (noun), 209: any region that is thinly populated, or remote from main centres.

désordre, 124, 1000: agitated or distracted state of mind.

détour, 697, 1269: wile, devious way.

développer, 930, Variants (52): to unfold, to unravel, to explain something that is obscure.

devoir (verb), with *devoir, falloir, pouvoir,* the imperfect and the perfect of the indicative can be used instead of the past conditional. 61: 'a dû' = 'aurait dû'; 153: 'j'ai pu' = 'j'aurais pu'; 970: 'vous deviez' = 'vous auriez dû'. See *croire.*

diligence, 271: exactness, attention to details, meticulous care.

en diligence, 1563: in haste.

discours, not necessarily: public speech, piece of oratory. 267: remark; 672, 729, 1066, 1249, 1434, 1438, 1653: talk, reflections; 935, 1146: reasonings, arguments.

disgrâce, 104, 911, 1151: loss of favour, and more generally, misfortune (cf. Italian: *disgrazia*).

disputer, 148: 'se disputer'.

distraire, with the full implications of the Latin: *distrahere,* to use force to pull apart. 1308: to alienate, to estrange. 1407: to deter.

se distraire, 400: to force oneself away from, to free oneself from an obsession. Not: to amuse oneself, or to seek relaxation from.

éclaircir quelqu'un, 1018: to enlighten someone on ('éclairer sur, instruire de').

s'éclaircir avec quelqu'un, 117: to enlighten oneself, to have it out with someone.

éclaircissement, 270: cf. *s'éclaircir.*

éclater, 196, 273: to appear in a clear, or a glaring light ('éclat' = flash, glare). With a subject or person: to manifest one's anger, grief, etc., with violence (753). Nowadays not used alone in that meaning. (But cf. 'éclater de rire', 'éclater en sanglots'.) 'Eclat' = burst.

économie, Epître au Duc de Chevreuse: order, arrangement.

effort, 1630: violent effect.

effusion, 1625: pouring, libation.

élever, 's'élever'.

éloigner, 1540: 's'éloigner'.

embrasser, 1314 etc.: to embrace, not: to kiss.

s'empresser à, 654: 's'empresser de'.

en (preposition), 'dans' would be more natural nowadays in a number of cases (290, 292, 642, 947, 985, etc.). 578: 'à' ('confier en').

en (pronoun), is used much more freely to refer to people: 'de lui, d'elle' (181, 1097, 1141, Première Préface: 'j'en ai fait une jeune fille très sage'). Like 'y' it may refer to a whole sentence, (870: to 'sa puissance ne peut être affaiblie'), or to a whole passage (1183: to the way in which Claudius died). It is used even more loosely in a number of expressions: Première Préface: 'en user', 777: 'mon cœur s'en est plus dit', 1020: 'n'en voilà que trop', 1425: 'si je m'en croyais', (cf. 926, 1516), 1515: 'je m'en fie'.

enchanteur (adj.), 429: acting like an enchantment, bewitching.

encor, spelling allowed only in poetry (323, 977, etc.).

ennui, 509: vexation. Usually has a much stronger meaning: grief, torment (1577), or even: despair (1641).

entendre, means more often than today: 'comprendre' (245, 1020, 1069), but also: to hear.

entreprise, 1079: daring project.

envier, 414: to begrudge, to deprive someone of something, to refuse.

envieux, 701: always ready to deprive, jealous, watchfully malevolent.

envisager, 1107: to look in the face.

épancher, 1624: to pour out (now rare in its literal sense).

espérer de, 696: 'j'espère de vous revoir' is archaic for: 'j'espère vous revoir'. But *espérer* can still be used with *de* if it is itself in the infinitive, as in: 'Puis-je espérer de vous revoir?' (Grevisse, 757, 3).

esprit, Seconde Préface: natural talent, 1569: disposition, feeling.

esprits, In Descartes's physiology: 'de petits corps légers, chauds et invisibles, qui portent la vie et le sentiment dans les parties de l'animal.' Hence 293, 1578: spirit, soul.

établir, With a stronger meaning: to make stable, unalterable (911).

éteindre, 612: 's'éteindre'.

étonné, still sometimes meant: as if struck by lightning (today: 'foudroyé') (321). Has in all cases a stronger meaning than nowadays: stunned, astounded, confounded (506, 1034).

étonnement, 397, 1638: See *étonné*.

exclus, excluse, 545: 'exclu, exclue' (cf. the modern spelling of 'inclus, incluse').

expliquer, 548, 554, 1709: to declare, fully to disclose, to develop. 1067: *s'expliquer*, to express one's feelings.

fâcheux, 489: Not: troublesome, but: difficult and unpleasant ('Les Alpes sont fâcheuses à traverser', Cayrou).

facile, 272, 1591: pliable, accommodating, obliging.

facilité, 1602: See *facile*.

faits, 1673: exploits.

feu(x), 1085: love, a cliché of seventeenth-century *galanterie*.

fidèle, 43: true to oneself.

fier, 36: wild, untamed, fierce, cruel (Latin: *ferus*). 393: rough, uncouth. (Can also mean: proud.)

fierté, 413: wild disposition. 952: shy reserve, aloofness. (Also: pride, haughtiness, 38, 1594.)

se fier sur, 607: 'se fier à', here with the meaning of: to look for reassurance.

flamme, 571: love (cf. *feux*).

flatter, 248, 550, 819, 972: to encourage, to favour; to give hopes, or false hopes. 282: to relieve. 1310: to spare, to treat gently.

se flatter, 635: to deceive oneself.

foi, 513, 1736: loyalty, faithfulness. 326, 720: loyalism, fidelity. 843, 1525: oath, promise of fidelity. 1457: 'manquer de foi à': to break one's promise to. 1485, 1588: truthfulness, sincerity, ('la foi de nos serments').

sur la foi de, 206: relying on, trusting. 146: 'laisser quelqu'un sur sa foi': to trust someone's word, or his judgment. (Furetière:'le laisser se conduire seul').

fortune, 144: rank, position. 689: fate, life.

front, 489, 1009, 1591: face, expression.

fureur, 41, 1718: raving madness (Latin: *furor*). Also in the ordinary meaning of: anger, rage (1382, 1685, 1704).

gêner, still retained the older meaning of: to torture, physically or mentally, but was already weakening (13, 1199): to be a cause of intolerable constraint.

généreux, 21: of noble race and noble feelings, magnanimous.

génie, 506, 800: nature, character, innate disposition.

gouverner quelqu'un, 814: to have under one's influence, to guide in all things.

gouverneur, Acteurs, 1162, Variants (16): archaic in the meaning of: tutor ('précepteur').

humeur, 36: moral and physical disposition, temper.

impatient, 11: with the Latin meaning of 'unable to bear': rebellious, restive.

impatience, 441: revolt, rebelliousness (or in the modern sense: 983).

impatiemment, Première Préface: cf. *impatient*.

impunément, may have an active as well as a passive meaning. 445: without inflicting a punishment. (Not: without being punished.)

indigne de, 785: who does not deserve (an insult, etc.). Also as today: shameful (1247); cf. *indignité* (611).

indiscret, 1425: unrestrained, inordinate.

indiscrétion, Première and Seconde Préfaces: lack of reserve or caution.

infidèle, 944: not to be trusted, perfidious.

infidélité, 1202: perfidy.

ingrat, ingrate, 902, 936: one who does not return someone's love (or with the wider modern meaning).

injure, 299, 1208: injustice, wrong suffered

inquiet, 377: restless, agitated (Latin: *inquietus*).

inquiétude, 1760: extreme, continuous agitation.

intelligence, 916, 992, 1543, Variants (64): concord, harmony. 'Être d'intelligence avec (1311, 1524) still means: to be in (secret) agreement with.

s'intéresser pour, 905, 1548: to take side whole-heartedly, to commit oneself in favour of someone.

s'intéresser dans, 656: 's'intéresser à'.

intérêt, vaguer than today, 31: what concerns someone; *mon intérêt*: the fact that I am involved in this affair.

irriter (*un sentiment*), 89, 418, 509, 833: to increase, to stimulate, to sharpen.

jusques, used indifferently as well as *jusque* (77, 481, 1257). Rare nowadays.

justifier, 962: 'se justifier'.

loi, 295: sometimes one particular command or order.

malice, 1600: has normally the strong meaning of: wish to harm, spitefulness (cf. 57: *malignité*).

marquer, 24: to show clearly, to prove. As today: to mark, often in a sinister way: to sully, to brand (227, 1142, 1686).

maxime, 1343, 1767: rule of conduct.

méconnaître, Première Préface: not to recognize. (Nowadays: not to acknowledge.)

même, could precede the noun where it now follows. (Epître au Duc de Chevreuse, 307).

ménager, 711, 1462: to make the best possible use of.

misérable, 760: worthy of compassion ('malheureux').

misère, 247, etc.: 'malheur'.

murmurer que, 971: 'murmurer de ce que'.

mystère, 635: pretence. 1619: dissimulation. Also, 930, in the modern sense of mystery, obscure, puzzling situation.

naissant, 29: youthful, adolescent. (Cf. 'Les dames aiment la jeunesse et vous êtes naissant', Mesnard, VIII, 334.)

négligence, 391: absence of ornament, informal simplicity.

neveux (plural), 1734: descendants.

nièce, 244: descendant. Also: niece (1131).

nouveau, 294: unheard of. 1403: recent, keenly felt, unhealed.

objet, 237, 1753: spectacle, sight that meets the eyes.

obséder, Variants (1): to beset, to be in continuous attendance.

occupé, may mean: absorbed, engrossed (405, 975, 1175).

on, may mean: 'je' (1287), or 'vous' (372, 815, 1090, 1114, 1288).

opprimé de, 734: 'opprimé par'.

où (relative pronoun), is used not only instead of 'dans lequel' but also of 'auquel' (575, 1064), 'sur lequel' (1128), 'chez lesquelles' or 'parmi lesquelles' (Première Préface), *d'où* = 'dont, desquels' (1598).

ouïr, no longer in common use for 'entendre' (1093, 1242). Most of its forms (except 'ouïr' and 'ouï') were already archaic in the seventeenth century.

paraître, Seconde Préface, 1515, 1532: to be obvious, manifest.

parmi, 695: 'au milieu de, au sein de'.

parricide, not only, as nowadays, murder of a father, but also of a brother (1431), sister, son, or king (fratricide, regicide). 1384: adjective.

partager, 268: To divide into two enemy parties.

à peine, 732: 'avec peine, avec difficulté' (cf. 'à grand'peine'). 1620: hardly (now usually followed by 'que').

penché, 1637: reclining ('couché').

perdre, 'faire périr, causer la ruine de' hence: *se perdre*, to cause one's downfall, or to perish by one's own hand (1764).

plaindre quelque chose, to deplore, to feel and to express sorrow (284, 840, 1371, 1741, Variants (5)). Also: to pity (464).

plus, Première Préface: *deux ans plus*, 'deux ans de plus'.

plusieurs, Epître au Duc de Chevreuse: 'nombreux'.

plutôt, 148, 830, Variants (81): 'plus tôt'.

pompe, 889, 1484, 1552: splendour, solemn pageantry; like *pompeux* it carries no critical, or ironical, undertone.

porter, Première Préface, 298: 'supporter'.

pouvoir, 153, 864: see *devoir*.

prendre, see *conseil*.

prendre part à, Epître au Duc de Chevreuse: to take an interest in.

préoccupé de, 251: prejudiced about, convinced without proof.

BRITANNICUS

présence, 540, 699: 'vue qu'on a d'une personne ou de quelque autre chose' (Richelet).

prêt à, 1216: 'près de'. In Racine's time 'prêt à' (ready for) and 'près de' (on the verge of) were often used one for the other.

presse, 1644: 'foule'.

presser, 655: 'oppresser'. Also, as in modern French: to hasten (1389), or: to urge (1730).

prétendre quelque chose, Not: to pretend = to make believe. 866: to lay claim (to a throne); to aspire to (157, 1259). Also, as in modern French: *prétendre à* (216).

prétendre+infinitive, to mean to do something (142, 625, 638, 1666); to be determined (361).

prétendre que+subjunctive or conditional, to have in the mind, to intend (301). To believe (wrongly), to hope (without reasonable ground) (1143, 1433).

prompt, 1444: ready, willing. Also in the ordinary meaning of: swift (1184).

que, 'pourquoi?' (474, 1563); 'où' ('le temps n'est plus que . . .' 91); 'sauf', 'sinon' (329, 552); 'à moins que', 'sans que' (Première Préface, 161); 'lorsque' (1199); 'de ce que' (*murmurer que*) 'à ce que' (*consentir que*).

querelle, 1348: 'parti, cause'.

qui (relative pronoun), used after a preposition, referring to things (582: 'aux mains/A qui (= auxquelles) Rome a commis . . .')

qui (interrogative), 735, 1323: 'qu'est-ce qui?' 743: '*A qui. . .?*' = 'A quoi'. . . ? (See Note).

qui (indefinite), 365: 'quelqu'un qui'+ conditional (*Qui suivrait leurs pas . . .* = 'si quelqu'un suivait' . . .)

race, 1691: generation of men.

ramener dans, 904: 'ramener á'.

rappeler, 1149: 'se rappeler'. 623, 784, 1666: to bring back, to revive.

rassembler, 1086: 'réunir' (Junie et Britannicus). Now normally used for more than two people.

ravaler, 879: to humiliate, to make someone fall from high estate ('faire déchoir').

se ravir, 1723: to flee, to tear oneself away.

réciter, 1476: normally a poem, not a song.

récompense, 67: compensation, counterpoise. (Cf. Bossuet: 'Récompensez le péché par d'excellentes vertus.')

reconnaître, 1397: to acknowledge gratefully. (Cf. 'reconnaître une faveur'.)

récrier, Première Préface: 'se récrier'.

remener, 1080: 'ramener'.

s'en remettre sur, 1669: 's'en remettre à'.

remplir, 1076: 'compléter' (to bring up to the required number). 618: to be equal to the demands of, to be worthy of.

reproche, 1023: offence.

respirer de, 201: to breathe again after being relieved from.

ressentir, 837: to resent. (Today: 'éprouver du ressentiment, de la rancune'.)

ressort, 1089: secret means, underhand stratagem, intrigue.

ressource, From 'resurgir', had a somewhat stronger sense in the seventeenth century: way of overcoming a serious situation, of solving a grave problem (827).

réunir, 264: 'réconcilier'.

réunion, 1626: 'réconciliation'.

révoquer, 918: to withdraw, to take back.

rire, 381: to be favourable ('sourire').

secret (noun), 138: private meeting, confidential talk.

secret (adj.), Applied to people, it means: reticent, circumspect, cautious (897).

séduire, 184, 364, 914, 1136, 1537: to deceive, to lead astray, to corrupt.

séjour, 1557: 'retard'.

servitude, 1444: 'servilité'.

seul, In the meaning of 'alone' is not distinguished from 'only' by its position: 1062 (*sa seule inimitié* = 'son inimitié seule'), 1670.

sévère, With an even stronger meaning than today: harsh, cruel (675, 990).

sévérité, 798: austere, rigid, unbending character.

simple, 'candide' (1244, here used ironically).

singulier, belonging to a single individual, characteristic of one thing (as today). Hence 1471: rare, unique, unequalled (used ironically).

soi, soi-même, now refers to 'on', or an indeterminate subject; not the case in 1685.

soigneux de+infinitive, taking great care to (653). Cf. *soin.*

soin, soins, a word used very frequently in the seventeenth century with a variety of meanings. From the modern one of: careful attention (Première Préface, 1012), one passes almost imperceptibly to the one of: solicitous care, constant application (285, 518, 805, 913, 1181, 1276, 1393, 1397, 1412, 1572, 1584, Variants (30, 41, 77). Hence the stronger sense of: worry, ('souci'), trouble, exertion, heavy duty, or heavy care imposed on someone: 591, 986, 889, 1197, 1224. By itself the word could mean: respects paid to any woman, or to a woman one loves; love, usually for a woman (600), exceptionally from a woman (465).

solide, Seconde Préface: serious, profound, not just pleasant. 624: real, weighty, lasting.

souffrir, 1714: 'tolérer'.

souhaiter quelqu'un, 705: to wish for the presence of someone, to long for.

soupir, 553, 966: especially in the plural, this word belongs to the language of *galanterie:* like *soins, feu, flamme, vœux,* it means: love. In 684, although this implication is not entirely forgotten, Racine brings the word back to its straight, literal meaning.

soupirer pour, 455, 476: to be in love.

souscrire à, 1368: in official matters is still found in the meaning of: to sign a document (here a death sentence). Or has the modern meaning of: to agree, 575, 1421.

succès, favourable or unfavourable issue ('Pompée, en la bataille de Pharsale, eut un succès malheureux'). Used alone it usually means: good success (Seconde Préface).

superbe, 494: arrogant.

surprendre, 887: to seize by stealth and unfair means.

tâcher à, 498: 'tâcher de' is the normal construction.

tandis que, 315: as long as, 'tant que'.

temps, 983: 'moment'.

toucher, has lost some of its force. 636, 1638: to move deeply; 637: to make oneself loved by.

transport, 765, 1765: violent outburst of feeling; 1500: joy. 1614: grief. In modern French not used alone ('transport de rage, de douleur', etc.).

traverser, 1041: to thwart ('contrarier, mettre obstacle à').

triste, with a much stronger meaning than today. Gloomy (271, 528), ill-starred, dejected (83, 1724: 'la triste Octavie'). Fateful, baleful, sinister (36, 99, 1705).

tristesse, 379: deep melancholy, gloom. Cf. in the Préface de *Bérénice:* '... cette tristesse majestueuse qui fait tout le plaisir de la tragédie'.

en user, Première Préface: to deal (with a problem). Nowadays more often 'en user (bien on mal) avec quelqu'un', to treat someone well or badly.

venin, 116: poison.

vertu, often preserves part of its Latin meaning (virile qualities): energy, mental and bodily strength (1471). Or more generally: moral greatness (1738); and in the modern sense.

vœux (plural), 558, 1077: love. 470: vows made to the gods, or simply 'wishes' (381), as today.

voir, see *croire.*

voix, 157, 1162: approval, support. Also as today: vote (Première Préface).

Y (pronoun), 'à lui, à elle, à cela'. May refer not to one particular word but to a whole sentence or a whole passage (599: to Nero's proposal).

yeux, 353, 601, 698, 708, 949: a seventeenth-century cliché to refer to the woman one loves, to her power over one's soul. But in *Britannicus* the real movements and changing expressions of 'les yeux', 'les regards' have an extraordinary importance (380, 387, 682, 713, 737, 1002, 1501, 1697, etc.).

APPENDIX I

TACITUS: *extracts from the 'Annals'*

BOOK XII, *chapter* 1. Messalina's death convulsed the imperial household. Claudius was impatient of celibacy and easily controlled by his wives, and the ex-slaves quarrelled about who should choose his next one. Rivalry among the women was equally fierce. Each cited her own high birth, beauty, and wealth as qualifications for this exalted marriage. [2] ... Pallas, proposing Agrippina, emphasized that the son whom she would bring with her was Germanicus' grandson, eminently deserving of imperial rank: let the emperor ally himself with a noble race and unite two branches of the Claudian house, rather than allow this lady of proved capacity for child-bearing, still young, to transfer the glorious name of the Caesars to another family.

[3] These arguments prevailed. Agrippina's seductiveness was a help. Visiting her uncle frequently—ostensibly as a close relation—she tempted him into giving her the preference and into treating her, in anticipation, as his wife. Once sure of her marriage, she enlarged her ambitions and schemed for her son Lucius Domitius Ahenobarbus, the future Nero, to be wedded to the emperor's daughter Octavia. Here criminal methods were necessary, since Claudius had already betrothed Octavia to Lucius Junius Silanus Torquatus. [4] ... Vitellius put an unsavoury construction on the unguarded (but not incestuous) affection between Silanus and his sister. Claudius, particularly ready to suspect the future husband of the daughter he loved, gave attention to the charge. Silanus, unaware of the plot, happened to be praetor for the year. Suddenly, though the roll of senators and the ceremonies terminating the census were long complete, an edict of Vitellius struck him off the senate. Simultaneously, Claudius cancelled Octavia's engagement with Silanus, and he was forced to resign his office. [5] ... Next year, rumour strongly predicted Claudius' marriage to Agrippina; so did their illicit intercourse. But they did not yet dare to celebrate the wedding. For marriage with a niece was unprecedented—indeed it was incestuous, and disregard of this might, it was feared, cause national disaster. Hesitation was only overcome when Lucius Vitellius undertook to arrange matters by methods of his own. He asked Claudius if he would yield to a decree of the Assembly and the senate's recommendation. The emperor replied that he was a citizen himself and would bow to unanimity. Then Vitellius, requesting him to wait in the palace, entered the senate and stating that it was a matter of the highest national importance, asked permission to speak first.

'In his exceedingly arduous duties,' Vitellius said, 'which comprise the whole world, the emperor needs support, to enable him to provide for the public good without domestic worries. Could there be a more respectable comfort to our Censor—a stranger to dissipation or self-indulgence, law-abiding since earliest youth—than a wife, a partner in good and bad fortune

alike, to whom he can confide his inmost thoughts, and his little children? [6]
... Marriage to a niece, it may be objected, is unfamiliar to us. Yet in other
countries it is regular and lawful. Here too, unions between cousins, long
unknown, have become frequent in course of time. Customs change as
circumstances change—this innovation too will take root.'

[7] At this, some senators ran out of the house enthusiastically clamouring
that if Claudius hesitated they would use constraint. A throng of passers-by
cried that the Roman public were similarly minded. Claudius delayed no
longer. After receiving the crowd's congratulations in the Main Square, he
entered the senate to request a decree legalizing future marriages with a
brother's daughter.... From this moment the country was transformed.
Complete obedience was accorded to a woman—and not a woman like
Messalina who toyed with national affairs to satisfy her appetites. This was a
rigorous, almost masculine despotism. In public, Agrippina was austere
and often arrogant. Her private life was chaste—unless power was to
be gained. Her passion to acquire money was unbounded. She wanted it as
a stepping-stone to supremacy.

[8] On the wedding-day Lucius Junius Silanus Torquatus committed
suicide. For that day finally terminated his hopes of life—or perhaps he
chose it deliberately to increase ill-feeling. His sister was banished from
Italy.... Agrippina, however, was anxious not to be credited with bad
actions only. So she now secured the recall of Lucius Annaeus Seneca from
exile and his appointment to a praetorship. She judged that owing to his
literary eminence this would be popular. She also had designs on him as a
distinguished tutor for her young son Lucius Domitius Ahenobarbus (the
future Nero). Seneca's advice could serve their plans for supremacy; and
he was believed to be devoted to her. [9] ... It was now decided to act
without further delay. A consul-designate was induced by lavish promises
to propose a petition to Claudius, begging him to betroth Octavia to Domitius—an arrangement compatible with their ages and likely to lead to higher
things.... The engagement took place. In addition to their previous
relationship, Domitius was now Claudius' future son-in-law. By his mother's
efforts—and the intrigues of Messalina's accusers, who feared vengeance
from her son—he was becoming the rival of Britannicus. [25] ... In the
following year the adoption of Lucius Domitius Ahenobarbus was hurried
forward. Pallas, pledged to Agrippina as organizer of her marriage and
subsequently her lover, took the initiative. He pressed Claudius to consider
the national interests, and furnish the boy Britannicus with a protector:
'Just as the divine Augustus, though supported by grandsons, advanced his
stepsons, and Tiberius, with children of his own, adopted Germanicus;
so Claudius too ought to provide himself with a young future partner in his
labours.' The emperor was convinced. Reproducing the ex-slave's arguments to the senate, he promoted Lucius Domitius Ahenobarbus above his
own son, who was three years younger.

[26] Thanks were voted to the emperor. More remarkable was the compliment that the young man received: legal adoption into the Claudian
family with the name of Nero. Agrippina was honoured with the title of
Augusta. After these developments no one was hard-hearted enough not

to feel distressed at Britannicus' fate. Gradually deprived even of his slaves' services, Britannicus saw through his stepmother's hypocrisy and treated her untimely attentions cynically. He is said to have been intelligent. This may be true. But it is a reputation which was never tested, and perhaps he only owes it to sympathy with his perils. [36] ... The war in Britain was in its ninth year. The reputation of Caratacus had spread beyond the islands and through the neighbouring provinces to Italy itself. These people were curious to see the man who had defied our power for so many years. Even at Rome his name meant something. . . . But there were no downcast looks or appeals for mercy from Caratacus. [37] ... Claudius responded by pardoning him and his wife and brothers. Released from their chains, they offered to Agrippina, conspicuously seated on another dais nearby, the same homage and gratitude as they had given the emperor. That a woman should sit before Roman standards was an unprecedented novelty. She was asserting her partnership in the empire her ancestors had won. [41] ... In the following year, that of Claudius' fifth consulship, Nero prematurely assumed adult costume, to qualify himself for an official career. The emperor willingly yielded to the senate's sycophantic proposal that Nero should hold the consulship at nineteen and meanwhile, as consul-designate, already possess its status outside the city, and be styled Prince of Youth. Furthermore gifts were made to the troops and public in Nero's name, and at Games held in the Circus he was allowed to attract popular attention by wearing triumphal robes whereas Britannicus was dressed as a minor. So the crowd, seeing one in the trappings of command and the other in boy's clothes, could deduce their contrasted destinies.

Now, too, all colonels, staff-officers, and company-commanders of the Guard who showed sympathy with Britannicus' predicament were eliminated on various fictitious grounds; sometimes promotion was the pretext. Even ex-slaves loyal to him were removed. The excuse for this was a meeting between the two boys at which Nero had greeted Britannicus by that name, but Britannicus addressed him as 'Domitius'. Agrippina complained vigorously to her husband. This was a first sign of unfriendliness, she said, a contemptuous neglect of the adoption, a contradiction—in the emperor's own home—of a national measure, voted by the senate and enacted by the people. Disaster for Rome would ensue, she added, unless malevolent and corrupting teachers were removed. Disturbed by these implied accusations, the emperor banished or executed all Britannicus' best tutors and put him under the control of his stepmother's nominees.

[42] Nevertheless, Agrippina did not yet venture to make her supreme attempt until she could remove the commanders of the Guard, whom she regarded as loyal to the memory of Messalina and to the cause of Messalina's children. . . . Thereupon the command was transferred to Sextus Afranius Burrus, who was a distinguished soldier but fully aware whose initiative was behind his appointment. Agrippina also enhanced her own status. She entered the Capitol in a carriage. This distinction, traditionally reserved for priests and sacred objects, increased the reverence felt for a woman who to this day remains unique as the daughter of a great commander and the sister, wife, and mother of emperors. . . .

[66] Agrippina had long decided on murder. Now she saw her opportunity. Her agents were ready. But she wanted advice about poisons. A sudden, drastic effect would give her away. A gradual, wasting recipe might make Claudius, faced with death, love her son again. What was needed was something subtle that would upset the emperor's faculties but produce a deferred fatal effect. An expert in such matters was selected—a woman called Locusta, recently sentenced for poisoning but with a long career of imperial service ahead of her. By her talents, a preparation was supplied. It was administered by a eunuch who habitually served the emperor and tasted his food.

[67] Later, the whole story became known. Contemporary writers stated that the poison was sprinkled on a particularly succulent mushroom. But because Claudius was torpid—or drunk—its effect was not at first apparent; and an evacuation of his bowels seemed to have saved him. Agrippina was horrified. But when the ultimate stakes are so alarmingly large, immediate disrepute is brushed aside. She had already secured the complicity of the emperor's doctor Xenophon; and now she called him in. The story is that, while pretending to help Claudius to vomit, he put a feather dipped in a quick poison down his throat. Xenophon knew that major crimes, though hazardous to undertake, are profitable to achieve.

[68] The senate was summoned. Consuls and priests offered prayers for the emperor's safety. But meanwhile his already lifeless body was being wrapped in blankets and poultices. Moreover, the appropriate steps were being taken to secure Nero's accession. First Agrippina, with heart-broken demeanour, held Britannicus to her as though to draw comfort from him. He was the very image of his father, she declared. . . . Blocking every approach with guards, Agrippina issued frequent encouraging announcements about the emperor's health, to maintain the army's morale and await the propitious moment forecast by the astrologers.

[69] At last, at midday on October the thirteenth, the palace gates were suddenly thrown open. Attended by Sextus Afranius Burrus, commander of the Guard, out came Nero to the battalion which, in accordance with regulations, was on duty. At a word from its commander, he was cheered and put in a litter. Some of the men are said to have looked round hesitantly and asked where Britannicus was. However, as no counter-suggestion was made, they accepted the choice offered them. Nero was then conducted into the Guards' camp. There, after saying a few words appropriate to the occasion—and promising gifts on the generous standard set by his father— he was hailed as emperor. The army's decision was followed by senatorial decrees. The provinces, too, showed no hesitation.

Claudius was voted divine honours, and his funeral was modelled on that of the divine Augustus—Agrippina imitating the grandeur of her great-grandmother Livia, the first Augusta. . . .

BOOK XIII, *chapter* I. The first casualty of the new reign was the governor of Asia, Marcus Junius Silanus. . . . Agrippina was afraid he would avenge her murder of his brother. Popular gossip, too, widely suggested that Nero, still almost a boy and emperor only by a crime, was less eligible for the throne than a mature, blameless aristocrat who was, like himself, descended from the Caesars. For Silanus was a great-great-grandson of the divine Augustus—and this still counted. So he was murdered. . . . Equally hurried was the death of Claudius' ex-slave Narcissus. I have described his feud with Agrippina. Imprisoned and harshly treated, the threat of imminent execution drove him to suicide. The emperor, however, was sorry: Narcissus' greed and extravagance harmonized admirably with his own still latent vices.

[2] Other murders were meant to follow. But the emperor's tutors, Sextus Afranius Burrus and Lucius Annaeus Seneca, prevented them. These two men, with a unanimity rare among partners in power, were, by different methods, equally influential. Burrus' influence lay in soldierly efficiency and seriousness of character, Seneca's in amiable high principles and his tuition of Nero in public speaking. They collaborated in controlling the emperor's perilous adolescence; their policy was to direct his deviations from virtue into licensed indulgences. Against Agrippina's violence inflamed by all the passions of ill-gotten tyranny, they united.

She, however, was supported by Pallas, who had ruined Claudius by instigating his incestuous marriage and disastrous adoption. But Nero was not disposed to obey slaves. Pallas' surly arrogance, anomalous in an ex-slave, disgusted him. Nevertheless, publicly, Agrippina received honour after honour. When the escort-commander made the customary request for a password, Nero gave: 'The best of mothers.' . . . [4] . . . Nero attended the senate and acknowledged its support and the army's backing. Then he spoke of his advisers, and of the examples of good rulers before his eyes. 'Besides, I bring with me no feud, no resentment or vindictiveness,' he asserted. 'No civil war, no family quarrels, clouded my early years.' Then, outlining his future policy, he renounced everything that had occasioned recent unpopularity. 'I will not judge every kind of case myself,' he said, 'and give too free rein to the influence of a few individuals by hearing prosecutors and defendants behind my closed doors. From my house, bribery and favouritism will be excluded. I will keep personal and State affairs separate. The senate is to preserve its ancient functions. By applying to the consuls, people from Italy and the senatorial provinces may have access to it. I myself will look after the armies under my control.'

[5] Moreover, these promises were implemented. The senate decided many matters. They forbade advocates to receive fees or gifts. They excused quaestors-designate from the obligation to hold gladiatorial displays. Agrippina objected to this as a reversal of Claudius' legislation. Yet it was carried—although the meeting was convened in the Palatine, and a door built at the back so that she could stand behind a curtain unseen, and listen. Again, when an Armenian delegation was pleading before Nero, she was just going to mount the emperor's dais and sit beside him. Everyone was stupefied. But Seneca instructed Nero to advance and meet his mother. This show of filial dutifulness averted the scandal.

[6] At the end of the year there were disturbing rumours that the Parthians had broken out and were plundering Armenia. . . . So in Rome, where gossip thrives, people asked how an emperor who was only just seventeen could endure or repel the shock. A youth under feminine control was not

reassuring. Wars, with their battles and sieges, could not be managed by tutors.

However, there was also a contrary view, which regarded it as better than if the responsibilities of command had fallen to the lazy old Claudius, who would have been ordered about by his slaves.... [8] ... [And] there was satisfaction because the man appointed to secure Armenia was Cnaeus Domitius Corbulo—a sign that promotions were to be by merit....

[10] In the same year the emperor requested the senate to authorize statues of his late father and guardian. He declined an offer to erect statues of himself in solid gold or silver.... He refused to allow the prosecution of a Roman gentleman outside the senate for favouring Britannicus. [11]... Nero pledged himself to clemency in numerous speeches; Seneca put them into his mouth, to display his own talent or demonstrate his high-minded guidance.

[12] Agrippina was gradually losing control over Nero. He fell in love with a former slave Acte. His confidants were two fashionable young men, Marcus Salvius Otho, whose father had been consul, and Claudius Senecio, son of a former imperial slave. Nero's secret, surreptitious, sensual meetings with Acte established her ascendancy. When Nero's mother finally discovered it, her opposition was fruitless. Even his older friends were not displeased to see his appetites satisfied by a common girl with no grudges. Destiny, or the greater attraction of forbidden pleasures, had alienated him from his aristocratic and virtuous wife Octavia, and it was feared that prohibition of his affair with Acte might result in seductions of noblewomen instead.

[13] Agrippina, however, displayed feminine rage at having an ex-slave as her rival and a servant girl as her daughter-in-law, and so on. She refused to wait until her son regretted the association, or tired of it. But her violent scoldings only intensified his affection for Acte. In the end, deeply in love, he became openly disobedient to his mother and turned to Seneca—one of whose intimates had screened the first stages of the liaison, by lending his own name as the ostensible donor of the presents which Nero secretly gave Acte. Agrippina now changed her tactics, and indulgently offered the privacy of her own bedroom for the relaxations natural to Nero's age and position. She admitted that her strictness had been untimely, and placed her resources—which were not much smaller than his own—at his disposal. This change from excessive severity to extravagant complaisance did not deceive Nero—and it alarmed his friends, who urged him to beware of the tricks of this always terrible and now insincere woman.... [14] ... Nero, exasperated with the partisans of this female conceit, deposed Pallas from the position from which, since his appointment by Claudius, he had virtually controlled the empire: the ex-slave left the palace with a great crowd of followers..... Agrippina was alarmed; her talk became angry and menacing. She let the emperor hear her say that Britannicus was grown up and was the true and worthy heir of his father's supreme position—now held, she added, by an adopted intruder, who used it to maltreat his mother. Unshrinkingly she disclosed every blot on that ill-fated family, without sparing her own marriage and her poisoning of her husband. 'But heaven

and myself are to be thanked', she added, 'that my stepson is alive! I will take him to the Guards' camp. Let them listen to Germanicus' daughter pitted against the men who claim to rule the whole human race—the cripple Burrus with his maimed hand, and Seneca, the deportee with the professorial voice!' Gesticulating, shouting abuse, she invoked the deified Claudius, the spirits of the Silani below—and all her own unavailing crimes.

[15] This worried Nero. As the day of Britannicus' fourteenth birthday approached, he pondered on his mother's violent behaviour—also on Britannicus' character, lately revealed by a small indication which gained him wide popularity. During the amusements of the Saturnalia the young men had thrown dice for who should be king, and Nero had won. To the others he gave various orders causing no embarrassment. But he commanded Britannicus to get up and come into the middle and sing a song. Nero hoped for laughter at the boy's expense, since Britannicus was not accustomed even to sober parties, much less to drunken ones. But Britannicus composedly sang a poem implying his displacement from his father's home and throne. This aroused sympathy—and in the frank atmosphere of a nocturnal party, it was unconcealed. Nero noticed the feeling against himself, and hated Britannicus all the more.

Though upset by Agrippina's threats, he could not find a charge against his stepbrother or order his execution openly. Instead, he decided to act secretly—and ordered poison to be prepared. Arrangements were entrusted to a colonel of the Guard who was in charge of the notorious convicted poisoner Locusta. It had earlier been ensured that Britannicus' attendants should be unscrupulous and disloyal. His tutors first administered the poison. But it was evacuated, being either too weak or too diluted for prompt effectiveness. Impatient at the slowness of the murder, Nero browbeat the colonel and ordered Locusta to be tortured. They thought of nothing but public opinion, he complained; they safeguarded themselves and regarded his security as a secondary consideration. Then they swore that they would produce effects as rapid as any sword-stroke; and in a room adjoining Nero's bedroom, from well-tried poisons, they concocted a mixture.

[16] It was the custom for young imperial princes to eat with other noblemen's children of the same age at a special, less luxurious table, before the eyes of their relations: that is where Britannicus dined. A selected servant habitually tasted his food and drink. But the murderers thought of a way of leaving this custom intact without giving themselves away by a double death. Britannicus was handed a harmless drink. The taster had tasted it, but Britannicus found it too hot, and refused it. Then cold water containing the poison was added. Speechless, his whole body convulsed, he instantly ceased to breathe.

His companions were horrified. Some, uncomprehending, fled. Others, understanding better, remained rooted in their places, staring at Nero. He still lay back unconcernedly—and he remarked that this often happened to epileptics; that Britannicus had been one since infancy; soon his sight and consciousness would return. Agrippina tried to control her features. But their evident consternation and terror showed that, like Britannicus' sister Octavia, she knew nothing. Agrippina realized that her last support was gone.

And here was Nero murdering a relation. But Octavia, young though she was, had learnt to hide sorrow, affection, every feeling. After a short silence the banquet continued.

[17] Britannicus was cremated the night he died. Indeed, preparations for his inexpensive funeral had already been made. As his remains were placed in the imperial mausoleum, there was a violent storm. It was widely believed that the gods were showing their fury at the boy's murder—though even his fellow-men generally condoned it, arguing that brothers were traditional enemies and that the empire was indivisible. . . . [18] . . . [Nero's mother] became Octavia's supporter. Constantly meeting her own friends in secret, Agrippina outdid even her natural greed in grasping funds from all quarters to back her designs. She was gracious to officers, and attentive to such able and high-ranking noblemen as survived. She seemed to be looking round for a Party, and a leader for it. Learning this, Nero withdrew the military bodyguard which she had been given as empress and retained as the emperor's mother, and also the German guardsmen by which, as an additional compliment, it had recently been strengthened. Furthermore, he terminated her great receptions, by giving her a separate residence. When he visited her there, he would bring an escort of staff-officers, hurriedly embrace her, and leave.

[19] People's veneration of power, when that power depends on someone else, is the most precarious and transient thing in the world. Agrippina's house was immediately deserted. Her only visitors and comforters were a few women, there because they loved her—or hated her. One of them was Junia Silana. . . . Silana now saw her chance of revenge. She put up two of her dependants to prosecute Agrippina. They avoided the old, frequently heard charges of her mourning Britannicus' death or proclaiming Octavia's wrongs. Instead they accused her of inciting Rubellius Plautus to revolution. This man, through his mother, possessed the same relationship to the divine Augustus as Nero did. Agrippina, the allegation was, proposed to marry Plautus and control the empire again. . . . [20] . . . Nero was so alarmed and eager to murder his mother that he only agreed to be patient when Burrus promised that, if she was found guilty, she should die. But Burrus pointed out that everyone must be given an opportunity for defence—especially a parent; and that at present there were no prosecutors but only the report of one man, from a household unfriendly to her. . . . [21] This calmed the emperor's fears. Next morning, Burrus visited Agrippina to acquaint her with the accusation and tell her she must refute it or pay the penalty. Burrus did this in Seneca's presence; certain ex-slaves were also there as witnesses. Burrus named the charges and the accusers, and adopted a menacing air. But Agrippina displayed her old spirit. 'Junia Silana has never had a child', she said, 'so I am not surprised she does not understand a mother's feelings! For mothers change their sons less easily than loose women change their lovers. . . . If Britannicus had become emperor could I ever have survived? If Rubellius Plautus or another gained the throne and became my judge, there would be no lack of accusers! I should then be charged, not with occasional indiscretions—outbursts of uncontrollable love—but with crimes which no one can pardon except a son!'

Agrippina's listeners were touched, and tried to calm her excitement. But she demanded to see her son. To him, she offered no defence, no reminder of her services. For the former might have implied misgivings, the latter reproach. Instead she secured rewards for her supporters—and revenge on her accusers. . . .

BOOK XIV, *chapter* 1. When the new year came, Nero ceased delaying his long-meditated crime. As his reign became longer, he grew bolder. Besides, he loved Poppaea more every day. While Agrippina lived, Poppaea saw no hope of his divorcing Octavia and marrying her. So Poppaea nagged and mocked him incessantly. He was an emperor under orders, she said—master neither of the empire nor of himself. . . . The appeal was reinforced by tears and all a lover's tricks. Nero was won. Nor was there any opposition. Everyone longed for the mother's domination to end. But no one believed that the son's hatred would go as far as murder.

[2] According to one author, Agrippina's passion to retain power carried her so far that at midday, the time when food and drink were beginning to raise Nero's temperature, she several times appeared before her inebriated son all decked out and ready for incest. Their companions observed sensual kisses and evilly suggestive caresses. . . . [3] . . . Finally, however, he concluded that wherever Agrippina was she was intolerable. He decided to kill her. . . . A scheme was put forward by Anicetus, an ex-slave who commanded the fleet at Misenum. In Nero's boyhood Anicetus had been his tutor; he and Agrippina hated each other. A ship could be made, he now said, with a section which would come loose at sea and hurl Agrippina into the water without warning. Nothing is so productive of surprises as the sea, remarked Anicetus; if a shipwreck did away with her, who could be so unreasonable as to blame a human agency instead of wind and water? Besides, when she was dead the emperor could allot her a temple and altars and the other public tokens of filial duty.

[4] This ingenious plan found favour. The time of year, too, was suitable, since Nero habitually attended the festival of Minerva at Baiae. Now he enticed his mother there. 'Parents' tempers must be borne!' he kept announcing. 'One must humour their feelings.' This was to create the general impression that they were friends again, and to produce the same effect on Agrippina. For women are naturally inclined to believe welcome news.

As she arrived from Antium, Nero met her at the shore. After welcoming her with outstretched hands and embraces, he conducted her to Bauli, a mansion on the bay between Cape Misenum and the waters of Baiae. Some ships were standing there. One, more sumptuous than the rest, was evidently another compliment to his mother, who had formerly been accustomed to travel in warships manned by the imperial navy. Then she was invited out to dinner. The crime was to take place on the ship under cover of darkness. But an informer, it was said, gave the plot away; Agrippina could not decide whether to believe the story, and preferred a sedan-chair as her conveyance to Baiae.

There her alarm was relieved by Nero's attentions. He received her kindly, and gave her the place of honour next to himself. The party went on for

a long time. They talked about various things; Nero was boyish and intimate
—or confidentially serious. When she left, he saw her off, gazing into her
eyes and clinging to her. This may have been a final piece of shamming—or
perhaps even Nero's brutal heart was affected by his last sight of his mother,
going to her death.

[5] But heaven seemed determined to reveal the crime. For it was a quiet,
star-lit night and the sea was calm. The ship began to go on its way.
Agrippina was attended by two of her friends. One of them, Crepereius
Gallus, stood near the tiller. The other, Acerronia, leant over the feet of her
resting mistress, happily talking about Nero's remorseful behaviour and his
mother's re-established influence. Then came the signal. Under the pressure
of heavy lead weights, the roof fell in. Crepereius was crushed, and died
instantly. Agrippina and Acerronia were saved by the raised sides of their
couch, which happened to be strong enough to resist the pressure. Moreover,
the ship held together.

In the general confusion, those in the conspiracy were hampered by the
many who were not. But then some of the oarsmen had the idea of throwing
their weight on one side, to capsize the ship. However, they took too long
to concert this improvised plan, and meanwhile others brought weight to
bear in the opposite direction. This provided the opportunity to make a
gentler descent into the water. Acerronia ill-advisedly started crying out,
'I am Agrippina! Help, help the emperor's mother!' She was struck dead
by blows from poles and oars and whatever ship's gear happened to be
available. Agrippina herself kept quiet and avoided recognition. Though she
was hurt—she had a wound in the shoulder—she swam until she came to
some sailing-boats. They brought her to the Lucrine lake, from which she
was taken home.

[6] There she realized that the invitation and special compliment had
been treacherous, and the collapse of her ship planned. The collapse had
started at the top, like a stage-contrivance. The shore was close by, there
had been no wind, no rock to collide with. Acerronia's death and her own
wound also invited reflection. Agrippina decided that the only escape from
the plot was to profess ignorance of it. She sent an ex-slave Agerinus to tell
her son that by divine mercy and his lucky star she had survived a serious
accident. ... [7] To Nero, awaiting news that the crime was done, came
word that she had escaped with a slight wound—after hazards which left no
doubt of their instigator's identity. Half-dead with fear, he insisted she might
arrive at any moment. 'She may arm her slaves! She may whip up the army,
or gain access to the senate or Assembly, and incriminate me for wrecking
and wounding her and killing her friends! What can I do to save myself?'
Could Burrus and Seneca help? Whether they were in the plot is uncertain.
But they were immediately awakened and summoned.

For a long time neither spoke. They did not want to dissuade and be
rejected. They may have felt matters had gone so far that Nero had to strike
before Agrippina, or die. Finally Seneca ventured so far as to turn to Burrus
and ask if the troops should be ordered to kill her. He replied that the
Guards were devoted to the whole imperial house and to Germanicus'
memory; they would commit no violence against his offspring. Anicetus,

he said, must make good his promise. Anicetus unhesitatingly claimed the direction of the crime. Hearing him Nero cried that this was the first day of his reign—and the magnificent gift came from a former slave! 'Go quickly!' he said. 'And take men who obey orders scrupulously!' . . . [8] . . . Anicetus surrounded her house and broke in. Arresting every slave in his path, he came to her bedroom door. Here stood a few servants—the rest had been frightened away by the invasion. In her dimly lit room a single maid waited with her. Agrippina's alarm had increased as nobody came from her son. If things had been well there would not be this terribly ominous isolation, then this sudden uproar. Her maid vanished. 'Are you leaving me, too?' called Agrippina. Then she saw Anicetus. Behind him were a naval captain and lieutenant. 'If you have come to visit me', she said, 'you can report that I am better. But if you are assassins, I know my son is not responsible. He did not order his mother's death.' The murderers closed round her bed. First the captain hit her on the head with a truncheon. Then as the lieutenant was drawing his sword to finish her off, she cried out: 'Strike here!'— pointing to her womb. Blow after blow fell, and she died. [9] . . . This was the end which Agrippina had anticipated for years. The prospect had not daunted her. When she asked astrologers about Nero, they had answered that he would become emperor but kill his mother. Her reply was, 'Let him kill me—provided he becomes emperor!' [10] But Nero only understood the horror of his crime when it was done. For the rest of the night, witless and speechless, he alternately lay paralysed and leapt to his feet in terror— waiting for the dawn which he thought would be his last. Hope began to return to him when at Burrus' suggestion the colonels and captains of the Guard came and cringed to him, with congratulatory handclasps for his escape from the unexpected menace of his mother's evil activities. Nero's friends crowded to the temples. Campanian towns nearby followed their lead and displayed joy by sacrifices and deputations. . . . [12] . . . Nevertheless leading citizens competed with complimentary proposals—thanksgivings at every shrine . . . the inclusion of Agrippina's birthday among ill-omened dates. It had been the custom of Publius Clodius Thrasea Paetus to pass over flatteries in silence or with curt agreement. But this time he walked out of the senate. . . . [13] Nero lingered in the cites of Campania. His return to Rome was a worrying problem. Would the senate be obedient? Would the public cheer him? Every bad character (and no court had ever had so many) reassured him that Agrippina was detested, and that her death had increased his popularity. They urged him to enter boldly and see for himself how he was revered. Preceding him—as they had asked to—they found even greater enthusiasm than they had promised. The people marshalled in their tribes were out to meet him, the senators were in their fine clothes, wives and children drawn up in lines by sex and age. Along his route there were tiers of seats as though for a Triumph. Proud conqueror of a servile nation, Nero proceeded to the Capitol and paid his vows.

APPENDIX II

ABRIDGED GENEALOGY OF THE IMPERIAL FAMILY

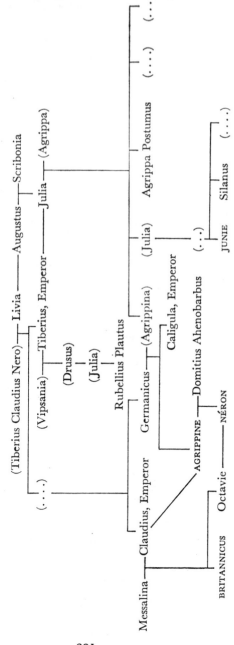